Heritage under Socialism

New Perspectives on Central and Eastern European Studies

Published in association with the Herder Institute for Historical Research on East Central Europe, Marburg, Germany

Series Editors
Peter Haslinger, Director
Heidi Hein-Kircher, Head of the Department Academic Forum

Decades after the political changes that accompanied the fall of the Soviet Union, the history and cultures of Eastern Europe remain very important for understanding the challenges of today. With a special focus on the Baltic states, Poland, the Czech Republic, Slovakia, and Hungary, *New Perspectives on Central and Eastern European Studies* investigates the historical and social forces that have shaped the region, from ethnicity and religion to imperial legacies and national conflicts. Each volume in the series explores these and many other topics to contribute to a better understanding of contemporary Central and Eastern Europe.

Volume 2
Heritage under Socialism: Preservation in Eastern and Central Europe, 1945–1991
Edited by Eszter Gantner, Corinne Geering, and Paul Vickers

Volume 1
Rampart Nations: Bulwark Myths of East European Multiconfessional Societies in the Age of Nationalism
Edited by Liliya Berezhnaya and Heidi Hein-Kircher

Heritage under Socialism

Preservation in Eastern and Central Europe, 1945–1991

Edited by
Eszter Gantner, Corinne Geering, and Paul Vickers

berghahn
NEW YORK · OXFORD
www.berghahnbooks.com

First published in 2022 by
Berghahn Books
www.berghahnbooks.com

© 2022, 2024 Eszter Gantner, Corinne Geering, and Paul Vickers
First paperback edition published in 2024

All rights reserved. Except for the quotation of short passages
for the purposes of criticism and review, no part of this book
may be reproduced in any form or by any means, electronic or
mechanical, including photocopying, recording, or any information
storage and retrieval system now known or to be invented,
without written permission of the publisher.

Library of Congress Cataloging-in-Publication Data

A C.I.P. cataloging record is available from the Library of Congress
Library of Congress Cataloging in Publication Control Number: 2021037698

British Library Cataloguing in Publication Data

A catalogue record for this book is available from the British Library

ISBN 978-1-80073-227-8 hardback
ISBN 978-1-80539-126-5 paperback
ISBN 978-1-80539-379-5 epub
ISBN 978-1-80073-228-5 web pdf

https://doi.org/10.3167/9781800732278

Contents

List of Illustrations vii

Acknowledgments ix

Introduction Heritage under Socialism: Trajectories of Preserving the Tangible Past in Postwar Eastern and Central Europe 1
Corinne Geering and Paul Vickers

Part I. Transfers and Exchanges in Heritage Policies and Practices

Chapter 1 The Past Belongs to the Future: Heritage in Soviet Policymaking on Cultural Development 35
Corinne Geering

Chapter 2 International Experts—National Martyrdom—Socialist Heritage: The Contribution of the Polish People's Republic to the Early UNESCO World Heritage Program 56
Julia Röttjer

Chapter 3 International Tourism and the Making of the National Heritage Canon in Late Soviet Ukraine, 1964–1991 78
Iryna Sklokina

Chapter 4 International Contacts and Cooperation in Heritage Preservation in Soviet Estonia, 1960–1990 105
Karin Hallas-Murula and Kaarel Truu

Part II. Canonizing and Contesting the Past: Heritage, Place, and Belonging under Socialism

Chapter 5 Socialist Royalty? The Ambiguities of the Reconstruction of the Royal Residence in Budapest in the 1950s 127
Eszter Gantner

Chapter 6 Justifying Demolition, Questioning Value: Urban Typologies and the Concept of the "Historic Town" in 1960s Romania 145
Liliana Iuga

Chapter 7 Making Sense of Socialism through Heritage Preservation: Stories from Northwest Bohemia 169
Čeněk Pýcha

Chapter 8 Socialism and the Rise of Industrial Heritage: The Preservation of Industrial Monuments in the German Democratic Republic 195
Nele-Hendrikje Lehmann

Conclusion Transnational Heritage Networks in Socialist Eastern and Central Europe 217
Corinne Geering

Index 237

Illustrations

Figures

Figure 0.1. Church of the Venerable Simeon Stylites on the Povarskaia next to a skyscraper on Novyi Arbat, Moscow (2014). Photograph by Corinne Geering. — 4

Figure 0.2. Restoration work during the construction of Kalinin Prospekt. Reprinted from the *UNESCO Courier* 20 (1967). Photograph © Paul Almasy / akg-images. — 5

Figure 5.1. Royal Palace, 1948. Source: Széchenyi Lánchíd újjáépítése, szemben a budai Vár / Reconstruction of Széchenyi Chain Bridge, opposite the Buda Castle (1948). Reproduced from Fortepan, Creative Commons CC-BY-SA 3.0. — 132

Figure 5.2. Construction works at the Royal Palace. Aerial image made by the Hungarian National Defense Association (MHSZ) (1963). Source: Légifotó a Budavári Palotáról (korábban Királyi Palota) / aerial photo of the Buda Castle (formerly the Royal Palace). Reproduced from Fortepan, Creative Commons CC-BY-SA 3.0. — 136

Figure 6.1. Historic Center of Brașov. The compact form of the medieval town is clearly evident. The town hall is located in the middle of the square, in the vicinity of the Gothic-style church. Source: Virgil Bilciurescu, "Studii pentru sistematizarea centelor istorice ale orașelor Brașov, Sibiu, Sebeș-Alba, Târgoviște," *Arhitectura* 14, no. 6 (1966): 53. Used with permission. — 151

Figure 6.2. Historic Center of Pitești. In the foreground, the Orthodox church is surrounded by trees and an elongated green area. Most buildings are relatively small-scale, late nineteenth-century constructions. The recently built modernist apartment blocks replacing some of these buildings on one side of the street are integrated into the scale of the old town. Source: Cezar Lăzărescu, "Studiu pentru sistematizarea zonei centrale Pitești," *Arhitectura* 14, no. 6 (1966): 51. Used with permission. — 157

Figure 7.1. Duchcovský viadukt, current state (2011). Photograph by Adam Pokorný. 181

Figure 7.2. Memorial to the killed workers, Duchcov (Duchcovský viadukt). Museum of Duchcov (sometime between 1954–63). © Museum Duchcov. Used with permission. 181

Figure 7.3. Transfer of the monument to the new site (1963). © Museum Duchcov. Used with permission. 182

Figure 7.4. A school class with the monument. Museum of Duchcov (after 1963). © Museum Duchcov. Used with permission. 182

Map

Map 7.1. Excerpt of the map of cultural monuments. The symbol near Duchcov refers to a "memorial of the struggles of the working class against capitalism." Reproduced from J. Hobzek, E. Šamánková, and V. Patera, *Mapa kulturních památek ČSSR: 1:500000*. Prague: Kartografické nakladatelství, 1968. Used with permission. 176

Acknowledgments

This book is based on research conducted in archives and libraries in at least ten countries, involving documents in as many languages. As editors, we are indebted to the knowledge and intellectual curiosity of our colleagues—the contributors—who offer innovative perspectives on a broad spectrum of actors, sites, and regions connected to the history of heritage under socialism.

The idea for this volume emerged during conversations in 2016, as we realized that what was missing from existing scholarship was a history of heritage practices within socialist Eastern and Central Europe. We were interested in a transnational approach that would address specific aspects of heritage under socialism, while at the same time paying close attention to the global processes informing heritage discourses, policies, and practices in the region in the period from the end of World War II until the dissolution of the socialist bloc in 1989–91. While legacies of socialism have already received more attention from researchers in heritage studies in the last decade, and historical research on individual socialist countries has also flourished, the ways in which experts, authorities, and other actors in socialist states—including individual Soviet republics—engaged with preserving the tangible past has not been explored in detail. What makes this volume's contribution to scholarship particularly insightful and innovative is how it sheds light on the ways in which actors from the region interacted with each other and how they were involved in the development of international discourses that crossed the Iron Curtain. The historical processes between 1945 and 1989–91 shaped the specific conditions of heritage management that continue to have an effect in many postsocialist countries and in international organizations today.

This book emerged from a collaboration between several institutions in Germany: the Herder Institute for Historical Research on East Central Europe in Marburg and the International Graduate Centre for the Study of Culture (GCSC) at the Justus Liebig University, Giessen, with additional support by the Imre Kertész Kolleg Jena and the Leibniz Research Alliance "Historical Authenticity." We wish to thank our colleagues at these institutions for their encouragement, assistance, and inspiring conversations. We are also grateful to the anonymous reviewers for their insightful comments on an earlier draft of this volume. Finally, we would like to thank the team at Berghahn for their always supportive, patient, and constructive collaboration on this volume, in particular Chris Chappell, Mykelin Higham, and Elizabeth Martinez.

Our dear colleague Eszter Gantner is sadly no longer with us to see this project come to fruition. Eszter passed away in summer 2019 while we were revising the chapter drafts. Her colleagues at the Herder Institute, Peter Haslinger and Heidi Hein-Kircher, along with Eszter's family, all helped in difficult circumstances to ensure her chapter could appear in this book. Eszter's insight on the topic of heritage, as well as her interest in engaging in research conversations across disciplines, countries, and historical periods, have shaped this volume. We hope that by completing the work that we started together, a suitable testimony to her passion and enthusiasm has emerged.

Corinne Geering and Paul Vickers
Leipzig/Regensburg, January 2021

INTRODUCTION
Heritage under Socialism
Trajectories of Preserving the Tangible Past in Postwar Eastern and Central Europe

Corinne Geering and Paul Vickers

On the cover of this book, a small, seventeenth-century, Orthodox church building stands right next to a large, paneled skyscraper in the city center of Moscow. The size of the church pales in comparison with one of the twenty-four story buildings that were erected on the new Kalinin Prospekt, today known as Novyi Arbat, between 1964 and 1968 as part of Moscow's urban development plan (figure 0.1). The arrangement of the two antithetic buildings may appear like a product of chance that saved a prerevolutionary, sacral building in the largest metropole of a state striving to build communism and promoting state atheism.

The images of the destruction of historic buildings, such as the detonation of the Church Christ the Savior in 1931 not far from this location, and the radical reconstruction envisaged by the Moscow General Plan of 1935, have become a crucial element of popular memory of the Soviet period.[1] By contrast, the small church on Novyi Arbat appears to have defied the destructive tendencies of state socialism and is thus reminiscent of holdouts situated in the middle of large-scale construction sites or new real estate developments. However, this scenario does not apply in this case, as the historical tradition expressed by the Orthodox building and the socialist vision of modernization reflected in the grand-scale, bulky design of socialist public spaces were not mutually exclusive. Instead, the community of church building and skyscraper was actually envisioned and promoted by the same socialist reconstruction plan in the 1960s. The Church of the Venerable Simeon Stylites on the Povarskaia, as the small church is called, was carefully restored during the construction of today's Novyi Arbat and repurposed to house an exhibition of applied arts.[2]

The apparent tension between tradition and modernization—embodied in the cover image of this book—also shaped the discourses and practices associated with heritage in the socialist states discussed in this volume. The contributions in this volume show that radical modernization indeed could be compatible with a commitment to preserving the heritage of the past. Historical sites, buildings, and objects from the era before socialism were integrated alongside modernist construction in accordance with socialist ideals within the same official discourses. Already in the immediate aftermath of the October Revolution in 1917, the waves of willful destruction motivated the new Bolshevik regime to issue a decree on the protection of monuments.[3] This fact was a source of Soviet patriotic pride, as publications issued in the postwar period connected the care of the Bolshevik regime for the past to the reconstruction of buildings destroyed in World War II, emphasizing that the act of preservation was a continuation of the victory in the so-called Great Patriotic War.

With the political transition to state socialism in Eastern and Central Europe following World War II, a number of new governments were confronted with the question of how to continue national historical narratives under the changed circumstances. At the same time, a general European trend was also in evidence as people were rediscovering the past during what can be described as a "historical turn" emerging from the 1960s.[4] This turn was marked in socialist states by the establishment of hundreds of new museums, the organization of festivals celebrating historical events, and the promotion of the study of local culture and local history through new voluntary associations.[5] While certain events assumed crucial importance in official public memory, such as World War II and socialist revolutions, the interpretation of the past also left room for discussion, negotiation, or even contestation, as well as personal reflection when dealing with specific historical sites, buildings, or objects.

Socialist ideas of heritage had not only local or regional resonance but were also of international significance, both within the region of Eastern and Central Europe and also transnationally, as these ideas shaped the nascent international organizations—among others, the United Nations Educational, Scientific and Cultural Organization (UNESCO)—dealing with heritage across the Iron Curtain. Thus, this volume points toward a broader global history of heritage, but within the more coherent spatial and temporal frames of postwar Europe. The example of the small church on Novyi Arbat reveals the relevance of the international sphere for socialist preservation practices, as heritage assumed a central position in the construction of the self-image of the Soviet Union and other socialist states after World War II. The restoration of the historical church building was not simply a by-product of the large-scale construction project; rather, the restored building was embedded in the overall representation of state-led efforts associated with modernization and striving toward communism in the Soviet Union. A picture of the final stages of construction of Kalinin Prospekt and restoration of the church unfolding right next to each other (figure 0.2) was reproduced for the global public in an article titled "U.S.S.R. Today" in a special issue of the *UNESCO Courier*, the monthly magazine of UNESCO. This special issue was published in 1967 in celebration of the fiftieth anniversary of the October Revolution and aimed to introduce an international readership to recent developments in the fields of education, science, and culture in the Soviet Union. Within this framework, the preservation of cultural heritage formed part of the achievements that Soviet officials sought to present to the world. Accordingly, the picture caption stated that the church was "preserved in its modern surroundings" and furthermore emphasized the increasing importance attributed to cultural heritage by socialist policies.[6]

This volume seeks to carefully examine the relation between nation-building and increasing internationalization in preservation in postwar Eastern and Central Europe, while also accounting for the role that local and regional actors, including voluntary societies and local residents, played in these processes. In an effort to move away from a homogenous conception of the so-called socialist bloc, this volume presents case studies from the Polish People's Republic, the Socialist Republic of Romania, the Czechoslovak Socialist Republic, the German Democratic Republic, the Hungarian People's Republic, and the Soviet Union, while also focusing on the Estonian and Ukrainian Soviet republics separately. International relations between these countries were consolidated by international agreements, such as the Council for Mutual Economic Assistance (COMECON) and the Warsaw Pact, while new international organizations like UNESCO provided avenues for experts from socialist countries to engage with global debates. The approach taken in this edited volume is thus a transnational history as the contributions pay particular attention to the international transfers and exchanges in the preservation and to uses of the historical built environment in postwar Eastern and Central Europe. These historical accounts on cultural heritage contribute to a reassessment of the relevance of the nation in the socialist period as well as of the influence and control in this region exerted by the political center in Moscow that has been emphasized in other accounts.[7] The transnational history in this volume instead seeks to shed light on the multiple actors that shaped preservation in the region and at the international level, both within the socialist bloc and transcending the ideological divide.

Figure 0.1. Church of the Venerable Simeon Stylites on the Povarskaia next to a skyscraper on Novyi Arbat, Moscow (2014). Photograph by Corinne Geering.

Heritage, Monuments, and Memorialization: Socialist Relations to the Past

The notion of heritage has emerged across the world as the primary concept driving today's management of and legislation on protection and preservation of movable, immovable, and intangible cultural property.[8] The differences of the concept of heritage to that of history and of memory and how they relate to place have been subject to considerable debate.[9] With the emergence of the field of heritage studies, scholarship appears to have settled on a consensus that understands heritage as a discourse and an interrelated set of sociocultural practices,[10] encompassing both tangible and intangible cultural expression as well as the natural environment, that are formed in the present and reflect concerns about the past.[11] The focus on present concerns also explains why scholarship on heritage has traditionally focused on contemporary societies rather than historical ones. This concern becomes ever more pressing when the present contrasts starkly from the past and thus urges societies to reorient themselves. Against this background, in the last three decades, scholarship dealing with heritage in the Eastern and Central European region has primarily engaged with ways of dealing with the socialist past during and after the political transition

Figure 0.2. Restoration work during the construction of Kalinin Prospekt. Reprinted from the *UNESCO Courier* 20 (1967). Photograph © Paul Almasy / akg-images.

of 1989–91. While earlier research has focused on the reinterpretation of socialist monuments,[12] postsocialist urban development,[13] dissonant heritage, and the question of how to come to terms with a difficult past,[14] more recent scholarship has reassessed the postsocialist nature of heritage and connected it to challenges of securitization in state-building processes in times of political upheaval.[15]

In contrast to scholarship dealing with postsocialist societies, where the focus has been on their ways of working through the socialist past, this book is concerned with how socialist societies related to the past between the end of World War II in 1945 and the dissolution of the socialist bloc in 1991. It discusses how experts of various backgrounds, government officials, and politicians, as well as tourists, visitors, and local residents, participated in the shaping of heritage in state socialist societies in Eastern and Central Europe. The contributions focus on the preservation of the tangible past, as manifested in legislation on protection, institution-building, and practices of restoration or reconstruction. The examples explored in this volume range from architecture, public infrastructure and sites, to other objects stemming from the historical periods preceding state socialism. The concept of heritage is used primarily as an analytical term, drawn from the more recent tradition of heritage studies, whereas other notions were employed more frequently by the historical actors at the time. In most languages concerned here, the concept generally used in source material would correspond to the English notion of *monument* (e.g., *pamiatnik* in Russian, *Denkmal* in German, *zabytek* in Polish, and *műemlék* in Hungarian). Valorization of heritage sites did not commence with the socialist era, of course; the new socialist governments had at their disposal national heritage registries that had been compiled over decades under different political conditions. While various actors, from ministries through academics to local administration and associations, exerted much effort in conceiving an officially sanctioned past compatible with socialism, this took into account existing historical layers, canons, and experiences of continuity and rupture.

The strong embeddedness of heritage registries in the national context, advanced by their function of representing a sanctioned account of national history, has often overshadowed the transnational links of members of governments and intellectual elites that shaped activities promoting heritage conservation in their respective countries, a process that emerged already in the nineteenth century.[16] During the Cold War era, too, the production of national culture through tangible remains from the past, known as monuments of history and culture, was an endeavor motivated by transnational links across ideological divides.[17] At the same time, the contributions here remain aware of the significance of the state as an actor in heritage policy and practice on the local, national, and international levels.[18] As the studies presented in the chapters of this volume show, socialist conceptions of heritage were not only manifested in specific sites and locations, but they also developed out of those sites, ultimately informing practices and discourses that took on international significance, in the shape of professional practices and discourses as well as international standard-setting instruments that remain in place to this day. For example, this is evident in the parallel development of the notion of industrial heritage in socialist and nonsocialist countries, as well as in the inclusion of dark heritage, such as concentration camps, in the international heritage canon. By inquiring into the socialist uses of the past, and the international responses to them at the time, this volume deepens the interlinkages of the fields of history, heritage studies, and Central and Eastern European studies. It seeks to further ongoing debates about the globally resonant concept of heritage where the socialist interpretations have so far played a marginal role.[19]

Recent inquiries have started delineating the characteristics of socialist conceptions of heritage, with a particular focus on the efforts by socialist regimes to create historical continuity over the political rupture of revolutions by including imperial structures like palaces and monasteries in the new socialist heritage canon. The October Revolution in 1917 also initiated a new time regime that later made it possible to extend the notion of heritage to include artifacts erected and created during socialism, such as modernist buildings and memorials.[20] Historical continuity not only provided a source of political legitimacy to the socialist regimes by effectively referring to established cultural canons, but also supported the transformation of citizens into "new men" through a cultural revolution that reassessed basic functions and notions of heritage.[21] For the region of Eastern and Central Europe, World War II presented a powerful caesura in multiple respects. For one, the transition to state socialism occurred in most countries in this region during and immediately after World War II. These states included, among others, the Estonian SSR as part of the USSR, the German Democratic Republic, the Polish People's Republic, the Socialist Republic of Romania, the Czechoslovak Socialist Republic, and the Hungarian People's Republic, which are all discussed in this volume. In some of these countries, the end of the war also led to a change in borders, thus subjecting new territories to socialist rule, which also applied to the Ukrainian SSR, a thitherto existing Soviet republic. Further, the massive destruction suffered across Eastern and Central Europe in World War II challenged the new and old socialist regimes to devise a reconstruction plan for historical places that accommodated both a longer national historical narrative and the political objectives of striving toward the communist future. The experiences of World War II provided the basis for postwar institutions responsible for preservation in many states in Europe as measures of safeguarding and reconstruction were implemented by public authorities in response to wartime destruction. Historical accounts have revealed that it was indeed Soviet republics other than the Russian SFSR that were pioneering in the field of preservation and thus also shaped measures taken by the political center in Moscow.[22] Moreover, studies on the reconstruction of cities in the Soviet Union, Poland, and the GDR have shown the extent of public debate and strong involvement of local actors, thus contrasting with narratives declaring a clear top-down decision-making process in state socialist societies.[23]

By focusing on heritage and practices of preservation, this book engages with broader themes in the historiography of postwar Eastern and Central Europe, such as the role of ideology, state propaganda, and historiographic revision in socialist societies.[24] The victory in World War II, called the "Great Patriotic War" in Russian, and the struggle against fascism have been central elements of official socialist historiography, education, and memory culture.[25] The substantial revisionism in these socialist narratives has been critiqued by important work highlighting blank spots and working through difficult pasts. Scholarship has revised socialist World War II accounts that focused on victims of antifascist struggle while ignoring Jewish suffering;[26] it has highlighted Communist crimes, such as the history of the Katyń massacre;[27] and, finally, it has rendered visible the multicultural history of borderlands and explored the history of regions affected by ethnic cleansing.[28] At the same time, however, rejection or disavowal of socialist-era historiography has been used to lend legitimacy to postsocialist nationalization of the past,[29] while also obscuring the ways in which socialist-era uses of the past have shaped regimes of memory that are still at work in the postsocialist present.[30] There are continuities in terms of what was deemed valuable and worthy of preservation from the past,[31] in aesthetic terms and in terms of values, at least where heroic and patriotic narratives are concerned.[32] This is not to suggest that Communist parties agreed on one interpretation of national symbols nor that they were necessarily successful in imposing it on the population, as the accounts in this volume highlight.[33]

In several countries in Eastern and Central Europe, the postwar period promoted the creation of ethnically homogenous nation-states (for example, Poland and the Czech part of the ČSSR), laying the foundations for the emergence of independent states after 1989. The authorities in Poland, for example, developed a mythology claiming that post-1945 Poland had been restored to its original location from around the turn of the second millennium, prior to Germanic aggression and the eastward shift in Poland's foreign policy that this necessitated, thus aggravating relations with

Eastern Slavic neighbors. Heritage played a role in legitimizing discourses, with sites relating to the medieval period—rather than later epochs—foregrounded in territories that had until the end of World War II formed part of the German Empire.[34] These sites provided the new regime with tangible symbols that the redrawn borders could only be protected from Western aggression by an alliance with the USSR, thus guaranteeing future prosperity in a modern socialist state.[35] The tangible past, then, was integral to the story not only of geopolitical security but also of future progress as projected by socialist-era accounts.

Examples such as this show that socialist modernity was manifested not only in factories, technological development, and, later, consumer products, but also in a modern form of nation-building that likewise under socialism involved "the invention of tradition."[36] Existing traditions were reframed and the canon mined for aspects of the past best suited to present-day needs for the purposes of official discourse. On the ground, whether among expert communities or "ordinary people," such as tourists or locals living near heritage sites, the official framing of the past could be subject to degrees of contestation[37]; while on the other hand, nonstate actors could also align with the state's heritage policy.

The role of states' use of heritage protection as part of cultural nationalism to aid political nationalism has been outlined in recent research linking nationalism studies and heritage studies.[38] Regime change in many of the states discussed here, as evident in the wake of the October Revolution and after World War II, generally entailed action to protect historical buildings.[39] This is borne out in many of the case studies in this volume, with wartime destruction often a key factor alongside socialist nation-building policies. However, since the chapters here go beyond the initial turbulence of the installation of Communist regimes, they delve further into continuities across regime changes, tracing not only the legacies in legislation and institutions of heritage protection, but also the influence of experts' intellectual inheritances, such as academic networks, local associations, and even family histories.

What this volume seeks to do, then, is to explore the extent to which heritage functioned within socialist nation-building efforts, but also to go beyond the focus on the effectiveness, or otherwise, of cultural nationalism for political legitimization. This is evident in the way the contributions draw on the perspectives of informal and formal networks that turned their attentions to local sites and their meaning for their users. In particular, the growing tourism sector and increasing opportunities to travel abroad for restorers and other experts offer insights into conflicting narratives and efforts toward extending the boundaries of more narrowly defined ideological foundations. By adopting approaches that highlight the ways in which the uses of the past under socialism were produced through individual and institutional activities, such as international travel, it becomes possible to trace not only forms of "permitted dissent"[40] but also the limited yet productive freedoms in the realms of conservation.[41] Thus, state policy in relation to heritage is revealed as a product of negotiation, disagreement, or individual initiative. It is also shown to be something guided only in part by political or cultural nationalism, with economic benefits and infrastructural development also becoming part of socialist heritage policy and practice. Against this background, the contributions here demonstrate the intersections of political order, ideology, expertise, localized practice, national canons and their reworkings, and local heritage sites as interlinked factors in the production of the diverse phenomenon of heritage under socialism.

Transnational Perspectives on Heritage under Socialism

From the very outset, socialism was conceived as an internationalist ideology that necessitated shared approaches to the past by individual nation-states, thus signaling the emergence of a new socialist realm of intensifying transnational exchange. However, socialism in postwar Eastern and Central Europe did not constitute a uniform ideology or a homogeneous practice. Recent research has stressed the diversity of the socialist experience across states and regions,[42] thus complicating a clear-cut definition of socialism. Nonetheless, socialism under different political, social, and cultural conditions shared similar trajectories, blueprints, and institutions.[43] They evolved in the course of transnational exchanges, which were facilitated by the politics of socialist internationalism and alternative processes of globalization centering in Eastern Europe.[44] Thus, the so-called Second World exhibited distinctive characteristics, which had evolved over time and which marked socialism itself as a historical product of transnational exchange.[45] These characteristics included the adoption of a variation of socialism as state ideology that involved the nationalization of property and the promotion of atheism. Socialist states were ruled by Communist parties whose congresses spearheaded a highly centralized form of governance. Party authorities controlled the censorship apparatus, issued travel permits, and expected varying degrees of ideological engagement from those working in public institutions. As a result, the state authorities were at the same time enablers of the international exchanges that made socialist heritage part of the global discussion on heritage. Indeed, as this volume shows, the ruling parties' gatekeeping practices were crucial to some of the more subtle reworkings and disagreements that come across in the historical source material discussed by the contributions in this volume. Such nuances can be revealed by an actor-centered, transnational perspective, even on the level of the production of legislation, where typically the domination of the center in Moscow or the respective state capitals has been underlined.

Socialism as an ideology and a form of rule did not remain consistent throughout the postwar period. The prevailing form of socialism in the different states was contingent on national contexts that were shaped over time by state reforms, intellectual debates over ideological foundations, and shifts in international alliances. While the early postwar period witnessed a consolidation of Communist rule in most of the countries examined in this volume, the death of Soviet leader Stalin in 1953 presented an important turning point, leading to the reforms of de-Stalinization during the Khrushchev Thaw. Though this period was characterized by efforts to liberalize the press, rehabilitate political prisoners, and renounce isolationist foreign policy, at the same time the Thaw period also witnessed more repression toward religious groups in the Soviet Union, as well as the Soviet interventions in Hungary in 1956 and in Czechoslovakia in 1968. In the 1970s, the politics of détente provided the basis for socialist countries to intensify international cooperation, especially within Europe, while against this background, opposition and protest movements gained ground, such as the Charter 77 in Czechoslovakia and Solidarność in Poland. Finally, the reforms of *perestroika* from the mid-1980s aimed at economic restructuring and more transparency in government institutions, laid bare in particular by the nuclear disaster in Chernobyl in 1986. In 1989–91, the socialist bloc ceased to exist, as states and Soviet republics followed through with declarations of independence, and with both peaceful and violent revolutions emerging during the political transition. What this very brief periodization of postwar Eastern and Central Europe shows are the shifts and tensions in the national and international policies of socialist states. They point to the need to scrutinize the specific historical setting of actors who articulated socialist conceptions of heritage and the policies relating to it.

These shifts had varying influences during the postwar decades in the socialist states, leading to different historical trajectories of preserving the tangible past. The burgeoning field of historical research on preservation under socialism has shed light on how socialist regimes in specific locations, from Cuba to the Soviet Union and Romania, appropriated the past from the prerevolutionary or prewar periods for their own purposes.[46] As highlighted by recent research on cultural heritage in socialist Africa during the Cold War, this also held true for international cooperation and transfer of socialist ideas from Eastern Europe in support of national liberation movements.[47] Notwithstanding shared socialist ideas, the appropriation and use of the past was no uniform process in different societies; instead, it involved negotiation, debate, and at times even contestation. Several case studies on particular locations in Soviet Russia have provided insight into preservation as a complex and long negotiation process between local residents, heritage experts from various fields, politicians, and members of state administration representing the interests of urban development and civil engineering.[48] In this respect, the preservation of sacral architecture under the conditions of state atheism, antireligious propaganda, and persecution, for example, have been of particular interest to scholarship.[49] Churches, monasteries, and other buildings associated with religion were included by Soviet authorities in state heritage registries and promoted as part of the state's cultural heritage. In many places, these buildings no longer served their previous religious function and were restored to house museums or tourist facilities, as it was the case in the aforementioned Church of the Venerable Simeon Stylites on the Povarskaia on today's Novyi Arbat in Moscow.

During the period between 1945 and 1991, heritage under socialism was also shaped by the increasing relevance of international cooperation. For one, there were regular meetings among socialist countries, in line with the ideology of socialist internationalism, to ensure coordination of their policies vis-à-vis the capitalist world. This also included meetings of the ministries of culture that oversaw the field of cultural heritage. At the same time, the global community saw the emergence of several new international organizations that were devoted to cultural policies and the preservation of cultural heritage as distinct fields of governance. The new legislation and standard-setting instruments adopted by international bodies both contributed to and drew inspiration from the policies of socialist states. These documents, such as the Venice Charter adopted by the Second International Congress of Architects and Specialists of Historic Buildings in 1964, built upon hitherto existing networks of the interwar period, while at the same time expanding the possibilities of international cooperation considerably. UNESCO, the International Council of Museums (ICOM), both established in 1946, and the International Council on Monuments and Sites (ICOMOS)—its establishment in 1965 was prompted by the Venice Charter—provided new platforms to engage in transnational discussion for experts from socialist countries, thus bringing practices developed in their home countries into the international community.

Actors from socialist states formed central constituents of the history of these international organizations. For instance, ICOMOS was founded in Warsaw in 1965 with the support of the Polish government; and from the moment of its inception, this organization was committed to promoting international cooperation and exchange across ideological divides during the Cold War. Subsequent to its meeting in Poland, ICOMOS alternated between locations in Eastern and Western Europe for the triennial general assemblies: the Third General Assembly was held in 1972 in Budapest, Hungary; the Fifth General Assembly in 1978 in Moscow and Suzdal', Russian SFSR; and the Seventh General Assembly in 1984 in Rostock, GDR. The support extended to this international organization and its work by socialist governments reflected the fact that transnational exchange through the channels of ICOMOS, as well as other international bodies, was fundamental for the development of preservation policies and practices in socialist countries in the postwar period.[50]

Against this background, processes unfolding under socialism cannot be confined easily within the framework of the nation-state and instead require both the transnational and subnational perspectives of the kind that this volume develops for the field of heritage. The volume thus contributes to a broader postwar history of transnational transfers and exchanges by discussing expert networks as well as less formal cross-border mobility (for example in tourism) outside the centers dominating transnational heritage discourse.[51] Heritage and more specifically the practice of preservation lend themselves particularly well to research examining processes across ideological and state borders during the Cold War, since it combines the two fields of culture and expertise. In the last fifteen years, several publications have revealed the active transnational networks of technology and cultural exchanges that transcended the Iron Curtain.[52] György Péteri was among the first scholars to reassess the separation and isolation associated with the systemic divide in the Cold War period. He suggested that it was necessary to reconsider the prominent metaphor of the Iron Curtain and instead reestablish it as a Nylon Curtain, one that "was not only transparent but . . . also yielded to strong osmotic tendencies that were globalizing knowledge across the systemic divide about culture, goods, and services."[53]

In the field of heritage, transsystemic transfers and exchanges promoted the use of culture as soft power and the development of mass tourism together with socialist consumer society. For example, the panel buildings framing the Kalinin Prospekt, mentioned above, included several shops and other services that catered to the needs of a new, socialist consumer society in the post-Stalin Soviet Union.[54] The fact that these processes unfolded in several countries, sometimes simultaneously, provided fertile ground for transnational discussions on the role cultural heritage was to assume in socialist societies. As the contributions to this volume demonstrate, transfers were often not unidirectional, solely a result of diktats and norms issued from the center in Moscow, but multidirectional, as ideas and practices from the Soviet republics and the Warsaw Pact states also exerted an influence on the development of shared preservation principles and of international heritage infrastructures.

Transfers and Exchanges across Socialist Eastern and Central Europe

Whereas the focus of existing studies has largely been on one socialist state, this volume inquires into preservation in Eastern and Central Europe on the regional scale by paying particular attention to transfers and exchanges. Thus, it seeks to complement earlier histories on international heritage cooperation in Eastern Europe that have emphasized contacts beyond the region, with Western Europe or the Global South, but in turn neglected internationalization within Eastern and Central Europe.[55] As several contributions in this volume highlight, the development of international contacts within the so-called socialist bloc preceded the involvement of socialist states in the relevant international heritage bodies and indeed even contributed toward the foundations for internationalization at the European and global levels. Moreover, this new realm of socialist internationalism in Eastern and Central Europe was established by professional communities in states that had, in most cases, inherited transnational expert networks as well as national legislation and policies from the interwar and imperial periods.

This book takes into account the diverse trajectories in heritage conservation under socialism when discussing the multilayered movement of heritage concepts and practices across borders and ideological divides. By pointing to central actors and sites involved, the contributions analyze the articulation of conceptions of heritage in and from socialist states, while also paying particular attention to the role of international organizations and various expert associations. The case studies reveal the dynamic nature of socialist interpretations of the tangible past and the negotiation of its meaning at the level of local, national, and international actors. Their focus on transnational transfers and exchanges also highlights the internationalization of preservation in the postwar period and the continuity of interwar international contacts under new political conditions. Exploring the internationalization of heritage policies and practices in postwar Eastern and Central Europe makes clear the place of socialist countries and actors in the broader European and global historical accounts dealing with heritage and uses of the past. In this volume, the region of Eastern and Central Europe is framed neither as peripheral to global processes nor as an isolated, self-enclosed region. Instead, it emerges as a region where ideas and practices related to heritage shaped the globalization of this field in the second half of the twentieth century, while also producing a particular mode of internationalizing preservation within the region. As this volume shows, heritage under socialism was a coconstitutive of the international heritage order that emerged after World War II.

The contributions offer insights relevant for intraregional comparisons on Eastern and Central Europe, thus diversifying the notion of the "socialist bloc," as well as cross-regional comparisons, demonstrating that heritage grew in significance on both sides of the Iron Curtain as part of a process shaped by transnational interactions. The focus on the broad scale and scope of the actors involved in negotiating and contesting the meaning of both heritage sites and the practice of preservation challenges ideas of heritage under socialism as a top-down, centrally dictated process. Instead, the volume is guided by an emphasis on the socialist construction of heritage sites and practices as a multidirectional and multisited process, taking place in intersecting local, national, regional, and international contexts.

The volume is divided into two parts that explore concepts of heritage and practices of preservation from a transnational perspective, first by tracing transfers and exchanges across state borders and the Iron Curtain, and second by looking into concrete manifestations of these processes at specific sites on the local and regional levels. The first part of this book, "Transfers and Exchanges in Heritage Policies and Practices," demonstrates how socialist conceptions of heritage were dynamic constructs that were also influential on the international level. The four chapters here concentrate on the versatile and multilayered relations between socialist heritage actors, practices, and policies across state borders and in particular in international organizations such as UNESCO and ICOMOS. The cases explored show how internationalization often went hand in hand with processes of nation-building under socialism. Recognizing how the state had a central role in heritage policies and practices also contributes to diversifying the socialist bloc in Eastern and Central Europe by moving the perspective away from Soviet authorities in Moscow toward actors in other places such as Poland, Estonia, and Ukraine that were participating in international debates. Transcending the ideological divide during the Cold War, period, ideas, and actors from the so-called Second World shaped heritage discourses and practices on the international level through formal and informal networks, including both scholarly exchange and tourism, as international travel increased rapidly in the postwar period. Like the volume generally, the chapters here highlight the contributions from this part of the world that have often been disregarded or ignored as a result of the rupture of 1989–91, thus continuing a general trend of epistemic asymmetry and moving Eastern European thought to the margins of analysis.[56]

The way heritage was incorporated in international exchanges while at the same time promoting ideas emerging from socialist conceptions of culture is demonstrated in Corinne Geering's opening chapter: "The Past Belongs to the Future: Heritage in Soviet Policymaking on Cultural Development." Her study of cultural policies in the Soviet Union highlights that heritage-making was not simply a case of transmitting state-sanctioned versions of the past and showcasing a vision of progress to the international community. Soviet policymakers and heritage experts harnessed tourism and official itineraries to conceive of heritage as a resource for economic development and public education in socialist countries. Geering shows how cultural heritage had been linked to the future already in the early Soviet policies, from 1917 and then throughout the 1920s, and highlights how this discourse took new shape in an era of intensifying international exchange from the 1960s onward. At the same time, international organizations began employing heritage for cultural development, with socialist practices and ideas contributing to what became the United Nations World Decade for Cultural Development, which, running from 1988–97, spanned the collapse of the USSR. The history presented in this chapter traces the build-up to this initiative, thus demonstrating beyond geopolitical rupture the continuities of ideas that ultimately outlasted state socialism.

The significant contributions of the Eastern and Central European region to global conceptions of heritage are particularly evident in the case of Poland. The second chapter in this section focuses on the activities of some of the same international bodies, in particular UNESCO, in the context of the Auschwitz-Birkenau Memorial and Museum, a globally recognized site bearing testimony to the Holocaust and Nazi persecution. Julia Röttjer's chapter, "International Experts—National Martyrdom—Socialist Heritage: The Contribution of the Polish People's Republic to the Early UNESCO World Heritage Program," shows how nascent international definitions of heritage were transformed by encounters with socialist conceptions of heritage, which drew on established cultural memory tropes. In the Polish People's Republic, Auschwitz was initially framed first and foremost as a site of national suffering and martyrdom, as well as an emblem of antifascist struggle, thus embodying socialist internationalist narratives of the past. An international group of experts' encounter with this site, which Poland proposed as one of the first UNESCO World Heritage sites in the late 1970s, contributed to a transformation of UNESCO's conception of sites of "outstanding universal value," thus broadening the initial focus on aesthetically and culturally valuable sites. Alongside the Old Towns of Warsaw and Kraków or the Wieliczka Salt Mine, Auschwitz was included in the UNESCO World Heritage List as a site embodying "negative historical values," thereby setting a precedent for inscription of sites dealing with the history of slavery and imprisonment. Röttjer notes that international visitors to the site during the socialist period were already struck by the care taken by the authorities for a site of dark heritage, which despite being framed with national interest in mind, ultimately transformed international parameters of UNESCO World Heritage.

In addition to demonstrating the contributions of the socialist bloc to the globalization of heritage institutions and discourses, this section highlights two particularly innovative aspects of this volume: firstly, the intraregional internationalization of heritage within the socialist bloc, and, secondly, individual Soviet republics' efforts to develop heritage practices and policies relatively independently of the Moscow center. Both of these aspects in turn fed back into socialist-era and postsocialist nation-building agendas that were particularly evident in the tourism sector. Iryna Sklokina's chapter, "International Tourism and the Making of the National Heritage Canon in Late Soviet Ukraine, 1964–1991," explores the growth of international visitors to Soviet Ukraine. From an initial focus on tourists associated with Soviet-approved émigré organizations in the mid-1960s, the scope of tourism expanded to include visitors not necessarily seeking affirmation of official narratives in itineraries that mixed traditions of historical state-building with industrial modernity. The entanglement of continuities with the past with projections of present successes and future transformations was most evident around Zaporizhia, where Cossack heritage, vast dams, and factories were woven into tour guides' narratives. As most tourists came from the North American diaspora or neighboring socialist states, particularly Poland, Hungary, and Romania, and had family connections to Ukraine, they demanded opportunities to visit relatives and former homelands. Especially in Western Ukraine, visitors increasingly sought recognition of their national group's contribution to what had been multiethnic spaces, and Jewish visitors to Kyiv challenged the absence of recognition of the Babyn Yar massacre. While officials sought to ensure tours reflected efforts to present heritage that was "national in form" and "socialist in content," this principle proved difficult to maintain, both at the scale of relations between tourists and guides, and at the level of tourist infrastructure. As Corinne Geering's chapter also shows, the commercialization of culture long before *perestroika* combined attempts to present socialist values to international audiences with infrastructural development. In tourism, it becomes clear that the financial benefits often could trump ideological demands and nationalist-oriented objectives.

A similar decentralizing perspective on heritage practices and policies in the Soviet Union is projected in Karin Hallas-Murula's and Kaarel Truu's contribution on Estonia, which in 1961 became the first Soviet republic to adopt a law on preservation. Their chapter, "International Contacts and Cooperation in Heritage Preservation in Soviet Estonia, 1960–1990," continues the themes of nation-building and international travel with a particular focus on contacts within socialist Eastern and Central Europe, especially those with Polish restorers. Hallas-Murula and Truu highlight the frictions, both productive and disruptive, of national and socialist aspects of heritage, as well as continuities with interwar networks of heritage experts. Estonian scholars maintained contacts with colleagues in other Baltic Soviet republics, as well as in Finland and Sweden, with these networks translating over time into nonstate organizations such as the Estonian Heritage Society, which laid foundations for an independent Estonia in 1991. Its emergence demonstrates the complex relations of conformity and disobedience that characterized officials' relations with the Soviet authorities whose permission was needed for the international networking trips that shaped the Estonian school of heritage, which alongside Lithuanian practices and policy was particularly pioneering in the USSR in protecting the urban built environment. This status enabled experts in the individual Soviet republics to maintain their own limited international relations and become visible on the international stage of professional and scholarly exchanges. The case study of Tallinn's Old Town highlights how the ready availability of local expertise produced tensions over both the construction of meaning of a site and the methods used to preserve it. The Polish Conservation Workshops (PKZ), seen as an international gold standard for restoration at the time, were brought to Tallinn for their first project in the USSR in preparation for the 1980 Moscow Olympics. The Polish restorers' methods were critiqued by Estonian colleagues who were confident in their own approaches that had been shaped by interwar and recent contacts with Scandinavia. Encounters like this highlight that intrabloc cooperation in the field of heritage could entail disagreement, or even rivalry, among members of the socialist bloc.

What emerges in this section from the study of cultural development, international standard-setting instruments like UNESCO World Heritage, the construction of national canons through tourism, and finally international contacts between restorers are processes of intraregional internationalization in Eastern and Central Europe. These international contacts at least partially continued along the trajectories of interwar expert networks, while at the same time carving out new realms for experts, state authorities, and other stakeholders to engage with the conscious shaping of socialist conceptions of heritage between 1945 and 1991. The canonization of sites that today continue to attract millions of visitors annually also involved discussion and, at times, contestation over the way the past should be interpreted and presented to this audience. The case studies explored in this section thus extend the analysis of issues into the socialist period that have otherwise been primarily the topic of research dealing with postsocialist heritage.

Heritage, Place, and Belonging under Socialism

Debate, negotiation, and contestation become evident when shifting the analysis onto specific heritage sites and discourses on the ground. How nationally and transnationally inflected heritage discourses and practices were both transformed and implemented at the local level is the central focus of the second part of this volume: "Canonizing and Contesting the Past: Heritage, Place, and Belonging under Socialism." The four contributions to this section explore the ways in which heritage contributed to place-making and creating a sense of belonging in local communities, demonstrating how approaches devised by heritage experts and state authorities were still in the making, thus also leaving some room for diverging ideas. The local processes intersected in various ways with top-down projections of ideology and nation-building projects in socialist states. The case studies from Hungary, Romania, Czechoslovakia, and the German Democratic Republic (GDR) demonstrate that the state apparatus in socialist countries enabled a degree of autonomy on community levels—whether in specific localities or institutions—and was influenced by both the expertise and demands of citizens. This section emphasizes the multiple actors involved in heritage-making and interpretation on the ground: administrators and politicians, heritage experts, institutions, and the visitors of heritage sites, including local residents and international tourists. The chapters here also suggest that it was not simply the case that the authorities could draw on national frameworks of identification to generate authority and legitimacy. Rather they had to engage with local, regional, or institutional specificities, including finding ways of incorporating legacies of troubling or officially delegitimized historical periods into popular narratives or expert knowledge.

Despite ideologies of progress toward a modernized socialist nation, prerevolutionary practices in preserving castles or visiting bourgeois stately homes, for example, remained part of official socialist cultural life. Neither the institutional and intellectual legacies of the interwar canons of heritage sites, including lists of protected sites and the value attached to them, nor the past generally could simply be remade according to a state-sanctioned grand narrative. Equally, shared visions of an internationalist utopian future were also shaped from the bottom-up through placemaking that could be related to a diverse array of sites. Royal palaces and parliament buildings, historical city centers, manor houses, and industrial heritage are offered as case studies in the chapters here. Under socialism, they could be reframed as part of efforts to align the past with present demands and future visions of nation-building, or they could offer an ideologically sound focus on proletarian labor and skilled craftsmanship. The outcome of such canonization processes, however, was often contested in the context of changing political, historical, and aesthetic circumstances, and always with reference to particular sites and their role in efforts to generate a sense of belonging to communities on various scales.

Eszter Gantner's contribution, "Socialist Royalty? The Ambiguities of the Reconstruction of the Royal Residence in Budapest in the 1950s," further develops the theme of international contacts within socialist Eastern and Central Europe from the first section of this volume. Her chapter embeds contacts between restorers from Hungary with those from neighboring countries in the story of how socialist regimes consciously emphasized particular historical layers when creating a sense of continuity with the socialist present through the reconstruction of heritage sites destroyed in World War II. Gantner shows how debates over the restoration of Buda Castle, the historical seat of royal power and a canonical site of Hungarian national history, involved a range of actors with competing interests, from Party leaders through journalists and academics to the general public, as well as international heritage experts. As in Tallinn, the Polish company PKZ was consulted on plans for reconstruction projects in Budapest. The site of Buda Castle was reconfigured both in terms of aesthetics and intended use several times in the postwar period, being shaped by shifting policies of socialist Hungary. While aesthetic values remained contested, often because of their bourgeois connotations, the Royal Palace's significance was framed each time in a manner that sought to maintain a sense of continuity with the past and build legitimacy for the policies of the ruling Communist authorities. A focus on opening up this site to the public, rather than reaffirming its exclusivity as the seat of power, came after the Hungarian uprising and Soviet intervention in 1956. Efforts to reverse this trend are becoming evident in today's Hungary, as Gantner shows. The history of the reconstruction of the Castle Hill complex illustrates the entanglements of socialist nation-building within Hungary, internationalization of heritage within the region, and the ongoing significance of a broader European history of art that, despite ideological wariness, remained central to socialist conceptions of heritage.

Urban heritage, the relation of expertise and ideology, and the relevance of interwar networks are further explored in Liliana Iuga's chapter dealing with socialist Romania. Her contribution, titled "Justifying Demolition, Questioning Value: Urban Typologies and the Concept of the 'Historic Town' in 1960s Romania," reveals how heritage experts negotiated recognition for Romania's diverse urban planning traditions stemming from the Ottoman and Habsburg Empires while also reflecting the arguments for radical reconstruction promoted by modernist architects in interwar Romania. Iuga sets ideas and practices of urban conservation in Romania in the context of international debates on the subject, with the architectural historian Gheorghe Curinschi proving a key actor in maintaining and developing knowledge in socialist Romania of discussions across Europe. His broad interests intersected with the country's regional diversity, which was shaped by the imperial past and challenged arguments for the existence of a single national architectural style. Instead, the debates in state institutions and professional organizations often drew on the interwar discourse of international modernist ideas for ideal cities and radical remodeling, thus demonstrating the extent of continuities in socialist conceptions of heritage that were ultimately realized in the construction of Bucharest's new city center under Ceaușescu. However, this canonical site of Romania's "socialist transformation of cities" was actually an outlier and exception. As Iuga shows, a singular Romanian model of urban heritage protection under socialism cannot be posited; instead, a patchwork emerges shaped by limited resources, competing discourses, and regional specificities, with value ascribed to urban heritage according to established European aesthetic values.

Regional difference and the intersection of the broader vision of modernist socialist transformation with efforts to rework official heritage canons are also elaborated in Čeněk Pýcha's chapter: "Making Sense of Socialism through Heritage Preservation: Stories from Northwest Bohemia." Largely inhabited by German populations before their expulsion in the wake of World War II, this area was doubly remade by ethnic cleansing and becoming part of a socialist state. As a single case study, the Duchcov viaduct and monument might illustrate ideologically motivated canonization of heritage sites in a socialist state, as a railway viaduct unremarkable in aesthetic and engineering terms was afforded the status of national cultural monument, making it an equal of Prague Castle. The viaduct was protected because an interwar workers' protest was violently crushed there. This event was subsequently incorporated into the Czechoslovak historical account of socialist revolution, leading to the erection of a memorial at the site. The Duchcov viaduct therefore combined two new forms of heritage-making, by, firstly, commemorating the workers' movement and, secondly, adding industrial heritage to the canon of sites deemed worthy of inclusion in the state's heritage registries. As a result, a local workers' protest was inscribed as a nationally significant event. Set in the comparative context, however, Pýcha demonstrates that the significance attached to heritage sites by their users was not easily determined from above by official canonization efforts. Visits to manor houses and gentry estates retained their long-established popularity despite the efforts to push through a new "authorized heritage discourse."[57] The limits of state power as an arbiter of what was deemed of national historical importance were laid bare by the failure to ensure the local grounding of the value of the site. Indeed, socialist modernization based on an extraction economy, with opencast mining tearing through the landscape, ultimately led to the disavowal of the significance of this site, a situation that was compounded by the collapse of socialism.

Industrial heritage remains one of the categories that is most readily associated with socialist aesthetics. That this type of heritage actually has a history reaching back into the pre-World War II period is one of the topics discussed in Nele-Hendrikje Lehmann's concluding chapter: "Socialism and the Rise of Industrial Heritage: The Preservation of Industrial Monuments in the German Democratic Republic." She shows how the prewar recognition of "technical cultural monuments" in Germany informed heritage policy and practices in the GDR and later the broader international discourse that developed out of diverse national traditions of preserving the industrial past. In the GDR, "industrial monuments" were already protected from the 1950s as a result of interactions between local authorities, *Heimat* (homeland) societies, a legacy of the prewar period, and centralized ideas of socialist nation-building that promoted different ideas and loci of belonging. Lehmann finds that over time, particularly in the 1970s, industrial heritage was no longer the focal point of the GDR nation-building project but one part of a broader canon that sought to reincorporate the key sites of German history, including Prussian history and the Lutheran Reformation. At the same time, the GDR was among the pioneers of the internationalization of industrial heritage; as one of a few states, alongside Poland and the United Kingdom, to systematically preserve the industrial past in the 1950s already, the GDR could take a leading role at the First International Congress on the Conservation of Industrial Monuments held in Ironbridge, United Kingdom, in 1973. The international committee organizing this event provided a forum where socialist heritage ideas could contribute to the development of international standards, while also being transformed by these international-level expert discussions, just as they had been by reinterpretations of established traditions on the level of local *Heimat* societies in previous decades. In the case of industrial heritage in the GDR, as well as for the issues discussed in preceding chapters, it becomes clear that socialist interpretations of the tangible past emerged from interactions between actors on the local, national, and international levels.

The discussions on industrial heritage in both Czechoslovakia and the GDR also point to the historical layers underlying efforts to create a new national canon under socialism that experts, authorities, and other actors were confronted with. Indeed, all the examples explored in this section also prompt a reassessment of what aesthetics and practices may be associated with the ideology of socialism, as traditions stemming from the interwar and imperial periods, as well as those connected to broader European or global processes, continued to shape heritage sites, expertise, and official discourses under socialism. As the contributions to this section make clear, specific sites and national canons, as well as heritage policy, were shaped not only by local particularities and national trajectories in the development of socialist ideology and rule in the respective locations. Processes of placemaking and canonization were also inflected by the kinds of transnational transfers and exchanges outlined in the first part of this book. And, of course, the reverse was also true—with expertise developed at sites such as Auschwitz, Warsaw and Tallinn Old Towns, Suzdal′, or Zaporizhia shaping international ideas and organizations.

Converging the Multiple Sites of Heritage under Socialism

One critique of the transnational turn has been that it can reinscribe the significance of the nation-state rather than overcome it. The contributions to this volume, in particular in the second part, show that turning to the local scale and particular places can be one way of challenging this shortcoming. In terms of the internationalization of heritage and formation of transnational heritage networks under socialism, however, the role of the state as a key actor cannot be ignored. Indeed, it was responsible for granting travel permits and organizing tours, for issuing contracts for restoration projects, and was the partner for participation in international organizations. It could be then that this volume also demonstrates the need to re-conceptualize the transnational turn to account for the role of the state in the so-called Second World, alongside the persistence of expert networks and informal contacts in the form of diasporic tourism. These themes are elaborated further by Corinne Geering in the conclusion: "Transnational Heritage Networks in Socialist Eastern and Central Europe." She discusses the central themes emerging from the transnational exchanges and interactions among heritage experts within Eastern and Central Europe, thus highlighting the overlapping and divergent spaces of internationalization in this region. While the logics of cultural diplomacy framed socialist states' activities on the international stage, it was ultimately specific actors, drawing on particular experiences and bodies of knowledge, who produced the transnational networks shaping the heritage discourses and practices in the respective countries. Moreover, by drawing on the significance of ideas and practices developed in the region for the formation of international heritage institutions, the conclusion also presents perspectives for future research on heritage under socialism.

While positing "socialist heritage" as a factor in international heritage discourse, the contributions here also highlight the local origins and intraregional dimensions of internationalization based on exchanges of ideas, practices, and expertise, as well as tourist contacts. The volume thus queries the notion of a singular socialist heritage. Instead, we find that it differed not only by national variations, but also within states, owing to subnational regional differences and also, temporally, as interpretations of socialism shifted. It is for this reason that this volume has as its central concept heritage under socialism, rather than socialist heritage. The historical contextualization guiding the volume points to both collaboration and contestation within and between socialist countries that accompanied the construction of the socialist heritage canon in the aftermath of war, genocide, and displacement in the region. What is clear from this volume is that nationalization and internationalization of heritage, likewise under socialism, are not mutually exclusive, but rather coconstitutive.

Indeed, the socialist period has left an institutional legacy in most countries, with the local, national, and international infrastructure of heritage policies shaped by events since 1945, and in particular since the 1960s. There is thus a significant portion of heritage sites that remain, at least partly, "socialist in form" from an institutional perspective, and indeed national in content as far as the narratives are concerned, just as was the case under socialism. The chapters illustrate that one way socialist rule sought legitimacy was by stressing continuities with national traditions and heritage canons. Today, though, there is a tendency toward framing heritage under socialism as a history of popular rejection of the socialist narratives rather than as a more complex interaction of contestation, reinterpretation, and acceptance. Indeed, rising nationalism and exclusionist memory politics in part of Eastern and Central Europe indicate the need to remain wary of historical accounts framing the socialist era as a time when expressions of national identity were repressed, censored, and opposed. Turning to the history of heritage shows that it was, in many cases, a time when the infrastructure, institutions, and contents forming national canons were developed further, particularly when it comes to their international recognition.

Corinne Geering leads a junior research group at the Leibniz Institute for the History and Culture of Eastern Europe (GWZO) in Leipzig. She received her PhD from the University in Giessen in 2018, where she was a doctoral fellow at the International Graduate Centre for the Study of Culture (GCSC). She has published on material culture, cultural politics, international cooperation during the Cold War, and the use of the past for regional development. She is the author of *Building a Common Past: World Heritage in Russia under Transformation, 1965–2000*.

Paul Vickers is manager of the Department for Interdisciplinary and Multiscalar Area Studies (DIMAS) and the Leibniz ScienceCampus Europe and America at the University of Regensburg, Germany. His book, *Making Popular Memory in Communist Poland*, is forthcoming.

Notes

1. See Sidorov, "National Monumentalization"; Zubovich, "The Fall of the Zariad'e."
2. Makarevich, *Prospekt Kalinina*, 48.
3. Stites, "Iconoclastic Currents in the Russian Revolution."
4. Historical research has revealed that socialist societies expressed profound interest in the past, especially from 1960s onward. See Clark, "Changing Historical Paradigms"; Haney, "The Revival of Interest in the Russian Past"; Kozlov, "The Historical Turn in Late Soviet Culture"; Colla, "The Politics of Time."
5. Campbell, "Preservation for the Masses."
6. "U.S.S.R. Today," n.pag.
7. For a more recent example of historiography that suggests that in the cultural sphere, too, Moscow could dictate policy in satellite states outside the USSR, see Babiracki, *Soviet Soft Power in Poland*.
8. See UNESCO, "What Is Meant by 'Cultural Heritage'?"
9. Ashworth, "From History to Heritage"; Nora, "Entre mémoire et histoire"; Lowenthal, "'History' und 'heritage.'"
10. L. Smith, *Uses of Heritage*.
11. Harvey, "Heritage Pasts and Heritage Presents"; Harrison, Fairclough, Jameson, and Schofield, "Introduction: Heritage, Memory and Modernity."
12. Forest and Johnson, "Unraveling the Threads of History."
13. Dmitrieva and Kliems, *The Post-Socialist City*; Kinossian, "Post-Socialist Transition."
14. Bartetzky, Dietz, and Haspel, *Von der Ablehnung zur Aneignung?*; Ingerpuu, "Socialist Architecture."
15. Plets, "Post-Soviet Heritages in the Making"; Demeter, "Regime Change and Cultural Protection."
16. See Swenson, "'Heritage,' 'Patrimoine' und 'Kulturerbe,'" 54.
17. Geering, *Building a Common Past*.
18. See Bendix, Eggert, and Peselman, *Heritage Regimes*.
19. See, for example, Harrison, *Heritage*; Falser and Juneja, *Kulturerbe und Denkmalpflege transkulturell*; Glendinning, *The Conservation Movement*.
20. Deschepper, "Between Future and Eternity."
21. Alonso González, "Communism and Cultural Heritage."
22. See Shchenkov, *Pamiatniki arkhitektury*.

23. Qualls, *From Ruins to Reconstruction*; Stangl, *Risen from Ruins*; Fuchs, *Städtebau und Legitimation*.
24. For an overview of how socialist regimes created historical memory and used the past as a source of legitimacy, see Mrozik and Holubec, *Historical Memory*.
25. See Plum, *Antifascism after Hitler*; Marples, *Historical Memory and World War II*; Qualls, "Where Each Stone Is History."
26. On Holocaust memory in socialist Czechoslovakia and Hungary, see Hallama, *Nationale Helden und jüdische Opfer*; Fritz, *Nach Krieg und Judenmord*.
27. See Etkind et al, *Remembering Katyń*.
28. For case studies of particular borderland cities and regions, see Amar, *The Paradox of Ukrainian Lviv*; Brodersen, *Die Stadt im Westen*; Glassheim, *Cleansing the Czechoslovak Borderlands*; Thum, *Uprooted*.
29. See Bernhard and Kubik, *Twenty Years after Communism*; Mink and Neumayer, *History, Memory and Politics*.
30. Mark, *The Unfinished Revolution*.
31. Rampley, *Heritage, Ideology, and Identity*.
32. On Poland, see Wawrzyniak, *Veterans, Victims, and Memory*. On Russia and the Soviet Union, see Wertsch, *Voices of Collective Remembering*.
33. For an argument making such claims, see, for example, Zaremba, *Communism, Legitimacy, Nationalism*.
34. This is outlined in Rączkowski, "'Drang nach Westen.'" The discourses were particularly prevalent in the initial postwar years and revived around the time of the Polish millennium in 1966.
35. Kamusella, *The Un-Polish Poland*, 103–4. The online exhibition of the Polish History Museum also offers a particularly clear, English-language outline of this narrative in Muzeum Historii Polski/ Polish History Museum, "Shifting Poland."
36. See Hobsbawm and Ranger, *The Invention of Tradition*.
37. Watson, "Memory, History and Opposition," 2. This contrasts with, for example, implication that contestation and public debates emerged only with communism's collapse and following "enforced official mnemonical stasis," as Maria Mälksoo's article on postsocialist East European memory politics suggests. Mälksoo, "The Memory Politics," 672, 659.
38. See the contributions in Thatcher, *The State and Historic Buildings: Preserving "The National Past."*
39. Thatcher, "Introduction: The State and Historical Buildings," 38.
40. Spechler, *Permitted Dissent*.
41. See Weiner, *A Little Corner of Freedom*.
42. Long, "Modernity, Socialism and Heritage in Asia."
43. Todorova, "Introduction: From Utopia to Propaganda and Back."
44. Mark, Kalinovsky, and Marung, *Alternative Globalizations*.
45. Babiracki and Jersild, *Socialist Internationalism in the Cold War*.
46. Alonso González, *Cuban Cultural Heritage*; Odom and Salmond, *Treasures into Tractors*; Grama, *Socialist Heritage*.
47. Telepneva, "A Cultural Heritage for National Liberation?"; Cowcher, "The Museum as Prison."
48. Donovan, *Chronicles in Stone*; Kelly, "'Ispravliat' li istoriiu?'"; Maddox, *Saving Stalin's Imperial City*.

49. Takahashi, "Church or Museum?"; S. A. Smith, "Contentious Heritage"; Kelly, *Socialist Churches*.
50. For the Soviet Union, see Bekus, "Transnational Circulation of Cultural Form."
51. See also Jalava, Nygård, and Strang, *Decentering European Intellectual Space*.
52. See, among others, Mikkonen and Koivunen, *Beyond the Divide*; Autio-Sarasmo and Miklóssy, *Reassessing Cold War Europe*; Mikkonen and Suutari, *Music, Art and Diplomacy*; Kohlrausch and Trischler, *Building Europe on Expertise*.
53. Péteri, "Nylon Curtain," 115.
54. The image of Kalinin Prospekt as a place of consumption and leisure is clear in contemporary presentation of the project. Cf. Makarevich, *Prospekt Kalinina*.
55. For example, Gfeller, "Preserving Cultural Heritage across the Iron Curtain"; Falser and Lipp, *Eine Zukunft für unsere Vergangenheit*. In his seminal study on the conservation movement, Miles Glendinning even differentiates between "a Western-bloc narrative, a socialist-bloc narrative and finally a growing internationalist narrative that mediated between the others," thus limiting the internationalist narrative to a space transcending the realm of one side of the Cold War divide. Glendinning, *The Conservation Movement*, 259.
56. See Trencsényi et al., *A History of Modern Political Thought*; Buden, "Translation and the East." This process has also been repeated elsewhere in the history of ideas. Offering an illustration from the field of economics, Johanna Bockman's transnational history draws attention to how Eastern and Central Europe served both as an empirical testbed and as a space from which ideas that have come to shape twenty-first century global norms have emerged. Bockman, *Markets in the Name of Socialism*.
57. L. Smith, *Uses of Heritage*.

Bibliography

Alonso González, Pablo. "Communism and Cultural Heritage: The Quest for Continuity." *International Journal of Heritage Studies* 22, no. 9 (2016): 653–63.

———. *Cuban Cultural Heritage: A Rebel Past for a Revolutionary Nation*. Gainesville: University of Florida Press, 2018.

Ashworth, G. J. "From History to Heritage: From Heritage to Identity: In Search of Concepts and Models." In *Building a New Heritage: Tourism, Culture and Identity in the New Europe*, edited by G. J. Ashworth and P. J. Larkham, 13–30. London: Routledge, 1994.

Amar, Tarik Cyril. *The Paradox of Ukrainian Lviv: A Borderland City between Stalinists, Nazis, and Nationalists*. Ithaca: Cornell University Press, 2015.

Autio-Sarasmi, Sari, and Katalin Miklóssy, eds. *Reassessing Cold War Europe*. London: Routledge, 2011.

Babiracki, Patryk. *Soviet Soft Power in Poland: Culture and the Making of Stalin's New Empire, 1943–1957*. Chapel Hill: University of North Carolina Press, 2015.

Babiracki, Patryk, and Austin Jersild, eds. *Socialist Internationalism in the Cold War: Exploring the Second World*. Basingstoke: Palgrave Macmillan, 2016.

Bartetzky, Arnold, Christian Dietz, and Jörg Hapsel, eds. *Von der Ablehnung zur Aneignung? Das architektonische Erbe des Sozialismus in Mittel- und Osteuropa*. Köln: Böhlau, 2014.

Bekus, Nelly. "Transnational Circulation of Cultural Form: Multiple Agencies of Heritage Making." *International Journal of Heritage Studies* 26, no. 12 (2020): 1,148–65.
Bendix, Regina F., Aditya Eggert, and Arnika Peselmann, eds. *Heritage Regimes and the State*. Göttingen: Universitätsverlag Göttingen, 2012.
Bernhard, Michael, and Jan Kubik, eds. *Twenty Years after Communism: The Politics of Memory and Commemoration*. Oxford: Oxford University Press, 2014.
Bockman, Johanna. *Markets in the Name of Socialism: The Left-Wing Origins of Neoliberalism*. Stanford: Stanford University Press, 2011.
Brodersen, Per. *Die Stadt im Westen: Wie Königsberg Kaliningrad wurde*. Göttingen: Vandenhoeck & Ruprecht, 2008.
Buden, Boris. "Translation and the East: There Is No Such Thing as an 'Eastern European Study of Culture.'" In *The Trans/National Study of Culture: A Translational Perspective*, edited by Doris Bachmann-Medick, 171–80. Berlin: De Gruyter, 2014.
Campbell, Brian. "Preservation for the Masses: The Idea of Heimat and the Gesellschaft für Denkmalpflege in the GDR." *kunsttexte.de* 3 (2004). Retrieved 13 April 2020. https://edoc.hu-berlin.de/bitstream/handle/18452/7671/campbell.pdf.
Clark, Katerina. "Changing Historical Paradigms in Soviet Culture." In *Late Soviet Culture: From Perestroika to Novostroika*, edited by Thomas Lahusen and Gene Kuperman, 289–306. Durham: Duke University Press, 1993.
Colla, Marcus. "The Politics of Time and State Identity in the German Democratic Republic." *Transactions of the Royal Historical Society* 29 (2019): 223–51.
Cowcher, Kate. "The Museum as Prison and Other Protective Measures in Socialist Ethiopia." *International Journal of Heritage Studies* 26, no. 12 (2020): 1,166–84.
Demeter, Laura. "Regime Change and Cultural Protection, a Matter of State Security." *International Journal of Heritage Studies* 25, no. 5 (2019): 522–35.
Deschepper, Julie. "Between Future and Eternity: A Soviet Conception of Heritage." *International Journal of Heritage Studies* 25, no. 5 (2019): 491–506.
Dmitrieva, Marina, and Alfrun Kliems, eds. *The Post-Socialist City: Continuity and Change in Urban Space and Imagery*. Berlin: Jovis, 2009.
Donovan, Victoria. *Chronicles in Stone: Preservation, Patriotism, and Identity in Northwest Russia*. Ithaca: Cornell University Press, 2019.
Etkind, Alexander, Rory Finnin, Uilleam Blacker, Julie Fedor, Simon Lewis, Maria Mälksoo, and Matilda Mroz. *Remembering Katyń*. Cambridge, MA: Polity, 2012.
Falser, Michael, and Monica Juneja, eds. *Kulturerbe und Denkmalpflege transkulturell: Grenzgänge zwischen Theorie und Praxis*. Bielefeld: Transcript, 2013.
Falser, Michael, and Wilfried Lipp, eds. *Eine Zukunft für unsere Vergangenheit: Zum 40. Jubiläum des Europäischen Denkmalschutzjahres (1975–2015)*. Berlin: Bässler, 2015.
Forest, Benjamin, and Juliet Johnson. "Unraveling the Threads of History: Soviet-Era Monuments and Post-Soviet National Identity in Moscow." *Annals of the Association of American Geographers* 92, no. 3 (2002): 524–47.
Fritz, Regina. *Nach Krieg und Judenmord: Ungarns Geschichtspolitik seit 1944*. Göttingen: Wallstein, 2012.
Fuchs, Jana. *Städtebau und Legitimation: Debatten um das unbebaute historische Warschauer Zentrum, 1945–1989*. Berlin: De Gruyter, 2020.
Geering, Corinne. *Building a Common Past: World Heritage in Russia under Transformation, 1965–2000*. Göttingen: Vandenhoeck & Ruprecht, 2019.

Gfeller, Aurélie Elisa. "Preserving Cultural Heritage across the Iron Curtain: The International Council on Monuments and Sites from Venice to Moscow, 1964–1978." In *Geteilt—Vereint! Denkmalpflege in Mitteleuropa zur Zeit des Eisernen Vorhangs und Heute*, edited by Ursula Schädler-Saub and Angela Weyer, 115–21. Petersberg: Michael Imhof Verlag, 2015.

Glassheim, Eagle. *Cleansing the Czechoslovak Borderlands: Migration, Environment, and Health in the Former Sudetenland*. Pittsburgh: University of Pittsburgh Press, 2016.

Glendinning, Miles. *The Conservation Movement: A History of Architectural Preservation, Antiquity to Modernity*. London: Routledge, 2013.

Grama, Emanuela. *Socialist Heritage: The Politics of Past and Place in Romania*. Bloomington: Indiana University Press, 2019.

Hallama, Peter. *Nationale Helden und jüdische Opfer: Tschechische Repräsentationen des Holocaust*. Göttingen: Vandenhoeck & Ruprecht, 2015.

Haney, Jack V. "The Revival of Interest in the Russian Past in the Soviet Union." *Slavic Review* 32, no. 1 (1973): 1–16.

Harrison, Rodney. *Heritage: Critical Approaches*. Abingdon: Routledge, 2013.

Harrison, Rodney, Graham Fairclough, John H. Jameson Jr., and John Schofield. "Introduction: Heritage, Memory and Modernity." In *The Heritage Reader*, edited by Graham Fairclough, Rodney Harrison, John H. Jameson Jnr, and John Schofield, 1–12. London: Routledge, 2008.

Harvey, D. C. "Heritage Pasts and Heritage Presents: Temporality, Meaning and the Scope of Heritage Studies." *International Journal of Heritage Studies* 7, no. 4 (2001): 319–38.

Hobsbawm, Eric, and Terence Ranger, eds. *The Invention of Tradition*. Cambridge, UK: Cambridge University Press, 1983.

Ingerpuu, Laura. "Socialist Architecture as Today's Dissonant Heritage: Administrative Buildings of Collective Farms in Estonia." *International Journal of Heritage Studies* 24, no. 9 (2018): 954–68.

Jalava, Marja, Stefan Nygård, and Johan Strang, eds. *Decentering European Intellectual Space*. Leiden: Brill, 2018.

Kamusella, Tomasz. *The Un-Polish Poland, 1989 and the Illusion of Regained Historical Continuity*. Cham: Palgrave, 2017.

Kelly, Catriona. "'Ispravliat' li istoriiu?' Spory ob okhrane pamiatnikov v Leningrade 1960–1970-kh godov." *Neprikosnovennyi zapas* 64, no. 2 (2009). Retrieved 1 April 2017. http://magazines.russ.ru/nz/2009/2/kk7.html.

———. *Socialist Churches: Radical Secularization and the Preservation of the Past in Petrograd and Leningrad, 1918–1988*. DeKalb: Northern Illinois University Press, 2016.

Kinossian, Nadir. "Post-Socialist Transition and Remaking the City: Political Construction of Heritage in Tatarstan." *Europe-Asia Studies* 64, no. 5 (2012): 879–901.

Kohlrausch, Martin, and Helmuth Trischler, eds. *Building Europe on Expertise: Innovators, Organizers, Networkers*. Basingstoke: Palgrave Macmillan, 2014.

Kozlov, Denis. "The Historical Turn in Late Soviet Culture: Retrospectivism, Factography, Doubt, 1953–91." *Kritika: Explorations in Russian and Eurasian History* 2, no. 3 (2001): 577–600.

Long, Colin. "Modernity, Socialism and Heritage in Asia." In *Routledge Handbook of Heritage in Asia*, edited by Patrick Daly and Tim Winter, 201–17. London: Routledge.

Lowenthal, David. "'History' und 'heritage': Widerstreitende und konvergente Formen der Vergangenheitsbetrachtung." In *Geschichtskultur in der Zweiten Moderne*, edited by Rosmarie Beier, 78–86. Frankfurt: Campus, 2000.

Maddox, Steven. *Saving Stalin's Imperial City: Historic Preservation in Leningrad, 1930–1950*. Bloomington: Indiana University Press, 2015.

Makarevich, G. V. *Prospekt Kalinina*. Moscow: Stroiizdat, 1975.

Mälksoo, Maria. "The Memory Politics of Becoming European: The East European Subalterns and the Collective Memory of Europe." *European Journal of International Relations* 15 (2009): 653–80.

Mark, James. *The Unfinished Revolution: Making Sense of the Communist Past in Central-Eastern Europe*. New Haven, CT: Yale University Press, 2010.

Mark, James, Artemy M. Kalinovsky, and Steffi Marung, eds. *Alternative Globalizations: Eastern Europe and the Postcolonial World*. Bloomington: Indiana University Press, 2020.

Marples, David R., ed. *Historical Memory and World War II in Russia and Ukraine*. Spec. Issue of *Canadian Slavonic Papers/Revue Canadienne des Slavistes* 54, no. 3/4 (2012).

Mikkonen, Simo, and Pia Koivunen, eds. *Beyond the Divide: Entangled Histories of Cold War Europe*. New York: Berghahn Books, 2015.

Mikkonen, Simo, and Pekka Suutari, eds. *Music, Art and Diplomacy: East–West Cultural Interactions and the Cold War*. Farnham: Ashgate, 2016.

Mink, Georges, and Laure Neumayer, eds. *History, Memory and Politics in Central and Eastern Europe: Memory Games*. Basingstoke: Palgrave Macmillan, 2013.

Mrozik, Agnieszka, and Stanislav Holubec, eds. *Historical Memory of Central and East European Communism*. New York: Routledge, 2018.

Muzeum Historii Polski/ Polish History Museum. "Shifting Poland." Google Arts & Culture. Retrieved 11 January 2021. https://artsandculture.google.com/exhibit/shifting-poland/QR9NfYtI.

Nora, Pierre. "Entre mémoire et histoire: La problématique des lieux." In *Les lieux de mémoire*, edited by Pierre Nora, 23–43. Paris: Quarto Gallimard, 1997.

Odom, Anne, and Wendy R. Salmond. *Treasures into Tractors: The Selling of Russia's Cultural Heritage, 1918–1938*, edited by Anne Odom and Wendy R. Salmond. Seattle: University of Washington Press, 2009.

Péteri, György. "Nylon Curtain—Transnational and Transsystemic Tendencies in the Cultural Life of State-Socialist Russia and East-Central Europe." *Slavonica* 10, no. 2 (2004): 113–23.

Plets, Gertjan. "Post-Soviet Heritages in the Making." *International Journal for History, Culture and Modernity* 7, no. 1 (2019): 1,080–88.

Plum, Catherine. *Antifascism after Hitler: East German Youth and Socialist Memory, 1949–1989*. New York: Routledge, 2015.

Qualls, Karl D. *From Ruins to Reconstruction: Urban Identity in Soviet Sevastopol after World War II*. Ithaca: Cornell University Press, 2009.

———. "Where Each Stone Is History: Travel Guides in Sevastopol after World War II." In *Turizm: The Russian and East European Tourist under Capitalism and Socialism*, edited by Anne E. Gorsuch and Diane P. Koenker, 163–85. Ithaca: Cornell University Press, 2006.

Rączkowski, Włodzimierz. "'Drang nach Westen'? Polish Archaeology and National Identity." In *Nationalism and Archaeology in Europe*, edited by Margarita Díaz-Andreu and Timothy Champion, 189–217. London: Routledge, 1996.

Rampley, Matthew, ed. *Heritage, Ideology, and Identity in Central and Eastern Europe: Contested Pasts, Contested Presents*. Woodbridge: Boydell Press, 2012.

Shchenkov, A. S, ed. *Pamiatniki arkhitektury v Sovetskom Soiuze: Ocherki istorii arkhitekturnoi restavratsii*. Moscow: Pamiatniki istoricheskoi mysli, 2004.

Sidorov, Dmitri. "National Monumentalization and the Politics of Scale: The Resurrections of the Cathedral of Christ the Savior in Moscow." *Annals of the Association of American Geographers* 90, no. 3 (2000): 548–72.

Smith, Laurajane. *Uses of Heritage*. London: Routledge, 2006.

Smith, S. A. "Contentious Heritage: The Preservation of Churches and Temples in Communist and Post-Communist Russia and China." In *Heritage in the Modern World*, edited by Paul Betts and Corey Ross. Spec. issue of *Past & Present* 226, no. 10 (2015): 178–212.

Spechler, Dina. *Permitted Dissent in the USSR: Novy Mir and the Soviet Regime*. New York: Praeger, 1982.

Stangl, Paul. *Risen from Ruins. The Cultural Politics of Rebuilding East Berlin*. Stanford: Stanford University Press, 2018.

Stites, Richard. "Iconoclastic Currents in the Russian Revolution: Destroying and Preserving the Past." In *Bolshevik Culture*, edited by Abbott Gleason, Peter Kenez, and Richard Stites, 1–24. Bloomington: Indiana University Press, 1985.

Swenson, Astrid. "'Heritage,' 'Patrimoine' und 'Kulturerbe': Eine vergleichende historische Semantik." In *Prädikat 'Heritage': Wertschöpfung aus kulturellen Ressourcen*, edited by Dorothee Hemme, Markus Tauschek, and Regina Bendix, 53–74. Münster: LIT Verlag, 2007.

Takahashi, Sanami. "Church or Museum? The Role of State Museums in Conserving Church Buildings, 1965–1985." *Journal of Church and State* 51, no. 3 (2009): 502–17.

Telepneva, Natalia. "A Cultural Heritage for National Liberation? The Soviet-Somali Historical Expedition, Soviet African Studies, and the Cold War in the Horn of Africa." *International Journal of Heritage Studies* 26, no. 12 (2020): 1,185–202.

Thatcher, Mark. "Introduction: The State and Historic Buildings: Preserving 'the National Past.'" *Nations and Nationalism* 24, no. 1 (2018): 22–42.

———. *The State and Historic Buildings: Preserving "The National Past."* Themed Section in *Nations and Nationalism* 24, no. 1 (2018): 22–147.

Thum, Gregor. *Uprooted: How Breslau Became Wrocław during the Century of Expulsions*. Princeton: Princeton University Press, 2011.

Todorova, Maria. "Introduction: From Utopia to Propaganda and Back." In *Post-Communist Nostalgia*, edited by Maria Todorova and Zsuzsa Gille, 1–14. New York: Berghahn Books, 2010.

Trencsényi, Balázs, Maciej Janowski, Monika Baar, Maria Falina, and Michal Kopeček. *A History of Modern Political Thought in East Central Europe*. Volume 1: *Negotiating Modernity in the "Long Nineteenth Century."* Oxford: Oxford University Press, 2016.

UNESCO. "What Is Meant by 'Cultural Heritage'?" UNESCO. Retrieved 27 June 2019. http://www.unesco.org/new/en/culture/themes/illicit-trafficking-of-cultural-property/unesco-database-of-national-cultural-heritage-laws/frequently-asked-questions/definition-of-the-cultural-heritage/.

"U.S.S.R. Today." *The UNESCO Courier* 20 (1967): n.pag.

Watson, Rubie S. "Memory, History and Opposition under State Socialism: An Introduction." In *Memory, History and Opposition under State Socialism*, edited by Rubie S. Watson, 1–20. Santa Fe: School of American Research Press, 1994.

Wawrzyniak, Joanna. *Veterans, Victims, and Memory: The Politics of the Second World War in Communist Poland*. Frankfurt am Main: Peter Lang, 2015.

Weiner, Douglas R. *A Little Corner of Freedom: Russian Nature Protection from Stalin to Gorbachëv*. Berkeley: University of California Press, 1999.

Wertsch, James V. *Voices of Collective Remembering*. Cambridge, UK: Cambridge University Press, 2002.

Zaremba, Marcin. *Communism, Legitimacy, Nationalism: Nationalist Legitimization of the Communist Regime in Poland*. Berlin: Peter Lang, 2019.

Zubovich, Katherine. "The Fall of the Zariad'e: Monumentalism and Displacement in Late Stalinist Moscow." *Kritika: Explorations in Russian and Eurasian History* 21, no. 1 (2020): 73–95.

PART I

Transfers and Exchanges in Heritage Policies and Practices

CHAPTER 1

The Past Belongs to the Future
Heritage in Soviet Policymaking on Cultural Development

Corinne Geering

"Without the heritage of capitalist culture, we are unable to build socialism," claimed V. I. Lenin as cited in a monograph by a Belarusian historian on historical and cultural monuments from 1978.[1] The author of this monograph, V. B. Korotkevich, argued that the more Soviet society focused on the future, the more defined its concern for the past would become. The quote by Lenin reflects this complex relationship between change and continuity in socialist attitudes toward the past that has recently attracted renewed scholarly interest.[2] While revolutionary movements tended to radically break with the past, they also sought to gain control over historical narratives and material traces of the past in order to legitimize and build the new political order. Therefore, rather than declare a blank slate, the goal of revolutionary governments was to display in a teleological fashion a historical tradition leading up to the present and into the future.[3] Against this background, and in line with Marxist–Leninist ideology, Soviet policymaking regarded the preservation and use of heritage as a resource in the continuous construction of the future communist society.[4] Throughout the twentieth century, these policies were articulated in a global climate saturated by a belief in progress, thus shaping what some researchers have referred to as the development century.[5]

This chapter discusses the Soviet conception of heritage in the context of policymaking on cultural development. The notion of cultural development here encompasses both the idea of developing culture (e.g., by providing a society with education) and the principle of increasing economic and social progress by means of cultural resources. Historical artifacts, buildings, and sites have been acknowledged by international organizations as a resource of economic development, especially in the context of the United Nations development initiatives from the 1960s onward. By focusing on the issue of development, this chapter seeks to analyze the socioeconomic dimensions of heritage-making, which have received considerably less attention in scholarship in comparison with accounts dealing with historical narratives and expertise. Due to the ideological focus on the social dimension of heritage-making, the case of socialist states, in particular the Soviet Union, offers insightful contributions to the discussion of how heritage served as a resource in cultural development in the twentieth century. The tensions between the Soviet regime's ideological foundation in European modernity and its "desire to offer alternatives to Western capitalism, nationalism, imperialism, and colonialism"[6] open up perspectives on heritage as a resource that extend beyond prevailing analytical frameworks in current research on heritage and cultural development. While historical research has revealed the role of postcolonial politics in international heritage debates in both the West and the Global South,[7] socialist states have so far received considerably less attention in this respect.[8]

Given the expansion of the concept of heritage in international policymaking since the 1960s that gradually integrated elements from different fields, the historical research in this chapter does not rely only on documents dealing specifically with preservation. The analysis also looks into documents dealing with education and culture more broadly in order to highlight the changes and continuities in heritage-making in the Soviet Union. Therefore, this chapter uses statements by Soviet experts as well as legal documents enacted by the Soviet state and its federal subjects. Further, UNESCO and their international forums, such as the roundtables and world conferences on cultural policies organized since 1967, reveal the changing role of heritage in the international arena that again shaped the Soviet understanding of cultural development. The sources used in this chapter indicate the crucial importance of development politics in the internationalization of heritage during the Cold War, while also shedding light on the role of socialist policymaking in this global history.

The following discussion is structured in three parts that analyze how heritage was presented and used as a resource for cultural development in Soviet policymaking between 1917 and 1991. It first introduces the notion of heritage as a resource and outlines the general role attributed to heritage in Soviet policies. In the second part, it shows how these policies were articulated in an era of intensifying international exchange after World War II and in the course of decolonization. The third and final part ends with the launch of the United Nations World Decade for Cultural Development (WDCD) in 1988. This program set the scene for initiatives that have since shaped present-day international heritage policies. Although socialist states had been instrumental in conceiving the WDCD, the simultaneous collapse of state socialism and the end of the Cold War contributed to the omission of the expertise from socialist states in subsequent historical accounts dealing with heritage policies. By tracing Soviet policymaking on heritage, this chapter thus reveals how socialist notions of heritage shaped international policies. It therefore addresses issues regarding the social, political, and economic role of heritage in the second half of the twentieth century that have so far been marginal to existing research.

Heritage as a Resource for Development in Policymaking

At first glance, heritage and development appear to be opposites, referring to two different temporalities of past-preserving and future-making. Accordingly, heritage as the discourse and practice of preservation would be perceived as a barrier to the further transformation of historical buildings, objects, and practices. However, researchers investigating historic conservation, urban planning, and environmentalism have pointed out that the concept and practices of heritage emerged as part of a new approach to planning and managing natural resources in the late nineteenth century. New building principles introduced policies in urban development aimed at permanence, while shortages of natural resources sparked debates on future resource management.[9] Against this background, the modern notion of heritage has been framed as "a resource of value to the present and the future, a driver or enabler of development," as Paul Basu and Wayne Modest have argued recently.[10]

Heritage had served as a driver of development for decades before, conversely, development found its way into policies dealing specifically with preservation following what has been termed the cultural turn in development.[11] Several international organizations—including the United Nations Educational, Scientific and Cultural Organization (UNESCO); the International Bank for Reconstruction and Development (World Bank); and the Council of Europe—started implementing heritage-related development projects in the postwar period. Especially in tourism, heritage has been used and promoted as a resource that could revive local and regional economies.[12] Against this background, global historiographies of heritage have shown that the preservation of objects, buildings, and sites—together known as monuments at the time—is not an end in itself. Rather, these monuments served the purpose of economic, political, social, and cultural development, and must thus be interpreted in the context of these histories.

The idea of cultural development emerged alongside economic and political development in the modern period when it was employed by states and empires to implement Enlightenment policies among the populace in their colonies and peripheral territories. From their inception, Soviet heritage policies focused on the economic relevance of heritage as property and its political role as a resource in education. Early Soviet policies therefore also drew on the idea and practice of the civilizing mission, in particular in the former tsarist colonies in Central Asia.[13] In the ideology of Marxism–Leninism, the cultural development of the Soviet people was inseparably linked to economic and political development. Once their culture had been transformed, this ideology claimed, the people would be able to build a new proletarian culture under communism.[14] In this understanding, cultural development is taken to mean a set of cultural initiatives aiming at far-reaching social transformation by adapting the populace to changing working conditions and technological innovation, and encouraging them to comply with the political objectives of socialism. Following the October Revolution, the preservation of cultural heritage was greatly affected by the efforts of the Bolshevik government to nationalize all property, which made the state the primary custodian of historical objects. The heritage of the past was declared to "belong to all people," and the revolutionary policies of the Council of People's Commissars regulated the movable cultural property of museums, libraries, educational facilities, and other public institutions including churches. The council issued several decrees on the collecting, registering, and protection of historical, scientific, and artistic objects.[15] While these decrees formally sought to protect cultural heritage from looting and illicit export, the registration procedure also allowed for the organized sale of valuable objects by the financially stricken Soviet Union in auction houses abroad.[16] The beginnings of heritage policies in the Soviet Union, often hailed by Soviet publications as the first systematic policies in Russia, were therefore driven by economic considerations and entailed the commodification of heritage, regardless of the new socialist economic policies.

The centralization of institutional competencies in heritage protection and preservation remained a work in progress until the disintegration of the Soviet Union, which reflected the competing claims of conservation, education and cultural policies, and spatial planning. In the early Soviet Union, heritage conservation initially formed part of education policies, as it was subsumed alongside other cultural institutions under the People's Commissariat of Enlightenment (Narkompros).[17] Thus, the domain of policies dealing with culture was considerably broader than the Soviet nationality policy's notion of cultural "blossoming" (*raztsvet*), which some researchers have also translated as cultural development.[18] Instead, the ultimate goal of cultural development was the education of the "new man" who would be able to build communism. In the 1920s and 1930s, this approach manifested itself in the large-scale literacy campaigns aimed at transforming the agrarian state into an industrial one. Attempts at establishing a separate Commissariat of the Arts to distinguish arts from education were at first rejected;[19] but eventually, a State Committee for Arts was established in 1936, which included a department overseeing the preservation of monuments. The destruction of historical buildings and the loss of artistic objects suffered in World War II demanded immediate safeguarding measures, thus leading to the establishment of new institutions dealing with preservation and reconstruction during the war already.[20] In 1948, the responsibilities were handed to the federal subjects of the Soviet Union, which was confirmed in the first all-union law on preservation in 1976.[21] The approach to preservation as a domain of both federal governance and local politics remained prevalent as a structure embedded in Soviet democratic centralism.

The lack of centralized competencies was reflected in the existence of several parallel institutions responsible for the preservation, documentation, and dissemination of cultural heritage. In addition to the State Committee for the Arts, a State Committee for Architecture was formed at the Soviet Council of Ministers in 1943, which oversaw the reconstruction projects in the Soviet Union following World War II. Thus, heritage increasingly became the concern of town planners, which was reflected in the integration of this committee into the State Committee for Construction in the Soviet Union (Gosstroi) in 1950. Finally, in 1953, the first all-union level institution dealing with culture as a distinct field of politics, the USSR Ministry of Culture, was established on the basis of the earlier State Committee of the Arts. In the following decades, this Ministry dealt with the preservation, documentation, and dissemination of monuments in collaboration with town and regional planning institutions, restoration workshops, the Academies of Sciences, and increasingly, in most Soviet republics, with voluntary preservation societies. The scope of responsibilities and the nature of cooperation between these institutions were the subject of several reforms in the post-Stalin Soviet Union and remained unclear until the union's disintegration.[22]

With the establishment of new institutions in the postwar years, the interest of the Soviet government in the issue of cultural heritage increased visibly during the 1960s. On the one hand, this was reflected in the expansion of collaboration with international organizations in this field, especially UNESCO and the International Council on Monuments and Sites (ICOMOS). On the other hand, the governing bodies of the Soviet republics turned to the preservation and popularization of cultural heritage against the backdrop of what researchers have referred to as the historical turn of the post-Stalin era. According to Victoria Donovan, after the 22nd Congress of the Communist Party in 1961, the official deployment of history became one component in the broader strategy of popular mobilization on the path toward communism. N. S. Khrushchev, the First Secretary of the Communist Party of the Soviet Union (CPSU), rejected the idea of preservation as an end in itself, instead maintaining that it should be put to use for ideological purposes.[23] Several studies have analyzed the historical narratives at play and examined specific cases of the preservation of selected towns and individual buildings, in particular in Leningrad.[24] However, further driving forces behind heritage preservation have received less attention, meaning that the Soviet approach to heritage has often been framed outside the context of the global trends of the period. This argument is substantiated here by looking at how the fields of education and tourism fostered the preservation and shaped the use of cultural heritage from the 1960s until the *perestroika* reforms in the 1980s.

International Development, Tourism, and Communist Education

The notion of cultural development as a distinct form of development found its way into international forums that were concerned with cultural policies in the late 1960s. This process was advanced by the first United Nations Development Decade adopted in 1961, which was one of a total of four to come through 2000. The content and practice of cultural development, as well as the relation to economy and politics, remain subjects of ongoing scholarly and political debate. For the postwar policies, we may distinguish between two modes of cultural development that emphasize the economy or education, respectively, although they often overlapped. The first mode of cultural development aimed at developing culture and in most states was considered until the 1960s part of education policies that were directed at the general population. The second mode used culture as a resource for socioeconomic development of specific territories. These two modes are outlined below with regard to the Soviet Union in order to discuss the role heritage played in cultural development policies, both in socialist states and in the international debates, in the postwar period.

In publications by Soviet scholars, in accordance with the framework of Marxist–Leninist ideology, issues of culture were not discussed as separate from those of politics and economy. To that effect, Soviet cultural theorist È. A. Baller argued in a treatise from 1968 that the issue of cultural heritage was to be regarded as being of utmost importance to the overall progress of socialist society. According to Baller, the prerevolutionary heritage of the Russian Empire was to be put to use and adapted for the impending communist future. His writings illustrate the political use and ideological eclecticism underlying socialist preservation discourse and practice. Baller conceived of preservation as an active process of adaptation to the conditions of the present, thus paying considerable attention to the question of defining adequate ways in which the Soviet people could relate to the heritage of past generations. He was interested in the criteria that could determine the selection from what he referred to as the treasures of world culture, and how socialist societies could also make use of the cultural achievements of contemporary capitalist societies.[25] While Baller's questions point to public debate about the scope and content of cultural heritage, there were also considerable restrictions to the scope of the questions he raised. Most importantly, the purpose of preserving historical monuments was always predefined as the building of communism.

The all-union law on preservation from 1976 specified the tasks of Soviet legislation in this field, using a similar approach to the ideas outlined in Baller's treatise. The law proclaimed that the protection and use of monuments should be regulated "with a view to preserving them for present and future generations and ensuring their effective use for scientific study and popularization in the interests of the Communist education of the working people."[26] Being a defining factor in postwar Soviet policymaking on cultural development, Communist education of the working people (*kommunisticheskoe vospitanie trudiashchikhsia*), to use the official terminology, also played a central role in preservation. Heritage as the material culture of the past served well the purpose of aesthetic and patriotic education in the formation of the socialist subject and thus continued the revolutionary policies from the early Soviet Union. Against the background of a wave of new museum-institutions being established, the Central Council of the Communist Party of the Soviet Union adopted a decree in 1964 on using museums for the Communist education of the working people. At the same time, the ministries of culture and the preservation societies promoted itineraries of heritage sites for educational purposes, in particular for young people, in order to inspire feelings of Soviet patriotism. Historical places that commemorated the foundation of the socialist state, the Revolution, World War II, and socialist internationalism were of particular interest. They were displayed, for example, during the all-union expedition of pioneers and schoolchildren entitled "My Fatherland—the USSR" in commemoration in 1972 of the fiftieth anniversary of the foundation of the Soviet state.[27] The aim of these expeditions was to increase the public awareness of preservation, which in 1976 was defined by the Soviet law on preservation as the duty of every Soviet citizen, by showcasing the country's cultural and natural heritage. The itineraries were thus ideologically driven, with this mode of cultural development forming part of the Soviet agenda of educating the masses.

The second mode of cultural development, which used culture as a resource for economic development, also relied heavily on the method of compiling itineraries. Beginning in the 1960s, international expert forums as well as the Soviet authorities turned to tourism as a way of deploying cultural heritage for the economic development of peripheral regions. The USSR became a member of the UN World Tourism Organization[28] in 1956 as tourism promised to be a lucrative strategy for revitalizing historic sites. The United Nations Conference on Tourism and International Travel held in 1963 in Rome discussed preservation as an investment in development projects; and consequently, the year 1967 was designated by the United Nations as the International Tourist Year. In 1969, an international committee of experts convened by UNESCO declared that the best way to preserve cultural heritage was to "integrate it in the economic and social life" of the time, and as a result, preservation could not be undertaken by a single specialized ministry but instead "must become part of regional planning."[29] The legacy of these ideas is still evident today, with heritage playing a central role in sustainable development projects involving the reappraisal of local resources aimed at reviving traditional economic sectors such as agriculture, fishing, and crafts.[30] Contrasting with the earlier initiatives of the 1960s, however, recent measures have increasingly sought to subvert the hierarchies of development and preservation by focusing on mutually compatible goals.[31]

The Soviet authorities' idea of using preservation for development was not limited to the USSR, but rather extended to other world regions as well. In the 1960s, these ideas also formed part of the logic behind Soviet efforts to promote development in Asia and Africa that regarded "the right use" of cultural heritage as a crucial factor in this process.[32] Soviet foreign policy quickly turned to the field of culture by providing educational materials and stipends for students from developing countries and promoting the establishment of libraries, museums, and festivals.[33] Development aid also found expression in large safeguarding campaigns for historical sites in the so-called developing countries. In particular, the UNESCO-coordinated International Campaign to Save the Monuments in Nubia (1960–80) and the campaign to preserve the Borobudur Temple Compounds in Indonesia (1972–83) cemented public perception of preservation as part of development projects. Contemporary media by Soviet institutions promoted this idea, too, although the involvement of the Soviet authorities in the international preservation campaigns themselves was limited.[34]

In a similar vein to international initiatives, the Soviet authorities showed interest in the promised benefits for regional economic development within the Soviet republics by integrating preservation into plans to promote tourism.[35] V. M. Kazakevich, the chairman of the USSR Academy of Sciences excursion bureau, referred to foreigners as convertible currency at a meeting of the All-Russian Society for the Protection of Historical and Cultural Monuments (VOOPIiK) in 1968.[36] This attitude seemed to have been widely shared among members of the Soviet elite, although, as Kazakevich claimed, they hardly knew anything else about the foreign tourists coming into the country. The use of monuments in tourism presented an attractive response to the challenge of how historical objects should be employed in the socialist present wherein many of them had been dissociated from their original social value. From the perspective of Soviet heritage experts, the preservation of cultural heritage was deemed as important as the question of what role they would or should play in contemporary society. A. G. Khalturin, the first president of the USSR National Committee of ICOMOS, aimed at a "harmonization" of past and present buildings. He claimed that the best option, among the various possibilities of using heritage for economic purposes and urban planning, was to make "cultural treasures known to the widest publics, both at home and abroad."[37]

The establishment of tourist centers and routes in historic small towns and in the countryside not only presented a feasible adaptation of historical structures to present conditions. It also complied with the socialist ideals of internationalism and mass education by displaying them to groups of domestic and international tourists. Against the backdrop of the abovementioned international initiatives of tourism promotion, the 1960s saw the advent of standardized mass tourism, when several elements of tourist infrastructure familiar to us today, for example in parts of Mediterranean Europe, were built. The Soviet authorities noted that the examples of other countries such as Bulgaria, Yugoslavia, Italy, and Spain showed that it was possible to use entire historic towns and not only individual historical buildings for touristic purposes.[38] This provided the basis for transforming the historic center of smaller towns, such as Suzdal´ in Vladimir Oblast, into what was termed a tourist center. The All-Union Central Council of Trade Unions together with the Department for Foreign Tourism at the USSR Council of Ministers organized the planning of roads, a bus station, hotels, camping sites, and restaurants in the historical structures including the Suzdal´ Kremlin and the surrounding monasteries.[39] Suzdal´ became a testbed for developing the first comprehensive tourist route in the Russian Soviet Federative Socialist Republic (RSFSR), which came to be known as the Golden Ring.

The revenues made from tourists reimbursed the cost of restoration and reconstruction of monuments and also guaranteed some additional earnings in desired foreign currency. The sources available on the planning of the tourist center in Suzdal´ show that the Council of Ministers carefully calculated the projected revenue from foreign tourists from lodging, eating at restaurants, and souvenir sales at state-owned shops.[40] In 1969, the Central Council of the Communist Party, the Council of Ministers, and the All-Union Central Council of Trade Unions provided the legal basis for developing tourist infrastructure in the decree "On the Means of Further Developing Tourism and Excursions in the Country." This document highlighted how the Soviet authorities understood tourism as a means of cultural development and political education of the population.[41] Cultural heritage was among the resources considered of interest to tourism alongside nature and the display of economic, scientific, and cultural achievements. As a result, the visits to historical sites by tourists were always accompanied by an array of public lectures on these topics. For example, tourists visiting Vladimir Oblast in 1975 could hear lectures on the region's economic development, the Soviet victory in the Great Patriotic War, the Soviet agrarian policies, and the development of Soviet culture in the current five-year plan, among other topics.[42]

The example of tourism shows that cultural heritage was always discussed by Soviet authorities in the context of its practical use and thus with respect to its role in the overall projected development toward communist society. While Soviet international development aid focused on education, the preservation and use of cultural heritage remained primarily the concern of domestic cultural development initiatives in the vast territory of the Soviet Union. It was only in the mid-1980s that the policies of *perestroika* and the United Nations World Decade of Cultural Development (1988–97) sparked greater interest, across the globe, in the issue of cultural heritage as a resource in cultural development. However, this apparent turning point at the end of the Cold War would not have been possible without the increasing interest in the cultural side of development since the late 1960s.

The World Decade for Cultural Development and the Legacies of Socialist Policies

During the first Development Decade of the 1960s, the issue of cultural development naturally received increasing attention from UNESCO as the specialized agency of the United Nations dealing with culture. The discussions within the UNESCO forums were characterized by a dynamic understanding of culture as a field subject to continuous change. Experts noted that culture not only played an increasing part in development, but that it was also equally affected by the changes brought about by development.[43] In accordance with this position, culture gradually emerged as a field of policymaking distinct from education. Cultural development was promoted on the basis of cultural sovereignty in order to avoid conflict or foreign domination, with this approach thus supporting UNESCO's primary objective of guaranteeing peace. Due to the emphasis on cultural sovereignty, the notion of development in cultural policies was rarely considered separate from preservation in the international debates unfolding from the mid-1960s. The entanglement of the preservation and the development of culture was particularly evident in the documents and initiatives that received major support from socialist governments. The Declaration of Principles of International Cultural Co-operation initiated by the UN Economic and Social Council (ECOSOC) and adopted by UNESCO in 1966 confirmed that "every people [had] the right and the duty to develop its culture."[44] In 1973, the UN resolution Preservation and Further Development of Cultural Values, initiated by Poland, urged governments to "make cultural values, both material and spiritual, an integral part of development efforts."[45] In 1974, UNESCO established the International Fund for the Promotion of Culture in order to provide financial resources to projects of cultural development after several states had voiced regret over the fact that those projects were not eligible for funding by the World Bank back then.[46] And finally, in 1976, the General Conference in Nairobi adopted the Recommendation on Participation by the People at Large in Cultural Life and Their Contribution to It. This document sought to encourage governments to ensure all individuals had access to cultural institutions and could participate in cultural activities.

Via these documents, the notion of cultural development entered the debates of the General Conferences of UNESCO within just a few years. In the first General Conferences, the delegates had focused on the narrower issues of arts education and the development of museums. In 1968, the topic of cultural policies was listed as a separate section in the resolutions of the General Conference, after the first roundtable on cultural policies had been organized by UNESCO the previous year. This international expert forum departed from the 1966 Declaration that had confirmed the right of every people to culture and subsequently turned to the question of what the extent of governments' involvement in people's culture should be. Many states formulated new cultural policies and appointed ministers of culture following the UNESCO meetings. This also included the Soviet Union and other socialist countries that regarded cultural development as a condition for progress. This view was stated by the USSR Minister of Culture, E. A. Furtseva, at the Intergovernmental Conference on Institutional, Administrative and Financial Aspects of Cultural Policies convened in Venice in 1970, later referred to as the first World Conference on Cultural Policies.[47] It inspired the formulation of guidelines concerning the cultural dimension in general development that also presented a definition of preservation reflecting the present and future concerns of societies. As part of these new guidelines, the final report of the conference rejected the objective to engage in preservationist efforts "for [their] own sake alone by scholars passionately interested in the past."[48] Instead, the report postulated that preservation had "become a part of social and cultural development."[49]

In line with this observation, the Second World Conference on Cultural Policies, convened in Mexico City in 1982, proposed to launch a World Decade dealing with cultural development by the United Nations with UNESCO as the lead agency.[50] The World Decade would concentrate several of the earlier initiatives, while cultural heritage was assuming an increasingly central role in the general framework of cultural development. G. V. Uranov, the general secretary of the USSR National Commission for UNESCO, acknowledged in a meeting in 1985 that the Major Program "Culture and the Future" launched by UNESCO the previous year clearly showed that by then most member states considered this program to be the foundation for preserving and developing humanity's cultural heritage.[51] He reiterated the position that the issue of cultural heritage could not be separated from general international cultural cooperation, thus confirming again the broad scope that heritage policies had assumed by the mid-1980s. Cultural issues gained further momentum in the international development agenda through the introduction of the concepts of sustainable development and sustained economic growth into the international public discourse where the role of preservation was also emphasized.[52]

The World Decade for Cultural Development (WDCD) was launched in 1988. The four objectives defined by the WDCD referred to the issues introduced by the international documents mentioned above: acknowledging the cultural dimension in development, asserting and enhancing cultural identities, broadening participation in cultural life, and promoting international cultural cooperation.[53] The WDCD was extremely popular with the Soviet authorities who viewed it as a bridge between the cultural development of the Soviet Union—in the context of the *perestroika* reforms—and the entire world.[54] The *perestroika* reforms brought culture, including the culture of socialist countries, to the fore as an essentially global issue that assumed increasing relevance in international relations. The great interest of the Soviet Union in the Decade was well received by members of the UNESCO Secretariat. After the United States, the United Kingdom, and Singapore had withdrawn from UNESCO in 1985, Henri Lopès, the Assistant Director-General for Culture, advised the Director-General of UNESCO to "ask the USSR to take up a leadership role" in the WDCD when meeting with the authorities on his field trip to Moscow.[55] The commitment to increase cooperation was consolidated in a memorandum concerning the cooperation between UNESCO and the USSR that was signed during the Director-General's trip on 16–20 July

1989. In this memorandum, all agreements in the field of culture were geared to the objectives of the WDCD.

At the same time, the WDCD was used by the Soviet authorities as a catalyst to promote the development of domestic cultural policies in the Soviet Union. On 9 June 1989, the decree by the USSR Congress of People's Deputies, "On the Fundamental Directions of Domestic and Foreign Policies of the USSR," instructed the Supreme Soviet and the USSR Council of Ministers to prepare a new program for cultural development, which concerned "the preservation and development of the cultural potential of society."[56] While Marxism–Leninism was still considered the inalienable foundation of Soviet state policies, the new program was to take into account the extensive transformation of Soviet society during *perestroika* and the changes in the cooperation of state bodies when formulating a new orientation in cultural policies.[57] The adoption of the program by the Council of Ministers was planned for the second half of 1991. However, the disintegration of the Soviet Union prevented the new state program on cultural development from seeing the light of day.

Conclusion

Most of the global impact of the World Decade for Cultural Development came after the disintegration of the Soviet Union, with experts from this region fading into the background of international debates. In 1992, the United Nations and UNESCO constituted the World Commission on Culture and Development, headed by the former UN Secretary-General Javier Pérez de Cuéllar. Its only member from the post-Soviet region was the Russian film director Nikita Mikhalkov, who had just become president of the new Russian Culture Fund. The Commission's report *Our Creative Diversity*, whose focus on cultural pluralism provided the basis for later legislation on the preservation of intangible heritage, was published in 1995, and by the early 2000s, the issue of cultural development had become an integral part of policies concerning cultural heritage.

Scholarship has described the greater attention on cultural development as part of "a new heritage paradigm" that focuses on the social production of heritage rather than on material things.[58] This "new paradigm" is exemplified by legal instruments such as UNESCO's Convention for the Safeguarding of the Intangible Cultural Heritage (2003) and the Council of Europe Framework Convention on the Value of Cultural Heritage for Society, the so-called Faro Convention (2005).[59] The approach to heritage as presented in these documents aligns well with publications from the field of heritage studies that have emerged over the last decades.[60] While most researchers seem to agree on the discursive nature of heritage and the growing need for community involvement, the scholarly interpretation of approaches to heritage as a resource has been more ambiguous. Some scholars celebrate the broad scope of new definitions of heritage for their inclusive and participatory character. Others criticize the neoliberal adaptability of heritage to changing market conditions since "anyone anywhere can claim some kind of cultural heritage."[61] What these different accounts have in common, however, is a compellingly presentist, ahistorical perspective on the phenomenon of heritage, only rarely going back beyond the turn of the millennium.

Contrasting with scholarship that stresses the recent emergence and novel character of these considerations, this chapter has shown how cultural heritage assumed an ever-greater role in general reflections on development both in Soviet policies and those promoted by international organizations over the course of several decades. Heritage had been deemed part of cultural policymaking in the international forum since the inception of cultural policymaking in the 1960s, and, in turn, preservation was not considered separately from development. Experts in and outside the Soviet Union argued for an intrinsic link between both preservationist and developmental approaches to culture. Tourism and participation in cultural life were the leading topics that framed both domestic and international discussions that preceded the well-known approaches to heritage in the present-day by almost half of a century. Moreover, the discussion in this chapter has challenged dominant notions of where actors commonly associated with the development of international heritage policies were located and which types of actors were involved. The Soviet Union represents an intriguing case for inquiring into the role of heritage in cultural development, since the Marxist–Leninist ideological underpinnings of heritage-making regarded the past as a resource in the building of the future communist society. This future-oriented transformative perspective on heritage was not an exclusive feature of state socialism, but rather a widely debated question in the international discussion on cultural aspects of development taking shape in the United Nations and its agencies from the 1950s. By focusing on the Soviet Union in the international forum, the discussion presented here has revealed approaches to heritage as a resource that extend beyond neoliberalism, which has framed claims of a "new heritage paradigm" in relation to recent international policies on intangible heritage and cultural diversity.

In the Soviet Union, heritage was constantly presented and used as a resource for cultural development in a variety of ways between 1917 and 1991. For one, it was harnessed for cultural development that sought to educate the masses along the lines of the "Communist education of the working people," by familiarizing them with the history of the Soviet state and the Revolution. Expedition itineraries like the all-union expedition of pioneers and schoolchildren entitled "My Fatherland—the USSR" in 1972 followed the blueprint provided by new tourism infrastructure. On the other hand, tourism promised to be an ideologically apt adaptation of historical structures to the socialist present that had otherwise ceased to fulfill their prerevolutionary functions (e.g., the building of a hotel in a monastic complex in Suzdal'). Yet, more importantly, it constituted a significant investment in the economic development of peripheral regions and smaller cities. By focusing on this socioeconomic dimension of heritage, rather than the historical narratives of sites, this chapter has highlighted how Soviet approaches to heritage may inform on the recent global history of heritage. The Declaration of Principles of International Cultural Co-operation of 1966 and the UN resolution Preservation and Further Development of Cultural Values of 1973 showed how socialist politics were integrated in the international discussion. Furthermore, a global perspective on cultural development also reveals that a revolution was not needed for projecting the past into the future during the twentieth century. Rather, that the past belonged to the future was considered common sense among the international community.

Corinne Geering leads a junior research group at the Leibniz Institute for the History and Culture of Eastern Europe (GWZO) in Leipzig. She received her PhD from the University in Giessen in 2018, where she was a doctoral fellow at the International Graduate Centre for the Study of Culture (GCSC). She has published on material culture, cultural politics, international cooperation during the Cold War, and the use of the past for regional development. She is the author of *Building a Common Past: World Heritage in Russia under Transformation, 1965–2000*.

Notes

1. V. I. Lenin, cited in Korotkevich, *Pamiatniki istorii i kul'tury*, 3.
2. On the changing perception of time in the course of the Russian Revolution, see Stites, *Revolutionary Dreams*. For a more recent perspective in relation to cultural heritage, see Alonso González, Comer, Viejo Rose, and Crowley, *Heritage, Revolution and the Enduring Politics of the Past*; in particular the contribution by Deschepper, "Between Future and Eternity"; see also Alonso González, "Communism and Cultural Heritage," 654–55.
3. Long, "Modernity, Socialism and Heritage in Asia," 206.
4. See "Law of the Union of Soviet Socialist Republics."
5. Macekura and Manela, *The Development Century*. The optimistic understanding of development is emphasised by Unger, *International Development*, 9.

6. Gorshenina and Tolz, "Constructing Heritage in Early Soviet Central Asia," 82–83.
7. See, e.g., Gfeller, "Anthropologizing and Indigenizing Heritage."
8. See Telepneva, "A Cultural Heritage for National Liberation?"; Cowcher, "The Museum as Prison."
9. See Holleran, *Boston's Changeful Times*, 3–4, 7; Lotz, "Expanding the Space for Future Resource Management."
10. Basu and Modest, *Museums, Heritage and International Development*, 8.
11. See Nederveen Pieterse, *Development Theory*, 64–82.
12. Gigase, Humair, and Tissot, eds. *Le tourisme comme facteur de transformations économiques*.
13. Already in the eighteenth and nineteenth centuries, cultural heritage had been used by colonial administrations to justify the civilizing mandate of the colonizer. Falser, "Cultural Heritage as Civilizing Mission," 4; Swenson, "The Heritage of Empire," 10. For the Bolshevik adaptation of the civilizing mission in Central Asia, see Teichmann, "Cultivating the Periphery."
14. Zvorykin, Golubtsova, and Rabinovich, *Cultural Policy in the Union of Soviet Socialist Republics*, 9.
15. Gavrilova, "Formirovanie pravovoi osnovy."
16. Semyonova and Iljine, *Selling Russia's Treasures*.
17. The full name of the commissariat in Russian was Narodnyi Komissariat Prosveshcheniia, shortened to Narkompros. The word *prosveshchenie* may be translated either as "education" or "enlightenment." See Fitzpatrick, *The Commissariat of Enlightenment*, 1.
18. Lane, *Soviet Society under Perestroika*, 188.
19. Fitzpatrick, *The Commissariat of Enlightenment*, 113.
20. Maddox, "These Monuments Must Be Protected!"
21. "Postanovlenie Soveta Ministrov SSSR ot 14 oktiabria 1948 g.," 65.
22. An overview of Soviet institutions in the field of heritage conservation is provided in Geering, *Building a Common Past*, 164–71.
23. Donovan, "'How Well Do You Know Your *Krai*?,'" 465; idem, *Chronicles in Stone*, 63.
24. Kelly, *Socialist Churches*; Maddox, *Saving Stalin's Imperial City*.
25. Baller, *Kul'turnoe nasledie i kommunizm*, 19.
26. "Law of the Union of Soviet Socialist Republics," Art. 2.
27. Romanova, "Iz opyta provedeniia vserossiiskogo smotra," 304–5.
28. Until 1975, the name of the organization was International Union of Official Travel Organisations (IUOTO).
29. Robert Brichet and Mario Matteucci, "Meeting of experts to establish an international system for the protection of monuments and sites of universal interest. Unesco House, 21–25 July 1969. Practical steps to facilitate the possible establishment of an appropriate international system," UNESDOC, 1969. Retrieved 23 March 2020, http://unesdoc.unesco.org/images/0021/002151/215153eo.pdf.
30. Kockel, *Regional Culture and Economic Development*, 166.
31. For a discussion see Winter and Daly, "Heritage in Asia," 13.
32. Some of the ideas underpinning the role of cultural heritage in development, in particular in Asia and Africa, were outlined by the archeologist and orientalist B. B. Piotrovskii in "Znachenie kul'turnogo naslediia v razvitii obshchestva i formy

ego sokhraneniia" (1975), Archive of the Russian Academy of Sciences (ARAN), f. 457, op. 1, d. 658, ll. 160–82, here l. 161.
33. Brichet and Matteucci, "Meeting of experts," 4.
34. *Vse Nadezhdy Mira.* Dir. B. Karpov. Tsentral'naia studiia dokumental'nykh fil'mov, 1986. Retrieved 20 January 2020, https://www.net-film.ru/film-9174.
35. The Soviet program to combine preservation with the development of tourism is outlined in A. G. Khaltourine [sic], "La conservation et l'exploitation des monuments compte tenu du développement du tourisme culturel en U.R.S.S." In *Cultural Properties and Tourism. Reports Submitted by the National Committees. Second General Assembly, Oxford, 6–12 VII 1969*, 1–14. ICOMOS Documentation Centre, Box Assemblée Générale ICOMOS II. For in-depth case studies of the Ukrainian SSR and Estonian SSR, see the articles by Iryna Sklokina, and Kaarel Truu and Karin Hallas-Murula, respectively, in this volume.
36. "Inostrantsy—èto valiuta." Minutes of the meeting on 18 December 1968 of the architectural and historical section [of VOOPIiK] on the question of the "Golden Ring." State Archive of the Russian Federation (GARF), f. A-639, op. 1, d. 207, ll. 33–89, here l. 74
37. Khalturin, "The Preservation of Monuments at the Present Day," 81.
38. Letter from the USSR Council of Ministers to A. N. Kosygin. GARF, f. A-259, op. 45, d. 5569, ll. 48–52, here l. 48; Geering, *Building a Common Past*, 137.
39. USSR Council of Ministers, "O sozdanii v g. Suzdale Vladimirskoi oblasti turistskogo tsentra." GARF, f. A-259, op. 45, d. 5569, ll. 42–44.
40. K. Krupin, "Spravka po invaliutnym postupleniiam ot inostrannogo turizma po turistskomu marshrutu Moskva–Vladimir–Suzdal', Moskva–Zagorsk–Pereslavl' Zalesskii–Rostov–Iaroslavl'" (1969). GARF, f. A-259, op. 45, d. 5570, l. 23
41. "Postanovlenie TsK KPSS, Soveta Ministrov SSSR i VTsSPS."
42. "Information on working with foreign tourists, performed by the voluntary society 'Znanie' of Vladimir Oblast in 1975." GARF, f. 561, op. 1, d. 1804, ll. 46–48.
43. UNESCO, *Problems of Culture and Cultural Values*, 9.
44. UNESCO, "Declaration of Principles of International Cultural Co-Operation," UNESCO, 1966. Retrieved 8 June 2021, http://portal.unesco.org/en/ev.php-URL_ID=13147&URL_DO=DO_TOPIC&URL_SECTION=201.html.
45. United Nations, "Resolution 3148 (XXVIII) Preservation and further development of cultural values. Twenty-eighth session of the General Assembly of the United Nations," United Nations, 1973. Retrieved 23 March 2020, http://www.unesco.org/culture/laws/pdf/UNGA_resolution3148.pdf.
46. The fund was an initiative of the government of Jamaica following the regional Caribbean Cultural Conference in 1970. See Davidson, "The New Unesco International Fund for the Promotion of Culture," 223.
47. McDermott, "Cultural Policy—A Modern Dilemma," 7.
48. UNESCO, *World Conference on Cultural Policies*, 5.
49. UNESCO, *Cultural Policy*, 38.
50. United Nations and UNESCO, *Rethinking Development*, 6.
51. G. V. Uranov, "Protokol zasedaniia Komissii SSSR po delam IuNESKO ot 24 dekabria 1985 goda." Russian State Archive of Literature and Art (RGALI), f. 2329, op. 35, d. 1807, ll. 114–32, here l. 120.

52. Garner, *The Politics of Cultural Development*.
53. World Decade for Cultural Development, Annex "Draft Plan of Action submitted by the Director-General of the United Nations Educational, Scientific and Cultural Organization (Unesco)" (1986). UNESCO Archives, World Decade for Cultural Development, Box 336, 008 A 183 "45-10".
54. "Ob uchastii SSSR vo vsemirnom desiatiletii razvitiia kul'tury" (1989). RGALI, f. 2329, op. 35, d. 3011, ll. 67–85, here l. 69. More information on how the Soviet authorities used the World Decade for Cultural Development to promote the objectives of the *perestroika* reforms is provided in Geering, *Building a Common Past*, 272–77.
55. Henri Lopès, "Follow up action to the proposals contained in the statement made by Mr. E. Chevardnadze, Minister of Foreign Affairs of the USSR at UNESCO on 12 October 1988" (1988). UNESCO Archives, Box 215, CLT/CH/02/1/534 (Part 2); Geering, *Building a Common Past*, 273.
56. "Postanovlenie S"ezda narodnykh deputatov Soiuza Sovetskikh Sotsialisticheskikh Respublik."
57. USSR Council of Ministers, "O predlozheniiakh po razrabotke Gosudarstvennoi programmy razvitiia kul'tury v SSSR" (1989). GARF, f. R-5446, op. 152, l. 792, ll. 1–3, here l. 2.
58. Fairclough, Dragićević-Šešić, Rogač-Mijatović, Auclair, and Soini, "The Faro Convention," 11.
59. For example, in Schofield, "Heritage Expertise and the Everyday," 4.
60. Smith, *Uses of Heritage*.
61. Scholarship dealing with contemporary international heritage policies tends to trace their emergence back to the UNESCO Universal Declaration on Cultural Diversity adopted in 2001. Logan, Kockel, and Craith, "The New Heritage Studies," 7.

Bibliography

Alonso González, Pablo. "Communism and Cultural Heritage: The Quest for Continuity." *International Journal of Heritage Studies* 22, no. 9 (2016): 653–63.

Alonso González, Pablo, Margaret Comer, Dacia Viejo Rose, and Tom Crowley, eds. *Heritage, Revolution and the Enduring Politics of the Past*. Spec. Issue of *International Journal of Heritage Studies* 25, no. 5 (2019).

Baller, Ė. A. *Kul'turnoe nasledie i kommunizm*. Moscow: Izdatel'stvo "Znanie," 1968.

Basu, Paul, and Wayne Modest, eds. *Museums, Heritage and International Development*. New York: Routledge, 2016.

Cowcher, Kate. "The Museum as Prison and Other Protective Measures in Socialist Ethiopia." *International Journal of Heritage Studies* 26, no. 12 (2020): 1,166–84.

Davidson, Alfred E. "The New Unesco [sic] International Fund for the Promotion of Culture." *Leonardo* 8, no. 3 (1975): 223–24.

Deschepper, Julie. "Between Future and Eternity: A Soviet Conception of Heritage." *International Journal of Heritage Studies* 25, no. 5 (2019): 491–506.

Donovan, Victoria. *Chronicles in Stone: Preservation, Patriotism, and Identity in Northwest Russia*. Ithaca: Cornell University Press, 2019.

———. "'How Well Do You Know Your *Krai*?' The *Kraevedenie* Revival and Patriotic Politics in Late Khrushchev-Era Russia." *Slavic Review* 74, no. 3 (2015): 464–83.

Fairclough, Graham, Milena Dragićević-Šešić, Ljiljana Rogač-Mijatović, Elizabeth Auclair, and Katriina Soini. "The Faro Convention, A New Paradigm for Socially—and Culturally—Sustainable Heritage Action?" *Культура/Culture* 8 (2014): 9–19.

Falser, Michael. "Cultural Heritage as Civilizing Mission: Methodological Considerations." In *Cultural Heritage as Civilizing Mission. From Decay to Recovery*, edited by Michael Falser, 1–32. Cham: Springer, 2015.

Fitzpatrick, Sheila. *The Commissariat of Enlightenment: Soviet Organization of Education and the Arts under Lunacharsky, October 1917–1921*. Cambridge, UK: Cambridge University Press, 1970.

Garner, Ben. *The Politics of Cultural Development: Trade, Cultural Policy and the UNESCO Convention on Cultural Diversity*. London: Routledge, 2016.

Gavrilova, M. F. "Formirovanie pravovoi osnovy v oblasti okhrany kul′turnogo naslediia v pervye gody sovetskoi vlasti." *Vestnik Kazanskogo gosudarstvennogo universiteta kul′tury i iskusstv* 4, no. 1 (2013): n.pag.

Geering, Corinne. *Building a Common Past: World Heritage in Russia under Transformation, 1965–2000*. Göttingen: Vandenhoeck & Ruprecht, 2019.

Gfeller, Aurélie Elisa. "Anthropologizing and Indigenizing Heritage: The Origins of the UNESCO Global Strategy for a Representative, Balanced and Credible World Heritage List." *Journal of Social Archaeology* 15, no. 3 (2015): 366–86.

Gigase, Marc, Cédric Humair, and Laurent Tissot, eds. *Le tourisme comme facteur de transformations économiques, techniques et sociales (XIXe–XXe siècles). Tourism as a factor of economic, technical and social transformations (XIX–XXth centuries)*. Neuchâtel: Éditions Alphil-Presses universitaires suisses, 2014.

Gorshenina, Svetlana, and Vera Tolz. "Constructing Heritage in Early Soviet Central Asia: The Politics of Memory in a Revolutionary Context." *Ab Imperio* 4 (2016): 77–115.

Holleran, Michael. *Boston's Changeful Times: Origins of Preservation & Planning in America*. Baltimore: Johns Hopkins University Press, 1998.

Kelly, Catriona. *Socialist Churches: Radical Secularization and the Preservation of the Past in Petrograd and Leningrad, 1918–1988*. DeKalb: Northern Illinois University Press, 2016.

Khalturin, A. "The Preservation of Monuments at the Present Day." *ICOMOS Bulletin* 2 (1971): 80–83.

Kockel, Ullrich. *Regional Culture and Economic Development: Explorations in European Ethnology*. Abingdon: Routledge, 2017.

Korotkevich, V. B. *Pamiatniki istorii i kul′tury*. Minsk: Nauka i tekhnika, 1978.

Lane, David. *Soviet Society under Perestroika*. London: Routledge, 1992.

"Law of the Union of Soviet Socialist Republics: On the Protection and Use of Historic and Cultural Monuments." In *Vth General Assembly of ICOMOS. Moscow/Suzdal, 21/27 May 1978*, edited by Soviet Committee of ICOMOS, n.pag. Moscow: Sovetskii khudozhnik, 1978.

Logan, William, Ullrich Kockel, and Máiréad Nic Craith. "The New Heritage Studies: Origins and Evolution, Problems and Prospects." In *A Companion to Heritage Studies*, edited by William Logan, Máiréad Nic Craith, and Ullrich Kockel, 1–25. Chichester: Wiley Blackwell, 2015.

Long, Colin. "Modernity, Socialism and Heritage in Asia." In *Routledge Handbook of Heritage in Asia*, edited by Patrick Daly and Tim Winter, 201–17. London: Routledge, 2012.

Lotz, Christian. "Expanding the Space for Future Resource Management: Explorations of the Timber Frontier in Northern Europe and the Rescaling of Sustainability During the Nineteenth Century." *Environment and History* 21, no. 2 (2015): 257–79.

Macekura, Stephen J., and Erez Manela, eds. *The Development Century: A Global History*. Cambridge, UK: Cambridge University Press, 2018.

Maddox, Steven. *Saving Stalin's Imperial City: Historic Preservation in Leningrad, 1930–1950*. Bloomington: Indiana University Press, 2015.

———. "These Monuments Must Be Protected! The Stalinist Turn to the Past and Historic Preservation during the Blockade of Leningrad." *The Russian Review* 70, no. 4 (2011): 608–26.

McDermott, Frank. "Cultural Policy—A Modern Dilemma." *The UNESCO Courier* 24 (1971): 5–17.

Nederveen Pieterse, Jan. *Development Theory*. London: SAGE, 2010.

"Postanovlenie S″ezda narodnykh deputatov Soiuza Sovetskikh Sotsialisticheskikh Respublik 'Ob osnovnykh napravleniiakh vnutrennei i vneshnei politiki SSSR.'" *Pravda*, 25 June 1989, 1–2.

"Postanovlenie Soveta Ministrov SSSR ot 14 oktiabria 1948 g., No. 3898. O merakh uluchsheniia okhrany pamiatnikov kul'tury." In *Okhrana pamiatnikov istorii i kul'tury*, edited by G. G. Anisimov, 65–67. Moscow: Sovetskaia Rossiia, 1973.

"Postanovlenie TsK KPSS, Soveta Ministrov SSSR i VTsSPS 'O merakh po dal'neishemu razvitiiu turizma i ėkskursii v strane' (30 maia 1969 g.)." In *Istoriia Rossiiskogo turizma (XIX–XX vv.)*, edited by A. A. Ivanov, 299–304. Moscow: Forum, 2011.

Romanova, L. M. "Iz opyta provedeniia vserossiiskogo smotra pamiatnikov istorii sovetskogo obshchestva, posviashchennogo 50-letiiu obrazovaniia SSSR." In *Voprosy okhrany, restavratsii i propagandy pamiatnikov istorii i kul'tury*, edited by N. K. Androsov and T. M. Sytina, 304–13. Moscow: Ministerstvo kul'tury RSFSR, 1976.

Schofield, John. "Heritage Expertise and the Everyday: Citizens and Authority in the Twenty-first Century." In *Who Needs Experts? Counter-Mapping Cultural Heritage*, edited by John Schofield, 1–11. Farnham: Ashgate, 2014.

Semyonova, Natalya, and Nicolas Iljine, eds. *Selling Russia's Treasures: The Soviet Trade in Nationalized Art, 1917–1938*. New York: Abeville Press Publishers, 2013.

Smith, Laurajane. *Uses of Heritage*. London: Routledge, 2006.

Stites, Richard. *Revolutionary Dreams: Utopian Vision and Experimental Life in the Russian Revolution*. New York: Oxford University Press, 1989.

Swenson, Astrid. "The Heritage of Empire." In *From Plunder to Preservation: Britain and the Heritage of Empire, c. 1800–1940*, edited by Astrid Swenson and Peter Mandler, 3–28. Oxford: Oxford University Press, 2014.

Teichmann, Christian. "Cultivating the Periphery: Bolshevik Civilising Missions and 'Colonialism' in Soviet Central Asia." *Comparativ* 19, no. 1 (2009): 34–52.

Telepneva, Natalia. "A Cultural Heritage for National Liberation? The Soviet-Somali Historical Expedition, Soviet African Studies, and the Cold War in the Horn of Africa." *International Journal of Heritage Studies* 26, no. 12 (2020): 1,185–1,202.

UNESCO. *Cultural Policy: A Preliminary Study*. Paris: UNESCO, 1969.

———. *Problems of Culture and Cultural Values in the Contemporary World*. Paris: UNESCO, 1983.

———. *World Conference on Cultural Policies: Mexico City, 26 July—6 August 1982. Final Report*. Paris: UNESCO, 1982.

Unger, Corinna. *International Development: A Postwar History*. London: Bloomsbury Academic, 2018.

United Nations, and UNESCO. *Rethinking Development: World Decade for Cultural Development 1988–1997*. n.p.: United Nations, 1994.

Winter, Tim, and Patrick Daly. "Heritage in Asia: Converging Forces, Conflicting Values." In *Routledge Handbook of Heritage in Asia*, edited by Patrick Daly and Tim Winter, 1–35. London: Routledge, 2012.

Zvorykin, A. A., N. I. Golubtsova, and E. I. Rabinovich. *Cultural Policy in the Union of Soviet Socialist Republics*. Paris: UNESCO, 1970.

CHAPTER 2

International Experts— National Martyrdom— Socialist Heritage

The Contribution of the Polish People's Republic to the Early UNESCO World Heritage Program

Julia Röttjer

The World Heritage Program that was officially launched by the United Nations Educational, Scientific and Cultural Organization (UNESCO) in the 1970s provided states with an opportunity for showcasing and disseminating common as well as competing concepts of cultural heritage. The proposal by socialist Poland to add the former German Nazi camp Auschwitz-Birkenau to the first World Heritage List in 1978 immediately provoked discussions within UNESCO's World Heritage Committee. Ultimately, though, the committee accepted the inclusion of "negative historical values"[1]—as they were then labelled—into the conception of World Heritage in 1979. The integration of Auschwitz-Birkenau into World Heritage has become a key pillar of UNESCO's conceptions of heritage and its narratives for the embodiment of these values. For World Heritage actors, the site with its socialist reading provided the first template for historical heritage independent of aesthetic categories and conventional cultural heritage concepts, as represented by the presence of cathedrals, old city ensembles, fortifications, or other classic topics of monument preservation on the list. At the same time, the original interpretation of Auschwitz-Birkenau as a site of *national martyrdom*, to use a term that was prevalent in the narrative produced in the context of socialist Poland and prominent in the nomination, persisted within the World Heritage discourse. Simultaneously with Auschwitz, Senegal's island of Gorée was likewise included solely due to its "associative values"; later examples of such sites, albeit in very different historical stages of the World Heritage program, were the Hiroshima Peace Memorial (1996), Mauritius' Aapravasi Ghat immigration depot (2006), and the Old Bridge Area of the Old City of Mostar (2006).

This chapter explores the site of Auschwitz-Birkenau within the context of its position among the portfolio of the five early World Heritage contributions of the Polish People's Republic (PRL). What emerges is a case study on how both the socialist and national framings of the heritage-related aspects of this site of national martyrdom were translated in a transnational context. The national and the socialist readings not only complemented each other—despite the internationalist ambitions of the latter—but the national frame was indeed necessary for the socialist narratives to gain acceptance. As Maciej Górny and Marcin Zaremba have elaborated, Polish Marxist historiography was dominated by national narratives from the beginning, with the ruling communists using constructions of national narratives strategically to legitimize their ideology and their power.[2] The case of Auschwitz was one central element in the memory politics of the ruling Polish United Workers' Party (PZPR), and its predecessor the Polish Workers' Party (PPR), since the communists took power in Poland in 1944–45. Its strategy in the realm of memory politics was embodied not least in the Museum, a central state institution that was founded on the site in 1947 as a memorial to the martyrdom of the Polish nation and other nations.[3]

What I consider here is how these particular claims and the global claims as to the meaning of Auschwitz as World Heritage existed alongside each other and interacted. I investigate the role of Polish institutions and experts participating in UNESCO's new program on "World Heritage" in the 1970s and early 1980s, examining the ways in which conceptions of heritage in the Polish People's Republic were employed in a transnational context across ideological divides. Auschwitz and Warsaw, two hotly debated sites framed by prevailing socialist interpretations of heritage, were inscribed into the World Heritage List within the first three years of its existence. Seen in the context of the other early Polish sites, the inclusion of Auschwitz as World Heritage can serve to reveal meanings ascribed to heritage in socialist Eastern and Central Europe more broadly while also demonstrating how these meanings were translated on and by the transnational stage, where these notions were integrated, rejected, or reinterpreted. At the same time, these processes can be discussed in the light of changing concepts, political agendas, and interactions of both Polish heritage experts and the socialist state administration within the framework of UNESCO and other international organizations. The case study of Auschwitz-Birkenau shows that socialist heritage conceptions found their way into international standards and that the results of these heritage policy transfers continue to have an impact today.

Socialist—National—International?
Proposing Auschwitz as World Heritage

The Convention Concerning the Protection of the World Cultural and Natural Heritage—the international treaty providing the basis for the World Heritage List—was adopted by the Seventeenth General Conference of UNESCO in 1972. The first states subsequently started ratifying the convention, and in 1977 the preparations for drawing up the initial entries to the World Heritage List took on more definite form. A World Heritage Committee, which would convene yearly, was formed as the international body within UNESCO for deciding on matters related to World Heritage. Poland was at that time very active in the internationalization of conservation. Polish experts had played an active part in the preparatory work leading to the 1972 Convention, including the Venice Charter of 1964, and in the subsequent establishment of the organization that would serve as an Advisory body to UNESCO on cultural matters: the International Council on Monuments and Sites (ICOMOS). Poland had ratified the World Heritage Convention in 1976 and was one of the fifteen member states elected to the first World Heritage Committee that same year. At the earliest possible opportunity, in 1978, Poland nominated the city centers of Kraków and Warsaw, the Wieliczka Salt Mine, and Białowieża National Park. The fifth nomination—Auschwitz-Birkenau—evoked a controversial discussion about what could be considered heritage. In 1978, these Polish nominations were among the first to reach UNESCO's cultural administration, along with twenty-one dossiers from other countries (Canada, Ecuador, Ethiopia, the Federal Republic of Germany, Senegal, Tunisia, and the United States), which were discussed on 8 and 9 June by the Bureau of the World Heritage Committee. The specialist on monument preservation entrusted with representing Poland in World Heritage affairs was Krzysztof Pawłowski, a lecturer (later professor) in architecture. At the time he was Poland's Deputy General Conservator and deputy head of the department of monument preservation and museums within the Ministry of Culture. It was he who drew up the first five Polish proposals.[4]

On behalf of the Ministry of Culture, Pawłowski collaborated with the authorities in charge of the respective sites—in the case of Kraków with the conservator responsible for the city, Jerzy Kossowski, and in Wieliczka with the administration of the Museum that had been established there in 1951.[5] In the case of Auschwitz, the partner was the State Museum Auschwitz-Birkenau in Oświęcim, responsible for running the memorial site (which in the Polish context is always referred to as "museum") since 1947 as a central state institution. While the origins of the idea to nominate Auschwitz are not completely clear, it is evident that there was no wider discussion concerning Auschwitz and the other (or possible alternative) candidates.[6] Existing research has attributed the original plan to nominate Auschwitz to the International Auschwitz Committee (IAC), an organization that had been founded in 1952 by survivors of Auschwitz-Birkenau. While representatives of this organization indeed reassured the UNESCO administration of their wholehearted support for the inscription, reading statements by the IAC itself[7] suggests that it is necessary to question the assumption that it had initiated the efforts. This narrative has retrospectively lent an "international touch" to the nomination process,[8] but it also overlooks the historicity and complexity of the International Auschwitz Committee and the role of its national member committees in the context of confrontation between the blocs as well as the entanglement of the Polish section with the Polish government.[9] Following standard procedure for World Heritage nominations, the Auschwitz proposal came from the responsible national government—in this case Poland. The Ministry of Culture and the Auschwitz State Museum, whose director Kazimierz Smoleń was also Secretary General of the IAC, were both involved, but the Ministry was the driving force behind this idea.[10] In the end, it seems as if Pawłowski, who had used also earlier opportunities to discuss possible sites with international colleagues, might have suggested some of the final decisions himself.[11] In any case, the nomination form was signed by Pawłowski as a high ranking official in heritage conservation within the Ministry of Culture, with the proposals then supported by the Ministry of Foreign Affairs. The description of the Auschwitz concentration camp in the form thus reflects the official Polish perspective on the site in 1978, with the nomination formulated in such a way as to ensure that both the site and the framing narratives could enter this new potential arena of worldwide representation as World Heritage.

The official text submitted to the Committee referred to the Museum as the nominated site. While there might have been pragmatic reasons for this, it also had implications for the reading of the site, as it also included the postwar institution and not only the National Socialist camp. Thus, the boundaries of the site were (almost) identical with those of the Museum: it comprised large parts of the complexes of Auschwitz I and Birkenau, while other important structures such as the camp and industrial plants at Monowitz, infrastructural connections, and other parts of the vast system of subcamps were left out. The nomination delivered, firstly, a physical inventory, and secondly, an inventory referring to the memorial, educational, and scientific work of the Museum, thus going far beyond the historical frame of the camp in order to underline the object's contemporary significance. On the level of physical objects, the grounds themselves and built structures such as barracks, watch towers, and drainage installations were listed, with special emphasis given to the five gas chambers and crematoria, the execution wall, the arrival platform, the prisoner cell blocks, and the mass burial pits. On the educational–memorial level, archival material, collections of historical items, objects of artistic interest, and numerous photographs, library volumes, visitor numbers, traveling exhibitions, lectures given, films shown, and works published were mentioned.[12]

One important function of this in both the Polish and international socialist context that was particularly prominent in the nomination were the demonstrations for peace, organized on behalf of the ruling PZPR, which involved more than 1.3 million participants from Poland and other countries. In order to underline the impact of the Museum, the extent of international scientific cooperation was emphasized. The educational and political work of the Museum was presented as an integral part of the site to be included into World Heritage. This also served to "to contribute to the strengthening of world peace"[13] and security. In the Polish socialist narrative, striving for world peace was given particular prominence, with the Auschwitz-Birkenau State Museum coming to embody the most important site of "martyrdom"[14] over the years and thus playing an important role in this battle for peace. In the nomination for World Heritage, this argument was well placed because it also addressed UNESCO's ideas of the World Heritage Program perfectly. The convention itself formulated the importance of international cooperation on cultural questions and thus by definition embraced ideas such as "the international community as a whole."[15] The interpretation presented by the Polish nominees was that Auschwitz-Birkenau and its stewards or custodians of interest, represented by the State Museum, were saving fragments and evidence of the past that carried a unique meaning for the understanding of the history of the world. They were actively promoting the sharing of these experiences and traces of the past with an international community. And they were doing so with a positive and peaceful message for the future that emerged from the historical lessons drawn from Auschwitz.

The nomination form included a short overview of the camp's history. It mentioned the total number of victims, which until 1990 was assumed to be approximately four million people.[16] It highlighted the first prisoners: Poles interned for political reasons. The description also mentioned other nationalities and included in this list "Jews in tremendous numbers."[17] The section concluded with an outline of the development of Auschwitz-Birkenau into the major center for the mass extermination of Jewish people, with most being sent to their deaths immediately upon arrival. The World Heritage nomination file ended with the justification for inscription. Arguments relating to delivering proof and evidence on the one hand and to representations of struggle on the other hand formed the two dominant strands of the text. The final argument referred to general statements going back to the foundation of the Auschwitz-Birkenau State Museum in 1947, which made clear that the struggle portrayed was understood first and foremost as a national one: "[t]he Auschwitz-Birkenau Memorial was established . . . as a monument to the suffering and struggle of the Polish nation and other peoples, on the site of the largest Hitlerite extermination camp where lie the ashes of some four million subjects of 24 countries."[18]

The Auschwitz concentration camp and its museum were presented to the World Heritage Committee by the Polish authorities as a place of Polish national martyrdom, where other nations had also perished, and as a large cemetery. The authors of the text did not fail to refer to the mass extermination of the Jews, but, as was also the case in both the Museum's exhibitions and in the prevailing official narrative in Poland, Polish national martyrdom was given greater prominence, while Jewish suffering was subsumed under both the national and internationalist narratives. Thus, the application text emphasized the nation of origin of the victims and not their being Jewish, while also stressing that that the camp was a place of heroic struggle and resistance performed by an internationalist community. This narrative overshadowed the fate of not only inmates who did not participate in this struggle for various reasons but also of those murdered soon after their arrival, which had been the fate of the overwhelming majority of Jewish victims.

Delivering evidence of and bearing witness to the Nazi crimes to the world was presented as one of the main objectives of the Museum. Indeed, framing Auschwitz as a place documenting the crimes perpetrated was central to the argumentation of the nomination. The Auschwitz-Birkenau State Museum was said to be "testimony to an historical event of particular importance in the history of mankind."[19] As the safekeeper of this heritage, its task was to work toward a better, peaceful future.

These arguments, based on the narratives of the Museum's exhibitions, showed the central role of the memory of Auschwitz in the national understanding of Polish history and memory politics. World War II was central to Polish socialist memory politics (as was the case in other countries), with a heroic narrative and the topos of martyrdom its most prevalent elements. As also exhibited in the Auschwitz Museum, the nomination text thus emphasized struggle and active resistance over passive suffering. This heroic reading of the past fitted well with the Marxist interpretation of history, where the Party was presented as being the decisive factor in the victory, thus providing the basis for the founding myth of the socialist state. The Marxist historical development emerged triumphant and, according to its teleological theory, could now pave the way toward a brighter future. The image of martyrdom was entangled with the ruling PZPR's memory politics, which focused on a heroic narrative. In this way, the communist narrative did not stray far from established national ones, other than in subduing and transforming direct religious references. According to this narrative complex, the martyrdom of the Polish people was at the same time meant to serve and redeem all people, something already suggested by the idea of Poland as the "Christ of nations" that had gained momentum in the nineteenth century and continued to be relevant. The concept gave expression in equal measure to mourning the loss of the nation during the partitions of Poland toward the end of the eighteenth century but also to the hope attached to its promised resurrection. This religious metaphor of the nation's place in history became a core narrative[20] closely tied to the idea that the Polish struggle in the national uprisings of the nineteenth century was a universal one, succinctly embodied in the slogan "For our freedom and yours." That this simultaneously martyrological and heroic formula could fit ideally into the communist arsenal of imagery was best illustrated by PZPR's first secretary, Edward Gierek, declaring that it was embedded in the Party's founding idea in his programmatic speech at the VIII Party Congress in 1980. Ideally, realizing this slogan would provide a way to unite national and universal notions: the modification of the religious concept of martyrdom found redemption in the form of communism, which—since the communists assumed power in Poland—had been presented as the only way to universally overcome National Socialist crimes against humanity.[21]

The nomination of Auschwitz took the other members of the World Heritage Committee by surprise, as the majority of them interpreted the concept as a reference to cultural achievements or even human genius.[22] But from a Polish perspective presenting Auschwitz on a worldwide platform seemed obvious, as it formed an essential part of national memory. The framework of World Heritage also provided an ideal opportunity to present a socialist take on the memory politics concerning World War II, thus emphasizing not only the socialist version of Poland's martyrdom narrative, but also the overall antifascist struggle embodied by socialism.

Socialist Poland's National Pantheon in an International Perspective

How can the nomination of Auschwitz-Birkenau be contextualized within the group of Poland's initial proposals to the World Heritage List: Warsaw, Kraków, Wieliczka, and Białowieża? The historical city center of Warsaw was presented to UNESCO as a symbol of the "renaissance" of Polish culture after its almost complete destruction by the Germans during World War II. The medieval quarters of the Old Town and New Town together with other parts of the historical city were reconstructed in an enormous project running from the end of the 1940s until the mid-1950s.[23] Rebuilding works on the Royal Castle that had started in 1971 as a significant and largely successful propaganda and mobilization project aiming to demonstrate the concern of the regime for national heritage[24] were ongoing at the time of nomination. All reconstruction was concentrated on the medieval parts of the inner city, with restoration reflecting the buildings' condition in the eighteenth century. The World Heritage application thus focused on this historical period. According to the narrative presented in the text, these buildings were "historically bound up with the most important national traditions of Poland."[25] The historical city, despite being almost entirely a reconstruction, was presented as an example to other nations of the value of developing "awareness of their cultural heritage."[26]

For Kraków, the nomination included the Wawel Castle and Hill, the historic city center, and the medieval district of Kazimierz, with its significance for the Polish nation emphasized less strongly. Instead, Poland's former capital was read as being of notable and unique consequence for European art, education, and trade. Kraków was characterized as a remarkable cultural complex representative of the idea of *Europe*. It was described as "one of the major centres of Central European trade . . . Cracow occupies an important place in European art . . . as a centre of western art which was in contact with cultural influences coming from the East."[27] In accordance with this positioning, the description stressed artistic influences drawn from Italian Renaissance architecture and from Brussels tapestries, although German connections were carefully left out of the narrative. The Jewish history of medieval Kazimierz was rather superficially mentioned in one paragraph of the history section that was almost three pages long.[28] In the application featuring Wieliczka Salt Mine as industrial heritage, its historical importance for the Polish state, broader European significance, and importance for world industry were stressed equally. The nomination file also justified the importance of Wieliczka by noting that it had been a tourist destination for centuries.

The fifth candidate, the national park comprising parts of the Białowieża primeval forest, was nominated as a natural world heritage site, but the application was nevertheless signed and handed in by Pawłowski as the representative of the Ministry of Culture. The idea of nominating this already long-established nature reserve to World Heritage originated among groups of nature experts actively involved in the UNESCO system, with the national park having been recognized as a UNESCO Biosphere Reserve in 1976 already. The nomination drew heavily on the importance of this habitat for the European bison. It did not contain direct arguments appealing to the cultural criteria of the World Heritage regulations, though the primeval forest—the *puszcza*—was undoubtedly laden with associations not only of unspoiled wilderness, medieval kings, and the bison as the ruler of the old Polish-Lithuanian forest, but also of the partisan fights and "bloodlands" of World War II.[29]

With this iconic group, the Polish delegation to UNESCO presented a national image before the international community that was framed as having European and even worldwide significance: *The* monument to national martyrdom—Auschwitz—was bound together with the capital city that embodied a national revival providing the foundation myth of the new political system after World War II. Kraków, the old royal city, was interpreted more as a famous European center of culture, learning, science, and trade, thus lending greater historical depth and a European dimension to the narrative.

How was this group of sites, and especially Auschwitz-Birkenau, received by the international actors of the Convention? The first official reaction came from ICOMOS as the advisory body for cultural sites, which sent its review with a recommendation to accept Auschwitz. But in this special case, there were also third parties showing their support, namely the International Auschwitz Committee. It sent direct appeals to UNESCO Director General Amadou M'Bow, who had visited Auschwitz-Birkenau in 1977 as part of his itinerary on a visit to Poland. Nevertheless, at its session in 1978, the World Heritage Committee temporarily rejected the former National Socialist concentration and extermination camp and deferred consideration to the following year. The reason given was that there were too many Polish candidates. It had been agreed that two sites per country would be the maximum permitted. Poland was the only state with three completely acceptable sites, namely Kraków, Wieliczka, and Auschwitz. The latter had indeed been a controversial nomination, with some delegates tending toward the view that the first World Heritage List at least should be the preserve of the cultural dimension as a showcase of human genius.[30] The process of inscribing cultural sites involved disputes over several more overarching points relating to the interpretation of decision criteria for World Heritage status.[31] The questions raised by the Auschwitz nomination were at the heart of these discussions. Michel Parent, Vice Chairman of the World Heritage Committee's Bureau, was asked to write a report-commentary with a discussion of these issues concerning the typology and categorization of the sites. An important topic of this report was debating "'positive' and 'negative' historical values."[32] It found that the envisaged inscription of Auschwitz could not be considered as just one addition to the list amongst others, nor should it be deemed a precedent enabling the inscription of further sites of "negative" historical values or even additional concentration camps. On the contrary, the report found, the inclusion of Auschwitz could and would shape and influence the character of Cultural World Heritage. The report accentuated: "Nevertheless, and in order to preserve its symbolic status as a monument to all the victims, Auschwitz should, it seems, remain in isolation . . . it should stand alone among cultural properties as bearing witness to the depth of horror and of suffering and the height of heroism, and that all other sites of the same nature be symbolized through it."[33] In the conclusion, this idea of singularity was underlined: "sites representing the positive and negative sides of human history will only be invested with real force if we make the most remarkable into *unique symbols*, each one standing for the whole series of similar events."[34]

Since the inscription of a site into World Heritage is a process rather than a single act with a definite, unchangeable result as to why exactly a certain object has been selected, more than one interpretation can prevail at the same time, gaining significance depending on the context. With the formal nomination, the argumentation ceased to be under total control of its authors. Since it was received and also reinterpreted by third parties, by the advisory body, and also by the other representatives of the UNESCO World Heritage Committee, the national component was diminished and universally adaptable narratives gained in importance. Nevertheless, the significant role of heroism stayed intact, which was important for the Polish national perspective.

This heroic reading of the national past was also reinforced by the other Polish nomination discussed in the report: the Old City Center of Warsaw. ICOMOS and the World Heritage bodies were troubled because of the high degree of wartime destruction and the more or less full reconstruction of the site. To address this issue was very important because discussions about authenticity as a condition *sine qua non* outshining all other selection criteria had emerged at the very outset of the World Heritage program.[35] Concerning Warsaw, the nomination solved the problem by shifting the temporal reference point of authenticity from the "original" historical epochs to the time of re-creation under socialism in 1949–55. Warsaw would finally be accepted in 1980, precisely because of the comprehensive urban reconstruction that, to quote the ICOMOS evaluation, symbolized "the will of the nation . . . to insure [sic] the survival of one of the prime settings of Polish culture. . . . [T]he historic center of Warsaw, tragically destroyed in 1944, is an exceptional examp[le] of the global reconstruction of a sequence of history running from the thirteenth to the twentieth centuries."[36] At the same time, the Bureau of the World Heritage Committee recommended that no other reconstructed cultural properties be accepted for inscription as World Heritage in the future.

The martyrdom of the Polish nation and its subsequent resurrection under the socialist government after World War II was the narrative that linked the nominations of Auschwitz-Birkenau and Warsaw. This message was not only sent by the Polish delegation submitting the proposals. It was also received, understood, and, to a certain degree, sanctioned by the recipients in the UNESCO realm, including the other national members of the World Heritage Committee and the supporting cultural administration of UNESCO.

Auschwitz Legacy—Auschwitz Heritage: International Perspectives in the Context of World Heritage

In the case of Auschwitz-Birkenau, however, the national interpretation was not the only one heard. Two weeks before the decisive meeting of the World Heritage Committee at the end of 1979, when it was already clear that the inscription had been deemed favorable by the Committee's Bureau, the Secretary General of the Jewish World Congress, Gerhart Riegner, wrote to Amadou M'Bow, lending his support for the inscription. The letter showed that the Jewish World Congress, which had a permanent delegate to UNESCO, recommended the proposal exactly as it had been drafted by the Polish state. Riegner stated that among the nearly four million victims (on this number, see above), the majority had been Jews. On the factual level, this statement did not seem to contradict in any way what the Polish side had written, but rather provided a general summary. However, Riegner also expressed the expectation that the Convention would ensure the protection of the historic site by the Polish authorities and that the diversity of the victims in terms of nationality, culture, and religion would be recognized.[37] This interpretation likewise strengthened the case for nomination but also stressed its specific Jewish history, opposing the narrative of unifying victims while also making demands of the Polish authorities responsible for the Auschwitz-Birkenau site. In Riegner's perspective, the inclusion of Auschwitz-Birkenau under this interpretation would particularly enhance the purposes of the Convention because he understood the perpetuation of the memory of Auschwitz as a universal, even sacred, legacy to be transmitted to future generations.

In October 1979, at its session in Cairo and Luxor, the World Heritage Committee decided "to enter Auschwitz concentration camp on the List as a unique site and to restrict the inscription of other sites of a similar nature."[38] The advisory body and the Committee followed the argumentation of the nomination and stressed the function of the Museum as a reservoir of testimony, a site of martyrdom, and a unique historical lesson and facilitator of world peace. While there had been some opposition to the Auschwitz proposal, this was partly because other Committee members had imagined the list would contain only examples of "human genius"; they did not want "barbaric" heritage included, at least not in the first round. But, as the reception process showed, the World Heritage concept could be transformed to also include "negative historical values," as long as it was clear that this was an exception. The prominent role of the Polish nation indeed was diminished in the official inscription process of the site. Emphasis was put on the international composition of the victims—among them "so many Jews"[39]—but the socialist topoi of martyrdom, internationalization, and resistance also remained in place.

The disclaimer that the inscription of similar sites should be restricted not only signified that initial doubts had been overcome, but also that it should not be considered as setting a precedent or standard. The disclaimer followed the wording of the Parent report, which had dealt with the problems of neatly categorizing sites, a system in which Auschwitz did not fully fit. Nevertheless, the discussion about what a case of "similar nature" to Auschwitz actually meant did recur within the World Heritage Committee whenever other sites referring to "negative historical values" were proposed. Simultaneously with Poland's nomination of Auschwitz in 1978, Senegal proposed the island of Gorée. It was included in the World Heritage List as a site representing centuries of history related to the slave trade. This proposal had not led to the World Heritage Committee posing the same questions as in the case of Auschwitz, and it had not been considered problematic by Parent. His argumentation referred mostly to the circumstance that, compared to Auschwitz, the object and also the logic of proposing Gorée fitted much better into classical categories of cultural heritage due to its architectural form. Since the parallel discussion of Gorée was much less controversial, it became obvious that the proclaimed singularity of Auschwitz did not mean there could be no integration of other sites of "negative historical values" into World Heritage. But the formula used by the Committee to highlight the moral singularity of Auschwitz remained vague and thus open to diverging interpretations in the future. Researchers have interpreted Auschwitz and other, later World Heritage entries such as Robben Island (1999) or Genbaku Dome in Hiroshima (1996) as a group of sites contributing to the World Heritage interpretation of intangible values.[40] However, this interpretation goes too far in grouping together cases not only with differing contexts and subtexts in themselves, but also from different times and phases in the World Heritage Program.[41] In a similar way, the discussions about reconstructions and authenticity kept returning to the sessions of the World Heritage Committee.[42]

The first five Polish World Heritage nominations, it turned out, were the only ones submitted by the Polish People's Republic. Indeed, the relations between the Polish delegation to UNESCO and the World Heritage Committee changed. Poland's original term on the Committee had been scheduled to run from 1976 to 1978. The Polish delegate had not only been successful in terms of nominations but was also much sought after for his expertise. He even acted as rapporteur of the second session and as such would have been a member of the Bureau of the Committee in 1979. Thus, Poland's reelection to the World Heritage Committee was expected. But, instead, Poland waived a new candidacy at the last minute in order to give way to another candidate from the socialist bloc: Bulgaria. Still, after Kraków and Wieliczka were inscribed in 1978, Auschwitz and Białowieża followed in 1979. In 1980, after many discussions over including a full reconstruction onto the list, Warsaw was finally accepted. Pawłowski, who was elected one of the vice presidents of ICOMOS at the Fifth General Assembly in Moscow in May 1978, continued to participate in this function as an observer to the World Heritage Committee. But the political situation in Poland had changed. Following the introduction of Martial Law on 13 December 1981 and given its repercussions, both the Polish General Conservator and his deputy Krzysztof Pawłowski left their positions, with the latter going on to teach at the Universities of Montpellier and Toulouse.[43]

The brain drain and declining significance of World Heritage for the Polish Ministry of Culture, as well as the damage done to the good relations between the Polish delegation and the World Heritage administration, became quite obvious. In the 1970s, Poland had been contributing with expertise to the preparation and construction of the World Heritage Convention. It also provided two of the initial twelve sites and had even managed to introduce with Auschwitz and Warsaw two highly debated sites, characterized by prevailing socialist interpretations of heritage, in the first three nomination rounds. But throughout the 1980s, the dealings of the Polish delegation with the UNESCO administration were dominated by preparations for small-scale and large-scale technical assistance to Wieliczka Salt Mine and requests for equipment or personal scholarships for restoration courses. There were no new approaches, methodical discussions on monument preservation, or plans for the inscription of new sites from Poland. Toward the end of the decade, when preparations for nominating the Old City of Zamość began, the process took a completely different form. The World Heritage administration had to guide the Polish delegation through every step of the process and send them the operational guidelines for nomination more than once. Despite this assistance, the application reached Paris on the wrong template and could not be accepted. After this ordeal, the site was finally ready for consideration in the World Heritage Committee of 1992, after the communist regime had collapsed and the Polish People's Republic had become the Republic of Poland.[44]

Conclusion: A Socialist Heritage?

The UNESCO World Heritage site of Auschwitz-Birkenau has remained a subject of international debate after 1989. A more recent major change at this World Heritage site demonstrates how national positions have been presented in this international arena. In 2007, following a request by the Polish government, the name of the World Heritage site was changed from "Auschwitz Concentration Camp" to "Auschwitz-Birkenau. Former Nazi German Concentration and Extermination Camp (1940–1945)." The decision had to be postponed from the previous session because the political motivation for the proposal provoked opposition in the World Heritage Committee, as voiced by the Israeli delegation. The ambition of the Polish government to show the German context already in the naming is deeply rooted in a debate about (mis)representations of German perpetrators and atrocities committed on Polish soil occupied by Germany. It is connected to the discussion about the role of Polish individuals and, at times, of Polish institutions in the Holocaust and about antisemitism in Poland. A decade later, when the so called "Polish death camp controversy" materialized in a Polish law criminalizing the use of this specific term or similar terms, Polish diplomacy endured a crisis as the country was accused of undermining the freedom of speech.[45] The socialist reading had put so much emphasis on the Polish national meaning of Auschwitz that the Polish name of the town, Oświęcim, had been used regularly as a synonym for the camp. The Polish socialist narrative reflected in the Museum and other sites of former concentration and extermination camps had spared the German Democratic Republic and pointed instead to the evils of "Hitlerism" that was framed as a precursor to the political system of the Federal Republic of Germany. The new name of the World Heritage site, spelling out not only "German" and "Nazi," but also the exact time frame, points to a shift in the national reading of Auschwitz that has taken place in comparison to the former socialist interpretation, which, in different variations, had remained valid until the 1980s.

Notwithstanding this recent name change, the legacy of the socialist interpretation of the site remains in place in the UNESCO World Heritage program. This chapter has explored how the socialist politics of the past has informed the interpretation of Auschwitz as UNESCO World Heritage. This account did not center on the relics of socialism that through postsocialist memory have been turned into heritage, as explored by recent scholarship, but instead it focused on the production of and dealings with heritage in socialist times in the domestic and international realms.[46] It shows how national interpretations with martyrological motives were interwoven with universalist claims in a socialist framing. Since its beginnings, the World Heritage program has provided a context for formulating and validating national meanings in an international context. The conditions of the production of the heritage group described here and of the choice of the individual sites were firmly rooted in Poland's socialist administration. Of the five heritage objects, three had already been defined as protected heritage sites in the People's Republic, with one national park (Białowieża) and two Museums (Wieliczka and Auschwitz). The historical city centers of Warsaw and Kraków were well established as monument preservationists' favorite projects. This group of nominated sites formed a small pantheon with high prestige in the People's Republic. The arguments supporting inscription, the written justifications, and the description of the objects reveal the values for which these objects were appreciated in their societal context. Auschwitz was an essential part of that national memory. The State Museum of Auschwitz-Birkenau at times was subject to close attention from central state and Party bodies, with particular focus on the representation of its ideological significance. This institution was the first in Poland among a group of Museums that indeed formed a separate socialist category, namely (International) Museums of Martyrdom. In the Polish People's Republic, this sector was under the auspices of the Council for the Protection of Struggle and Martyrdom Sites (ROPWiM), which meant that it existed to some degree separately from the other large national museums and objects of monument preservation and was integrated much more closely into Party-controlled politics of history and memory.

The integral values and topics that formed the basis of this Polish presentation of heritage were largely derived from national narratives for which universal translation, or at least acknowledgment, was sought. The cases of Warsaw and especially of Auschwitz showed the close interconnection between socialist and national interpretations. The resurrection of the "martyred" capital city was a national topos, but it was inseparable from the socialist state's founding myth and its power over the framework for the memory of destruction and reconstruction as both its organizer, provider, and central actor. Auschwitz-Birkenau was framed as an embodiment of that national martyrdom.

The way this national sacrifice was presented, the line of argument subsuming and marginalizing the experience of others, the idea of an internationalist heroic struggle, and the staging of world peace were all derived from common socialist paradigms and practices of commemorational politics. National martyrdom was at the same time considered a universal value, with any heroic struggle always being internationalist and antifascist. Both martyrdom and heroism formed the heart of national Polish memory of World War II. This was the founding myth of the Polish People's

Republic, meaning that it was judged the worthiest frame of reference for presenting heritage in an international setting as formed by the idea and program of World Heritage.

Julia Röttjer holds a master's degree in Eastern European History, Medieval and Modern History, Political Science and Art History from Kiel University, Germany. Her research interests include cultures of memory, history policies, public history and studies of material culture, urbanism and architecture, World Heritage, and international history. She works as a researcher at the German Institute of Polish Affairs in Darmstadt and is an affiliated scholar at the Leibniz Institute of European History in Mainz. Her PhD project is titled "Challenging the Concept of UNESCO's World Heritage? The History of the Former Concentration Camp Auschwitz-Birkenau as World Cultural Heritage."

Notes

1. Parent, "UNESCO World Heritage Committee," 21.
2. Zaremba, *Komunizm, legitymizacja, nacjonalizm*; idem, *Im nationalen Gewande*; idem, *Communism – Legitimacy – Nationalism*; Górny, *"Die Wahrheit ist auf unserer Seite"*; idem, *Przede wszystkim ma być naród*; idem, *The Nation Should Come First*. For an earlier perspective in political sciences, see Zwick, *National Communism*; cf. also Kemp, *Nationalism and Communism in Eastern Europe*. With special emphasis on the developments from 1944 until 1960, see Curp, *The Politics of Ethnic Cleansing in Western Poland*; Meyer, *Zwischen Ideologie und Pragmatismus*; Fleming, *Communism, Nationalism and Ethnicity in Poland*.
3. "Pomnik Męczeństwa Narodu Polskiego i innych Narodów"—*naród* could be translated as either "nation" or "people." The changes in Polish Auschwitz discourses and thus in the Auschwitz-Birkenau Museum are discussed in Huener, *Auschwitz, Poland and the Politics of Commemoration*; Wóycicka, *Arrested Mourning*; Hansen, *"Nie wieder Auschwitz!"*; see also Steinlauf, *Bondage to the Dead*; Kucia, *Auschwitz jako fakt społeczny*; Forecki, *Reconstructing Memory*.
4. "UNESCO World Heritage Committee. Second Session."
5. Pawłowski, "30 lat Listy Dziedzictwa Światowego UNESCO," 94.
6. These are my findings after thorough research in the respective collections of the Internal Archive of the Polish Ministry of Culture and National Heritage (Archiwum Zakładowe Ministerstwa Kultury i Dziedzictwa Narodowe) and in the Archive of the Polish Ministry of Foreign Affairs (Archiwum Ministerstwa Spraw Zagranicznych), both in Warsaw.
7. Foremost among them, the Committee's information bulletin, which did not mention the preparations for proposing Auschwitz to the World Heritage program nor the program itself (even in contexts in which UNESCO was mentioned), nor the handing in of the proposal. The first and only appearance is a one-hundred-word article about the acceptance of Auschwitz on the World Heritage List in

November 1979, which stated that the IAC had "also supported" the nomination. "Auschwitz-Birkenau auf der Liste des Welterbes," 1.

8. Lennon and Foley gave an incorrect chronology of the process and initially named the IAC as the author of the nomination based on one sentence in an article published retrospectively fifteen years later by former IAC president Maurice Goldstein; other researchers took this information from them. Lennon and Foley, *Dark Tourism*, 49.
9. Stengel, *Herman Langbein*, 143–459; Wóycicka, "Auf dem Weg zu einer gemeinsamen Erinnerung?"; Wawrzyniak, *Veterans, Victims, and Memory*.
10. According to correspondence in the files of the Auschwitz-Birkenau State Museum's Conservation Department.
11. Pawłowski, "30 lat Listy Dziedzictwa Światowego UNESCO."
12. "World Heritage List. Auschwitz—Concentration Camp, Poland. Nomination Form."
13. Ibid.
14. In 1947, the Museums in Auschwitz-Birkenau and Majdanek were officially founded by the Central Government. Wóycicka, *Arrested Mourning*; Peters, *Revolution der Erinnerung*, 77–80. A guidebook published by the central institution for memorial policy, the Council for the Protection of Struggle and Martyrdom Sites (Rada Ochrony Pomników Walk i Męczeństwa) lists almost two thousand entries: Schutzrat für Kampf- und Märtyrerdenkmäler, *Stätten des Kampfes und des Märtyrertums*.
15. UNESCO, *Convention Concerning the Protection of the World Cultural and Natural Heritage*, Art. 6.
16. Piper, *Ilu ludzi zginęło w KL Auschwitz*; idem, "The Number of Victims."
17. "World Heritage List. Auschwitz."
18. Ibid.
19. Ibid.
20. On the concept in the nineteenth century, its connection to earlier ideas of *antemurale christianitatis* and its later function as the basis for identity in face of the "other," and for ethnic division, cf. Zubrzycki, *The Crosses of Auschwitz*, 40–57.
21. Peters, *Revolution der Erinnerung*, 38–49, 72–80; cf. Górny, *"Die Wahrheit ist auf unserer Seite,"* esp. 340–64 on the ambivalent Marxist reading of the uprisings; Wawrzyniak, *Veterans, Victims, and Memory*, 19–26; Wóycicka, *Arrested Mourning*.
22. Interview with Krzysztof Pawłowski, conducted by the author (Warsaw, 11 April 2014); Beazley, "Drawing a Line," 81–86; "UNESCO Intergovernmental Committee for the Protection of the World Cultural and Natural Heritage, Second Session."
23. Hryniewiecki, "Rebirth of a Shattered City"; Crowley, "People's Warsaw"; Kohlrausch, "Die Zentralität der Apokalypse nach 1945"; Popiołek, "Keine Stunde Null."
24. Zaremba, *Im nationalen Gewande*, 364–368.
25. "World Heritage List. Nomination submitted by Poland."
26. Ibid.
27. "World Heritage List. Cracov's [sic] Historical and Architectural urban Centre."
28. Ibid. The wording also exposed a colonial perspective that categorized this layer of history as rather marginal: "The old city of Kazimierz contained a Jewish ghetto

which dated back to the end of the 15th century and which, in the 16th and 17th centuries was a centre of Jewish culture and science. The ghetto retained its specificity and local colour until the Second World War . . ."
29. Bohn, Dalhouski, and Krzoska, *Wisent-Wildnis und Welterbe*. The term bloodlands was coined by Snyder, *Bloodlands*.
30. Interview with Krzysztof Pawłowski, conducted by the author (Warsaw, 11 April 2014); Beazley, "Drawing a Line around a Shadow?," 81–86; "UNESCO Intergovernmental Committee for the Protection of the World Cultural and Natural Heritage."
31. Inscription was tied to a set of criteria, of which six related to cultural and four to natural properties. Auschwitz was later to be included under criterion vi, which read at the time: "each nominated property should . . . be most importantly <u>associated</u> with ideas or beliefs, with events or with persons, of outstanding historical importance or significance"—emphasis in the original. "Operational Guidelines for the Implementation of the World Heritage Convention."
32. Parent, "UNESCO World Heritage Committee," 21.
33. Ibid.
34. Ibid., 24—emphasis in the original.
35. Smith, *Uses of Heritage*, 87–114; Cameron, "From Warsaw to Mostar," 19–24; Rehling and Paulmann, "Historische Authentizität jenseits von 'Original' und 'Fälschung'"; Mager, *Schillernde Unschärfe*; Röttjer, "Authentizität im UNESCO-Welterbe-Diskurs."
36. ICOMOS, "Evaluation to World Heritage List proposal no. 30. The historic center of Warsaw." Paris, May 1980. ICOMOS Documentation Centre Paris. World Heritage Sites, Box 30 "Centre Historique de Varsovie."
37. Letter from Gerhart M. Riegner, World Jewish Congress Secretary-General, to UNESCO Director General Amadou-Mahtar M'Bow (Genf 4 October 1979). UNESCO Archive Paris, Sig. 069:7 (100) A 218/101/103 (438).
38. "UNESCO World Heritage Committee, Third Session."
39. ICOMOS, "Evaluation to World Heritage List proposal no. 31. The National Museum of Auschwitz-Birkenau."
40. E.g., Beazley, "Drawing a Line around a Shadow?"; Cameron and Rössler, *Many Voices, One Vision*, 223–25.
41. For more on the issue of inscription and categorization, see Röttjer, "Safeguarding 'Negative Historical Values.'"
42. See endnote 30 above.
43. Interview with Krzysztof Pawłowski, conducted by the author. Warsaw University of Technology, 11 April 2014.
44. Correspondence in UNESCO Archive Paris, Sig. 069:7 (100) A 218/101/103 (438).
45. Cherviatsova, "Memory as a Battlefield"; cf. Wolff-Powęska and Forecki, *Der Holocaust in der polnischen Erinnerungskultur*; idem, *World War II and Two Occupations*; Forecki, *Reconstructing Memory*.
46. For examples and reflections of this theme, see Rampley, *Heritage, Ideology, and Identity in Central and Eastern Europe*; Mink and Neumayer, *History, Memory and Politics in Central and Eastern Europe*; Sindbæk Andersen and Törnquist-Plewa, *Disputed Memory*.

Bibliography

"Auschwitz-Birkenau auf der Liste des Welterbes." *Comité International d'Auschwitz: Informationsbulletin* [German version] 224, no. 11 (1979): 1.

Beazley, Olwen. "Drawing a Line around a Shadow? Including Associative, Intangible Cultural Heritage Values on the World Heritage List." PhD diss., Australian National University, 2006.

Bohn, Thomas M., Aliaksandr Dalhouski, and Markus Krzoska. *Wisent-Wildnis und Welterbe: Geschichte des polnisch-weißrussischen Nationalparks von Białowieża.* Cologne: Böhlau, 2017.

Cameron, Christina. "From Warsaw to Mostar: The World Heritage Committee and Authenticity." *APT Bulletin* 39 (2008): 19–24.

Cameron, Christina, and Mechtild Rössler. *Many Voices, One Vision: The Early Years of the World Heritage Convention.* Farnham: Routledge, 2013.

Cherviatsova, Alina. "Memory as a Battlefield: European Memorial Laws and Freedom of Speech." *The International Journal of Human Rights* (2020): 1–20.

Crowley, David. "People's Warsaw / Popular Warsaw." *Journal of Design History* 10, no. 2 (1997): 203–23.

Curp, T. David. *The Politics of Ethnic Cleansing in Western Poland, 1945–1960.* Rochester, NY: Rochester University Press, 2006.

Fleming, Michael. *Communism, Nationalism and Ethnicity in Poland, 1944–1950.* London: Routledge, 2009.

Forecki, Piotr. *Reconstructing Memory: The Holocaust in Polish Public Debates.* Frankfurt am Main: Peter Lang, 2013.

Górny, Maciej. *"Die Wahrheit ist auf unserer Seite": Nation, Marxismus und Geschichte im Ostblock.* Cologne: Böhlau, 2011.

———. *The Nation Should Come First: Marxism and Historiography in East Central Europe* Frankfurt am Main: Peter Lang, 2013.

———. *Przede wszystkim ma być naród: Marksistkowie historiografie w Europie Środkowo-Wschodniej.* Warsaw: TRIO, 2007.

Hansen, Imke. *"Nie wieder Auschwitz!" Die Entstehung eines Symbols und der Alltag einer Gedenkstätte 1945–1955.* Göttingen: Wallstein, 2014.

Hryniewiecki, Jerzy. "Rebirth of a Shattered City." *UNESCO Courier* 14 (March 1961): 4–13.

Huener, Jonathan. *Auschwitz, Poland and the Politics of Commemoration, 1945–1979.* Athens: Ohio University Press, 2003.

ICOMOS. "Evaluation to World Heritage List proposal no. 31. The National Museum of Auschwitz-Birkenau." *UNESCO World Heritage Centre*, n.d. Retrieved 8 August 2018. http://whc.unesco.org/archive/advisory_body_evaluation/031.pdf.

Kemp, Walter A. *Nationalism and Communism in Eastern Europe and the Soviet Union: A Basic Contradiction?* Houndmills: Macmillan, 1999.

Kohlrausch, Martin. "Die Zentralität der Apokalypse nach 1945: Städtebauliche Kontinuitätslinien und die internationale Rezeption des Wiederaufbaus von Warschau." In *Wiederaufbau europäischer Städte: Rekonstruktionen, die Moderne und die lokale Identitätspolitik seit 1945*, edited by Georg Wagner-Kyora, 179–201. Stuttgart: Franz Steiner, 2014.

Kucia, Marek. *Auschwitz jako fakt społeczny: Historia, współczesność i świadomość społeczna KL Auschwitz w Polsce.* Kraków: Universitas, 2005.

Lennon, J. John, and Malcolm Foley. *Dark Tourism: The Attraction of Death and Disaster.* Andover: Cengage Learning, 2010.
Mager, Tino. *Schillernde Unschärfe: Der Begriff der Authentizität im architektonischen Erbe.* Berlin: De Gruyter, 2016.
Meyer, Stefan. *Zwischen Ideologie und Pragmatismus: Die Legitimationsstrategien der Polnischen Arbeiterpartei 1944–1948.* Berlin: Wissenschaftlicher Verlag, 2008.
Mink, Georges, and Laure Neumayer, eds. *History, Memory and Politics in Central and Eastern Europe: Memory Games.* Hampshire: Palgrave Macmillan, 2013.
"Operational Guidelines for the Implementation of the World Heritage Convention (adopted by the Committee at its first session and amended at its second session)." *UNESCO World Heritage Centre,* n.d. [1978]. Retrieved 8 August 2018. http://whc.unesco.org/archive/opguide78.pdf.
Parent, Michel. "UNESCO World Heritage Committee. Report by Vice-Chairman and Rapporteur: Comparative Study of Nominations and Criteria for World Cultural Heritage." Paris, 20 September 1979. Retrieved 8 August 2018. http://whc.unesco.org/archive/1979/cc-79-conf003-11e.pdf.
Pawłowski, Krzysztof. "30 lat Listy Dziedzictwa Światowego UNESCO" In *Współczesne problemy teorii konserwatorskiej w Polsce,* edited by Bogusław Szymgin, 93–100. Warsaw: Wydawnictwo Politechniki Lubelskiej, 2008.
Peters, Florian. *Revolution der Erinnerung: Der Zweite Weltkrieg in der Geschichtskultur des spätsozialistischen Polen.* Berlin: Ch. Links, 2016.
Piper, Franciszek. *Ilu ludzi zginęło w KL Auschwitz: Liczba ofiar w świetle źródeł i badań.* Oświęcim: Państwowe Muzeum Oświęcim-Brzezinka, 1992.
———. "The Number of Victims." In *Anatomy of the Auschwitz Death Camp,* edited by Yisrael Gutman and Michael Berenbaum, 61–76. Bloomington: Indiana University Press; Washington, DC: United States Holocaust Memorial Museum, 1994.
Popiołek, Małgorzata. "Keine Stunde Null: Das Wiederaufbauprogramm für die polnischen Altstädte nach dem Zweiten Weltkrieg von Jan Zachwatowicz." In *Geteilt—Vereint! Denkmalpflege in Mitteleuropa zur Zeit des Eisernen Vorhangs und heute,* edited by Ursula Schädler-Saub and Angela Weyer, 129–39. Petersberg: Michael Imhof, 2015.
Rampley, Matthew, ed. *Heritage, Ideology, and Identity in Central and Eastern Europe: Contested Pasts, Contested Presents.* Woodbridge: Boydell Press, 2012.
Rehling, Andrea, and Johannes Paulmann. "Historische Authentizität jenseits von 'Original' und 'Fälschung': Ästhetische Wahrnehmung—gespeicherte Erfahrung—gegenwärtige Performanz." In *Historische Authentizität,* edited by Martin Sabrow and Achim Saupe, 91–125. Göttingen: Wallstein, 2016.
Röttjer, Julia. "Authentizität im UNESCO-Welterbe-Diskurs: Das Konzentrations- und Vernichtungslager Auschwitz-Birkenau." In *Authentizität als Kapital historischer Orte? Die Sehnsucht nach dem unmittelbaren Erleben von Geschichte,* edited by Axel Drecoll, Thomas Schaarschmidt, and Irmgard Zündorf, 35–55. Göttingen: Wallstein, 2019.
———. "Safeguarding 'Negative Historical Values' for the Future? Appropriating the Past in the UNESCO Cultural World Heritage Site Auschwitz-Birkenau." *Ab Imperio* 4 (2015): 130–65.
Schutzrat für Kampf- und Märtyrerdenkmäler, ed. *Stätten des Kampfes und des Märtyrertuzms 1939–1945: Jahre des Krieges in Polen. Guide.* Warsaw: Sport i Turystyka, 1965.

Sindbæk Andersen, Tea, and Barbara Törnquist-Plewa, eds. *Disputed Memory: Mediation, Emotions, and Memory Politics in Central, Eastern and South-Eastern Europe.* Berlin: De Gruyter, 2016.

Smith, Laurajane. *Uses of Heritage.* London: Routledge, 2006.

Snyder, Timothy. *Bloodlands: Europe between Hitler and Stalin.* New York: Basic Books, 2010.

Steinlauf, Michael C. *Bondage to the Dead: Poland and the Memory of the Holocaust.* Syracuse: Syracuse University Press, 1997.

Stengel, Katharina. *Herman Langbein: Ein Auschwitz-Überlebender in den erinnerungspolitischen Konflikten der Nachkriegszeit.* Frankfurt am Main: Campus, 2012.

UNESCO. *Convention Concerning the Protection of the World Cultural and Natural Heritage.* Paris: UNESCO, 1972.

"UNESCO Intergovernmental Committee for the Protection of the World Cultural and Natural Heritage. Second Session. Washington D.C. 5–8 September 1978. Final Report of the rapporteur [Krzysztof Pawłowski]." Paris, 9 October 1978. Retrieved 8 August 2018. http://whc.unesco.org/archive/1978/cc-78-conf010-10rev_e.pdf.

"UNESCO World Heritage Committee. Second Session. Washington, D.C. 5–8 September 1978. List of nominations to the World Heritage List and of requests for technical cooperation." Paris, 15 July 1978. Retrieved 10 June 2019. https://whc.unesco.org/en/sessions/02COM/documents/.

"UNESCO World Heritage Committee. Third Session. Cairo and Luxor, 22–26 October 1979. Report of the rapporteur [Michel Parent]." Paris, 30 November 1979. Retrieved 8 August 2018. http://whc.unesco.org/archive/repcom79.htm#31.

Wawrzyniak, Joanna. *Veterans, Victims, and Memory: The Politics of the Second World War in Communist Poland.* Frankfurt am Main: Peter Lang, 2015.

Wolff-Powęska, Anna, and Piotr Forecki, eds. *Der Holocaust in der polnischen Erinnerungskultur.* Frankfurt am Main: Peter Lang, 2013.

———. *World War II and Two Occupations: Dilemmas of Polish Memory.* Frankfurt am Main: Peter Lang, 2016.

"World Heritage List. Auschwitz—Concentration Camp, Poland. Nomination Form." Warsaw, 2 May 1978. Retrieved 8 August 2018. http://unesdoc.unesco.org/images/0003/000377/037749eb.pdf.

"World Heritage List. Cracov's [sic] Historical and Architectural urban Centre. Nomination Form." Warsaw, 2 May 1978. Retrieved 8 August 2018. http://whc.unesco.org/uploads/nominations/29bis.pdf.

"World Heritage List. Nomination submitted by Poland. Warsaw Historical Centre." Warsaw, 2 May 1978. Retrieved 8 August 2018. http://unesdoc.unesco.org/images/0003/000377/037760eb.pdf.

Wóycicka, Zofia. *Arrested Mourning: Memory of the Nazi Camps in Poland, 1944–1950.* Frankfurt am Main: Peter Lang, 2014.

———. "Auf dem Weg zu einer gemeinsamen Erinnerung? Die Internationalen Auschwitz- und Buchenwald-Komitees in den Jahren von 1952 bis 1989/1990." In *Von Mahnstätten über zeithistorische Museen zu Orten des Massentourismus? Gedenkstätten an Orten von NS-Verbrechen in Polen und Deutschland,* edited by Enrico Heitzer, Günter Morsch, Robert Traba, and Katarzyna Woniak, 74–83. Berlin: Metropol, 2016.

Zaremba, Marcin. *Communism—Legitimacy—Nationalism: Nationalist Legitimization of the Communist Regime in Poland*. Berlin: Peter Lang, 2019.

———. *Im nationalen Gewande: Strategien kommunistischer Herrschaftslegitimation in Polen 1944–1980*. Osnabrück: fibre, 2011.

———. *Komunizm, legitymizacja, nacjonalizm: Nacjonalistyczna legitymizacja władzy komunistycznej w Polsce*. Warsaw: TRIO, 2001.

Zubrzycki, Geneviève. *The Crosses of Auschwitz: Nationalism and Religion in Postcommunist Poland*. Chicago: The University of Chicago Press, 2006.

Zwick, Peter. *National Communism*. Boulder, CO: Westview, 1983.

CHAPTER 3

International Tourism and the Making of the National Heritage Canon in Late Soviet Ukraine, 1964–1991

Iryna Sklokina

Tourism is traditionally discussed in nationalism studies as a classical tool of nation-building.[1] As such, tourism helps to strengthen visual imaginaries of the nation's past, creates mental geographical borders, fosters national pride, and as a collective practice helps to build shared identifications. However, as Hyung-yu Park has noted, while the role of institutions in the selection and promotion of particular objects as elements of national heritage has been widely studied, much less attention has been paid to "unofficial and informal mechanisms of national identity formation via heritage tourism practices" and "how personal perceptions and individualized meanings, and subjective sentiments concerning collective social memories contribute to the long-standing tourism appeal of heritage institutions."[2] This remark is especially relevant for research on socialist countries because their official institutions are usually seen by scholars in terms of controlling and structuring individual experiences of the past, including heritage tourism.

Here I would like to focus on the interaction of official institutions and the grassroots level of tourism as a performance conducted by the guides and visitors.[3] My aim is to analyze how individual and group encounters between the visitors, places, and hosting professionals of the tourist sphere under state socialism contributed to making and negotiating the national heritage canon. How was the selection of particular objects as heritage influenced by the tastes and expectations of diverse publics? What possibilities for negotiating the meanings of particular heritage objects were present on the grassroots level? How special was tourist-based nation-making under socialism, and how were different versions of being Ukrainian negotiated by diasporic and nondiasporic visitors?

Recent scholarly works on tourism in post-Stalinist Soviet society situate this phenomenon in the context of the rise of consumerism and growing interactions and competition between the capitalist and socialist blocs during the Cold War and détente.[4] Indeed, scholars have mostly noted the modernizing and westernizing aspects of the Soviet tourism. It is therefore understandable that the issue of socialist heritage-making through tourist practices is still an understudied field, with few scholars highlighting aspects of tourism such as its contributions to national and imperial ideologies. In fact, the processes of internationalization and nationalization went hand in hand and involved multiple actors and discourses based around expertise, ideology, and practice. One of the most important works on this subject, by Zbigniew Wojnowski, explores Soviet international tourism as part of the cultural diplomacy between the USSR and countries of the socialist bloc. He highlights in particular Soviet ambitions for creating supremacy and imperial dominance through foreign tourism and the specific Soviet-Ukrainian patriotism emerging from interactions with the eastern European "Other."[5] Sergei Zhuk's article on Soviet travel agencies is another balanced account of how profit-oriented late Soviet tourism adopted advertising tools that mimicked Western-style rock music mixed with a national Ukrainian flavor.[6] Rachel Applebaum's research has illustrated the problem of Soviet international tourism's imperial dimensions, specifically in relation to Czechoslovakia.[7] The pioneering book by Victoria Donovan, meanwhile, is one of the first attempts to bring together the postwar Soviet politics of heritage, patriotism, and tourist practices, with a focus on the region of the historical Northwest of Russia.[8] A closer look at tourist practices offers insight into the broader processes of the local turn, regionalism, and nation-building in the late Soviet Union. Despite the homogenizing attempts to create a "Soviet nation" (*sovetskii narod*), separate nations consolidated within the institutional frameworks of socialist republics, with local Party elites forming paternalist clans, while the local intelligentsia employed the potential of *kraevedenie* (local studies) and tourism for more freedom in cultural production.[9]

In this text I would like to focus on international tourism as a sphere highly dependent on professional expertise, knowledge infrastructures, and ideological frameworks, where actors positioned on different levels of administration and practice were engaged in dialogue. This dialogue involved discussion on heritage-related issues within expert milieux, with their audiences, and with the authorities. This dialogue was marked not only by conformism and adaptation to the supposed expectations, but also by disagreements and inventiveness. I examine both modernizing and nationalizing aspects of tourism under socialism using several groups of sources: archives of tourist organizations (primarily tourist guides' reports about their conversations with audiences; minutes from the conferences for the specialists in the branch; texts of excursions; plans of newly created tourist routes; and correspondence with Party organs and local, republican, and central bodies),[10] tourist guidebooks, memoirs of travelers, and materials of specialized press.[11] In this way I combine both publicly circulated representations of socialist tourism as well as materials intended for the internal use of tourist agencies and their communication with state organs. The broader problem behind this study is the interrelation between consumer culture, Soviet modernization, the sphere of heritage tourism, and the making of late Soviet Ukrainian identity.

International Tourism to the Ukrainian SSR

The growing importance of international tourism to the USSR from the 1960s to the 1980s affected the structure of state control and management organs, fostering the development of tourist infrastructure in individual republics. In 1964, new state organs (offices for international tourism) were created in every union republic and attached to the respective Councils of Ministers. On the practical level, trips were organized by three main agencies: Inturist (most prominent one), trade unions, and the Sputnik travel agency. In the Ukrainian SSR, the divisions and agencies of Inturist grew exponentially, from seven in the 1960s (located only in the biggest tourist destinations—Kyiv, Kharkiv, Lviv, Odesa, Yalta, Uzhhorod, and Zaporizhia) to twenty-four (in every region) by the late 1980s.[12] By the late 1970s, almost one third of all international visitors to the USSR traveled to Ukraine.[13]

International tourism to the Ukrainian Soviet Socialist Republic had some specific features, most notably the presence of numerous diaspora groups. The territories forming today's Ukraine were part of the multicultural borderlands of the Russian and Austro-Hungarian Empires in the nineteenth and early twentieth centuries, where (most prominently) Polish, Jewish, Russian, Ukrainian, Hungarian, Romanian, and Tatar groups lived. For a long period, these agrarian lands were a source of migrants who left for many countries around the world. Some of those who identified as Ukrainian participated in the creation of lively community organizations, such as cultural clubs, cooperative firms and businesses, and political organizations, contributing to the formation of Ukrainian national (and nationalist) identification, especially after the wave of nationally minded migrants arrived after the period of revolution and state-building in 1917–21.[14]

From 1958 the Soviet political leadership permitted the Ukrainian diaspora from capitalist countries to visit their (or their parents') country of origin, both as individual travelers and members of organized groups (traveling with commercial tourist companies or other organizations, such as, for example, the left-leaning Association of United Ukrainian Canadians and the League of American Ukrainians). Gradually, tourists from the capitalist West became an important target group for Inturist's efforts to generate profit, with the most numerous groups among them treated separately as specific categories, including, for example, Canadian Ukrainians. It was also possible for Jews from the United States, Israel, and Latin America, as well as Hungarians, Poles, and Romanians to visit Soviet Ukraine as their former native country.[15] With the development of the tourist industry, the idea of differentiated approaches to the target groups became increasingly important. In some cases specific itineraries were created for visitors of Ukrainian origin,[16] with the round trip Lviv–Kyiv–Lviv, for example, enjoying enormous popularity among this category of visitors.[17] There were also separate groups of visitors of Jewish Ukrainian origin from Canada and the United States, groups from both the Federal Republic of Germany and the German Democratic Republic, and groups from France (Frenchmen and Frenchwomen, as well as émigrés from the former Russian Empire). There were also parties from the socialist "near abroad" grouped by countries (and very often professions). Visitors from the capitalist countries became more numerous year after year. In 1960 only 160 Canadian Ukrainians visited Ukraine (in six groups),[18] while in 1975 there were almost five thousand.[19] In the cities in the west of the Republic, Ukrainian diaspora tourists prevailed among foreign visitors; in 1972, they constituted more than half of the foreign visitors to Lviv and almost all the foreign visitors to Ternopil.[20]

The Performance of the National Identities in Soviet Ukrainian Heritage Tourism

The Soviet Inturist organization targeted international visitors, especially from the diaspora, both for ideological reasons (as potential future friends of the USSR in the West) and in order to secure hard currency income. Thus, the whole enterprise was marked by the inevitable contradiction between the wish to convey propaganda messages and to please the visitors. However, there was at least one point where both goals aligned, namely in the national coloring of the tourist service as both political strategy (to highlight the "friendship of the nations" and respect of national rights in the USSR) and its commercial strategy that made entertaining and exoticizing use of national aspects. Here I will show how these two interrelated goals were pursued in constant dialogue with audiences, and how this dialogue impacted on the selection of the heritage objects for the tours and their (re)interpretation. I argue that in this dialogue national identities were constructed, performed, and interpreted.

Diaspora visitors posed several challenges to the Soviet hosts. Mostly the tourists wished to visit ancient monuments, churches, and their rural places of origin.[21] However, the rural areas were largely closed to tourist groups, while the accent on ancient heritage in the tourism industry provoked anxieties among the Soviet bureaucrats who faced requirements "to reduce the share of Historicism" in the excursions in favor of modern buildings and Soviet monuments.[22] Heritage tourism was presented as a more progressive and "cultured" activity in comparison to visits to relatives in the villages. As an alternative, visits were organized to the "advanced" collective farms or to *skansens*, open-air museums of folk architecture and everyday life, for example, in Lviv (opened in 1971), Uzhhorod (1970), or near Kyiv in the village of Pyrohiv (1976). But only in bigger cities did the Inturist guides have all the possibilities at their disposal to demonstrate the marvels of industry and modern services (or, as the propaganda slogan put it, "the achievements of the Soviet people"[23]). For those who insisted on seeing relatives, Inturist proposed special meeting rooms in the bigger cities, or the relatives were taken on the organized tour together with the foreign guests.[24]

Another challenge was the international tourists' criticism of Soviet nationality policy. They raised the issue of the dominance of the Russian language in the public sphere, the Soviet historical narrative, its canon of national heroes, the reasons for the deportation of Crimean Tatars in 1944, and rights for Jewish emigration to Israel, among other things.[25] In response, the managers of tourism and international exchange, both on the local and republican levels (from the Party organs and professionals of the tourist sphere), called for increasing the presence of the Ukrainian language in tourism-related services and including more "national" landmarks on the itineraries. Of course, this shift was only possible due to the fact that the category of the nation remained one of the backbones of the Soviet system, offering support for the formal state attributes of the republics, including strictly controlled cultural diplomacy.[26] While the Ukrainian SSR had no real power in decision-making on the international issues, despite formally having a separate seat in the United Nations, its bureaucrats from the Commission for Foreign Affairs of the Supreme Council took seriously the need for the republic to be represented in international exchanges as a distinct actor with its own national pride, innovative industry, and authentic culture. In the context of de-Stalinization around 1956–57, the Commission started discussing ways to enhance the distribution of Ukrainian cultural products abroad, including books, press, souvenirs, and creative arts performances, while also noting the need to greet foreign delegations in Ukrainian.[27] Similarly, in discussions relating to hospitality infrastructure for foreign tourists to Ukraine, the members of the Commission stressed the need to produce more national-themed souvenirs and play Ukrainian music in the restaurants, for example. A resolution of the Central Committee of the Communist Party of Ukraine from 1965 also included several points on the presence of national culture in tourist services for foreigners.[28]

Staff working in the tourist industry were responsible for the practical implementation of these measures. From the 1960s, the reports of the regional Inturist departments began mentioning themed Ukrainian cuisine and restaurants, designed and built with the support of the Ministry of Trade.[29] The Moscow-based journal *Travel to the USSR* targeted international audiences and promoted the "exotic" (*ekzoticheskii*) Ukrainian-themed restaurants as well.[30] In 1973, the Department for International Tourism in Kyiv recommended implementing new forms of "cultured service" for foreign visitors, including "national arts festivals, theatrical shows staged at historical and architectural monuments and art museums,"[31] following the global demand for new forms of entertainment such as historical reenactments with local and national flavor. In 1976, the Department requested that the cafés and restaurants of the Inturist system report any use of what they called national and exotic[32] styles in their interior design.[33] The use of national flavor went so far that Ukrainian-themed restaurants were established not only in cities in the Ukrainian SSR, but also in Sochi, where the Ukrainian restaurant "Staraia melnitsa" was advertised along with the Caucasus-themed restaurant "Kavkazskii aul," as well as some other places where one could listen to *tsyganskie pesni* ("Gypsy songs"), see performances of the Balalaika ensemble, and eat Russian *bliny*.[34] It was of clear commercial significance, as were other new forms of tourist activity—for example, *ukrainski vechornytsi* (Ukrainian evening parties) organized in Lviv and Ternopil. These two western Ukrainian cities were very important for the tourist industry, as visitors from the Ukrainian diaspora were particularly prevalent there. Other national groups of visitors to western Ukraine were also supposed to be impressed by demonstrations of the respect of minority rights—for example, one Romanian-language school in Boyany village in Chernivtsi became a favorite destination for Romanian tourists,[35] while the collective farm Ukraina in the Zaporizhia region (with 80 percent of its inhabitants being Czech) became an important destination for tourists from Czechoslovakia.[36]

Importantly, the request of the republican Department for International Tourism that the guides should speak in the native language with visitors of Ukrainian origin had an additional impact: using the common language that was mostly preserved in the domestic, rather than public, sphere created a sense of closeness, frankness, and simplicity (key values proclaimed during the Khrushchev era). Speaking Ukrainian to the diaspora tourists also made perfect sense given the shortage of tourist guides with good skills in foreign languages. Thus, a nationalizing trend accompanied efforts toward creating a more personalized service, with reports on the "meetings with Soviet people in an informal atmosphere," along with visits to the homes of "ordinary Soviet people," becoming common in the tourist industry in the 1970s and 1980s.[37] The culmination of this strategy came in 1987 when the State Committee on International Tourism in Moscow recommended introducing tea parties in the homes of Soviet families as part of the tours.[38]

The national coloring of the tourist experience also went hand in hand with renegotiations of the understanding of industrial pride as an essential Soviet characteristic and as part of the national character of the cities, likewise in the east of the republic. The case of Kharkiv, one of Ukraine's largest cities, which is located near the border with Russia, is especially telling here. For foreign tourists, Kharkiv was presented as a place where modern consumer and leisure practices could be pursued, as was illustrated by pointing to the more comfortable hotels, the subway, entertainment in Gorky Park, the children's railway, pioneer palace, and modern medical facilities.[39] If proletarian tourism before World War II presented Kharkiv as primarily a city of newly built giant plants, in the 1960s through to the 1980s illustrations of production were supplemented by a much stronger accent on leisure and entertainment. At the same time, the national coloring of Kharkiv became much more important.

While the memoirs of diaspora tourists often mention the city's "Russified" character, the tourism managers tried to introduce more national and exotic elements into the tours. In 1966, a typical critique of the shortcomings of work with international tourists in Kharkiv was that "Ukrainian dishes, fruits and vegetables are absent . . . sales of the Ukrainian themed souvenirs for hard currency are poorly organized."[40] To improve the impression, the city was included in the 1960s on the itinerary of a tour for foreigners called "Hopak" (a Ukrainian national dance), which was aimed at those fond of folklore. Featuring the cities of Uzhhorod, Lviv, Rivne, and Kharkiv, the route served as an attempt to highlight that genuine folk culture was preserved in different parts of Ukraine, from the west to the east. Including Kharkiv (and specifically its research institutes in biology) into the itineraries of the participants of the international congresses of beekeepers also served as proof of the preservation of traditional Ukrainian crafts in this city.[41] Including sites related to Taras Shevchenko, the most prominent nineteenth-century Ukrainian national bard, was another way of stressing the Ukrainianness of Kharkiv. The monument to Shevchenko, as well as the two sacral objects, the seventeenth-century Pokrovsky (Intercession of the Theotokos) Cathedral in the Ukrainian Cossack Baroque style and the Baroque and neoclassicist Uspensky (Assumption) Cathedral that was constructed in the eighteenth and nineteenth centuries, were must-sees. Finally, when the central Moscow-based Inturist asked its local departments to introduce new themed tours as a supplementary commercial service for foreign visitors in the *perestroika* period, the Kharkiv Inturist department already had a tried-and-tested solution, namely themed lunches with Ukrainian traditional meals accompanied by a *bandurist* (traditional Ukrainian instrument player).[42] Adding Ukrainian national coloring was characteristic for other big urban centers primarily associated with industry, including, for example, Donetsk.[43]

Similar evidence comes from Odesa, a city generally associated with the architectural heritage of the Russian Empire, World War II heroism, and Russian high culture. The Odesa Inturist department reported in 1967: "Given that year in year out Odesa is the biggest tourist center of the republic, we consider it reasonable to organize a professional Ukrainian [folk] singing and dancing band . . . this will have a wholesome effect on the cultural services for tourists and guests and will stimulate the flow of tourists."[44] As for restaurants, Odesa had both Ukrainian and Russian-themed establishments.[45]

The encounter with the foreigners led tour guides to express their own understandings of what it meant to be Ukrainian and what constitutes its heritage canon. In 1967, an analytical report on the shortcomings of the tourist services in Izmail (in the south of the Odesa region, on the border with Romania) described the situation thus: "As a shortcoming, I note the small quantity of Ukrainian-themed souvenirs, especially children's embroidered shirts . . . there are no cards and envelopes with the views of the city of Izmail as a city of glory of the Russian arms [*slavy russkogo oruzhiia*]. There are no souvenir badges of Izmail either."[46] What is noteworthy here is the purely ethnographic vision of the notion of Ukrainian, whereas Russian and local is associated with military and state glory. It is also (unsurprisingly) a vision of Ukrainianness where it makes perfect sense for Izmail to be both Russian and Ukrainian. In 1973, the huge diorama presenting the siege of the fortress Izmail by the imperial Russian general Suvorov in 1790 was unveiled in the city, enabling Inturist to offer a visit to Izmail for a supplement.[47] This understanding of Ukrainianness as essentially folklore-related was quite common among the tour guides. As one of them noted, "like opera belongs to Italians, folklore, by right, belongs to Ukrainians."[48]

Another example of the role of imperial discourse in the tours related to the Masandra winery in Crimea.[49] Although mainstream Soviet discourse promoted the resorts of Crimea as evidence of the Soviet policy of caring for the toiling masses in contrast to the oppressive tsarist policy,[50] there was nevertheless some scope for praising selected achievements of the imperial period. In advertisements from the 1970s, Masandra was called the "cradle of Russian wine-making," thus including the imperial period in its historical canon.[51] During *perestroika*, alternative visions of the past were sought and thus Masandra was presented, additionally, as a site of imperial glory and the cradle of the civilizing efforts of the Russian aristocrats (Prince Golitsyn) and tsars, who took care of the local peasants while taming the region's wild and exotic nature. Wine-tasting and singing popular songs in unofficial settings consequently became the most important way of promoting "friendship of nations" in Masandra.

However, an increasingly "pro-Ukrainian" and ethnically oriented trend emerged in the tours of Crimea as well.[52] As the regional Crimean division of Inturist highlighted, the American tourists of Ukrainian origin constituted a special category of visitors, distinguished from those of Russian and Jewish origin. The guides from Inturist were selected on the basis of having Ukrainian language skills. In this way, the local Inturist administrators fulfilled the requirements from above to differentiate approaches to the audiences.[53] As one of the tourist guides from Yalta complained in his 1972 report, in every group of Ukrainians from Canada or the United States there had always been at least one person "obsessively looking for everything Ukrainian" and "obsessively speaking about our [Soviet] shortcomings," so the work was not easy.[54] However, as a resort, Crimea offered opportunities to satisfy this specific interest in Ukrainian heritage because many important cultural figures (later appropriated by different national canons) visited it in the nineteenth and twentieth centuries. Thus, Ukrainian tourists had a chance to visit the places where the famous poet Lesia Ukrainka and other important cultural figures had lived or stayed in health resorts. One of the important destinations where it was possible to speak of Russian or Ukrainian heritage depending on the group of visitors was the Polikurivskyi Memorial in Yalta. It was created in 1967 as a necropolis out of the remnants of a cemetery that was destroyed during the Nazi occupation. The memorial included eighteen tombstones and a memorial plaque bearing seven additional names of "Russian, Ukrainian, and Byelorussian" artists, scientists, and political activists from the period before 1917.[55] Another good place to demonstrate the "friendship of nations" in Yalta was the Hill of Glory with a memorial dedicated to two groups at once: those who died fighting on the side of the Bolsheviks in battles between 1918 and 1921, and those fighting for the Soviets in World War II.[56]

In some cases, this formal Ukrainianization for tourist (and commercial) purposes coincided with the efforts of the grassroots movement of the

Soviet Ukrainian patriots. This was the case in Zaporizhia, one of the most mythologized places in the Ukrainian (both nineteenth-century and Soviet) national narrative, as it is considered the cradle of the Cossack movement of the fourteenth to eighteenth centuries.[57]

Soviet tourism of the 1920s and early 1930s presented this place as related exclusively to the achievements of Soviet industrialization, primarily the construction of a giant dam and hydroelectric station (Dniprohes, or Dneproges in Russian) on the River Dnieper. The route for children designed in 1933 offered the following description: "The backbone of the route is Dneproges, this giant of the five-year plan, this pride of the USSR working class, and here Dneproges is seen not as isolated object. Dneproges is not only a dam . . . it means also the plants of Zaporizhia steel, grandiose aluminum works, it is the experimental electrification station for the agriculture at Khortitsa island, it is the blossoming socialist city where there had been steppe."[58] By contrast, with the consumerist turn in the USSR in the 1960s, it became a place of struggle for the creation of the nature reserve and a theme park dedicated to Ukraine's glorious Cossack past. In contemporary Ukrainian historiography, this struggle is presented exclusively as proof of the Ukrainian intelligentsia's patriotic views while at the same time benefitting from the protection offered by the regional and republic-level Party leadership.[59] However, the interest in the heritagization of this place came from less "patriotic" and more profit-oriented circles, too. The instructor of the republican council on tourism, Kharchiladze, stated in the Moscow-based *Turist* journal in 1968:

> The Ukrainian tourist council created a grandiose project for the tourist reserve "Zaporizka Sich" on Khortytsia island. The island should become a reconstruction of the Zaporizhian Cossacks military camp—with *kureni* [special huts] and taverns, shops and square for meetings. Coming to such a settlement, the tourist feels as if taken back to those glorious times when our ancestors defended our Motherland from nomadic raids, and listens to the wonderful songs of *Zaporozhtsi*. The interior of the buildings will be furnished with the most modern equipment. We would like our tourists who travel by the roads of Ukraine not only to fall in love with the steppes and woods, but also to learn the heroic history of the republic.[60]

This orientation toward historicizing Zaporizhia and giving it a national flavor is likewise obvious in the journal *Travel to the USSR*. A 1977 article[61] (presumably by Johannes Thomas, an author from the GDR who visited the city and shared his impressions) presented the tour of Zaporizhia as offering a combination of experiencing Cossack history and visiting the Dniprohes dam, which the author saw not only as a monument to the USSR's industrial might but also as a place of World War II battles. The article specifically highlighted the obelisk to a soldier who lost his life following efforts to prevent the dam from being blown up. Toward the end of the Soviet era, both elements—industrial pride in Dniprohes and the heroic national Ukrainian past—were closely entangled.[62]

However, this mixing of modernity and tradition did not go as smoothly as planned. Foreigners' visits to Zaporizhia could become an occasion for discussing Ukrainian national identity in relation to tradition and modernity. In 1966 a Soviet tourist guide from Zaporizhia described a problematic discussion with a certain Doris Yanda from Canada, who criticized the Russification of Ukraine and lack of genuine folk traditions. In his reply, the guide made fun of the wish to see Ukrainians as retrograde peasants and highlighted how Ukraine had undergone comprehensive transformations; thus instead of Cossack mud huts, "now the Dniprohes sends its light to the whole Ukraine." But, "if you wish to see a Ukrainian who loves *horilka*, dumplings with cheese, and *halushky* (national dishes)—here I am. I am a real flesh and bone Ukrainian."[63] It is clear that through this discussion some kind of new construction of modern Ukrainian identity emerged, one combining both industrial pride and a nativist understanding of nationality. Notably, the visitors seemed to share this kind of banal nationalism fused with consumerist leisure, with its accent on national beverages. Interestingly enough, another "anti-Soviet" Canadian Ukrainian tourist criticized the Soviet Union for suppressing everything Ukrainian by referring to the fact that Ukrainian *horilka* is exported abroad under the trademark "Russian vodka."[64]

Quite evidently, the formation of the heritage canon was not a simple process dictated from the center. The guides and the audiences were involved in negotiations over it. As the local experts in the republics were the bearers of specific competencies and knowledge, they had to decide what objects and places should be selected for the tourists and how to compose a coherent narrative out of this selection. When in 1970 the Moscow-based journal *Travel to the USSR* decided to prepare a special issue on traveling to Ukraine for international audiences, the editorial board sent a draft of the issue to Yosyp Zatiahan, head of the Department for International Tourism at the Council of Ministers of Ukrainian SSR. It included a mix of old architectural monuments (such as St. Sophia's Cathedral in Kyiv), the centuries-old "Cossack" oak tree on Khortytsia island, Soviet achievements (both industrial and consumerist—newly constructed districts in the capital, Dniprohes water power plant, new hotels), an advanced collective farm, national poet Taras Shevchenko's house museum, traditional folk art (*hopak* dance), and entertainment with a national flavor (cooking national dishes, visiting themed ethnic restaurants, and souvenirs). However, the presentation of high culture was supposed to include a painting by the Russian Valentin Serov from the Kyiv Art Museum. Zatiahan was critical, making several suggestions: replacing Serov with a Ukrainian artist; that western Ukrainian cities should also be included; presenting *hopak* dances with several dance collectives from different cities, including articles on visiting the *skansens* (open air museums) of Ukrainian rural architecture.[65] In this case, the official from the Ukrainian SSR turned out to be an ideologically skillful actor with better understanding of how to achieve balance and present all the regions of the republic as home to genuinely Ukrainian folk culture in order to thus convince foreign tourists that national rights are respected in the USSR. The final version of the publication in 1971 in *Travel to the USSR* (see no. 4) had a stronger accent on Ukrainian culture.

Similar negotiations, this time between the republican tourist manager and a rank-and-file tourist guide, on the balancing of different cultural elements in the heritage canon can be found in documents from Kyiv in 1968. Guides there were asked for creative ideas on potential new forms of engaging visitors and one suggested reenactments of Russian traditions, such as "Farewell to Winter" and riding *troika*, as well as producing a wider choice of souvenirs such as *matreshka* dolls and traditional Russian wooden spoons. They also stressed the need to avoid "delivering long lectures" to the tourists and let them walk freely in the woods to pick mushrooms and berries. However, another official (most likely from the republican Department for International Tourism) made handwritten corrections to these proposals. Unsurprisingly, "Russian" was corrected into "Ukrainian," *matreshkas* into ethnically neutral "dolls," and the "Farewell to Winter" was replaced with the Ukrainian *koliadky* (Christmas carols modified for atheist tastes).[66] In this case, the tour guide had suggested the most stereotypical images of Russian folk culture (those probably best-known abroad), whereas the more ideologically prepared official preferred the Ukrainian version of Sovietness that was necessarily dominant in the Ukrainian SSR, in accordance with the Soviet policy of ethnic particularism and nativism.[67]

Border Regions: Dialogue and Contestation

Many visitors from Poland, Romania, Czechoslovakia, and Hungary with family roots in the border regions of western Ukraine were quite challenging for the Soviet tour managers because they refused to visit particular places, wanted to stay with relatives (using tourist visas merely as a pretext), and engaged in political disputes, especially around the time of crisis moments related to Soviet policy in the "near abroad."[68] The dialogue embedded in tourism-based encounters could easily turn into contestation. One of the most telling examples is Lviv, the formerly Polish city, annexed by the USSR in 1939. Mass wartime and postwar deportations of ethnic Poles from the city and the Holocaust dramatically changed its ethnic composition. For the migrants and their descendants, Lviv became a painful memory and lost paradise shrouded in nostalgia.[69] While open political contestation of the new border was impossible in the socialist era, some polemical overtones were evident, albeit somewhat hidden, in the cultural sphere. This was the case, for example, in the differences between tourist guidebooks produced in Polish in the USSR for visitors from Poland and those published in the Polish People's Republic (PRL). While produced for the same audience by two neighboring countries, these two types of guidebooks presented quite different narratives. Whereas the guidebook from socialist Poland explains that "[f]rom the very beginning it was a multicultural city, where in different periods Poles, Armenians, Jews, Germans, Russians settled next to the innumerable Ukrainian population,"[70] its Soviet counterpart states that "it is clear that among the inhabitants the indigenous population (calling themselves Rusyns [an old name for Ukrainians]) dominated. It is enough to mention that in ducal [*kniazhyi*] Lviv there were only two Roman Catholic and three Armenian churches, but more than ten Orthodox churches."[71] The Polish guidebook concentrates on the flourishing of the city under the protection and privileges afforded by the Polish kings and on nineteenth-century Polish cultural figures and institutions (most prominently the Ossolineum library and scientific institute), whereas the Soviet guidebook stresses the most distant (presumably "Ukrainian") period of Lviv's history (the Principality of Galicia-Volhynia). The Soviet guidebook lists the oldest monuments owned by the Orthodox and Greek Catholic communities as examples of "Ukrainian" art and architecture, while Roman Catholic buildings also receive recommendations and extensive description but only as examples of respective international architectural styles: Gothic, Renaissance, Baroque, Historicist, and so on.

It came as no surprise, therefore, that Polish visitors to Lviv could have radically different views on the history and heritage of Lviv compared to their Soviet guides, who were supposed to demonstrate symbolic power and maintain a sense of being more knowledgeable and ideologically sound. This became especially obvious during *perestroika*. A report by the Lviv tourist guide L. Alekseeva from 1989 is especially telling in this respect as she stressed her extensive professional experience while giving her colleagues practical recommendations. In her report, "Propaganda of the role of culture in the life of the Soviet society among tourists from the socialist countries," she generalized as follows:

The tourists from the People's Republic of Poland—not only particular individuals but entire groups—react badly to the historical material from the excursions around the city. Repeatedly, at the very start of the excursion, when the guides say, "I will introduce the history and the present of our city to you," they hear indignant shouts: "Not your city, but OURS," or "we are interested only in the traces of Polish culture." Some tourists deny outright the East Slavic character of Galicia and Volhynia and their belonging to Kievan Rus. Some tourists note, "I feel as if I am in Kraków."[72]

Consequently, this experienced guide recommended paying more attention to Galician-Volhynian and Kievan Rus periods by drawing on quotations from Rus chronicles and epic poetry. As for the later period, the history of Lviv should be presented, she argued, as a time when three cultures—Ukrainian, Polish, and Armenian (Jews were notably not included in the list)—developed side by side. She thus highlighted the idea of Lviv's "unique" character, which seems to have been a good strategy for relegating the significance of its Polish historical layer.[73] However, the tourist guide also concluded her report with the suggestion that it would be great to offer more acknowledgment of the Polish past in Lviv's public space, for example through memorial plaques. In this case, once again, the guide sought to assert her authority over the tourists, yet the tourists succeeded in contributing to the agenda and changing opinion on the Soviet side.

Of course, many other tourists visiting formerly contested borderlands chose different strategies, avoiding confrontation in favor of dialogue and cooperation (at least superficially) with the tour guides.[74] In 1987, during a visit to a village with mixed Ukrainian and Moldovan populations, tourists from Romania gained insight into Leninist national policy while also enjoying Ukrainian and Moldovan meals together with locals to the accompaniment of the folk music band from the local textile factory; they visited *kolkhozniks*' houses; and received gifts of roses that they laid at the monument of soldiers who fell in World War II.[75] This was another enactment of the tried and tested mix of pride in labor and World War II memory combined with a more personalized tourist experience, informal communication, and stronger emphasis on entertainment. The guide described the overwhelmingly positive reaction of the leader of the Romanian group: "Folk songs, dances, original national dresses offer further proof that Bukovina is essentially a Slavic land." In this case, what was important was not whether visitors genuinely supported Soviet discourse nor even the Soviet guide demonstrating the effectiveness of tour guides' endeavors, but rather the guide's firm belief that the Romanian visitor's ideologically correct statement came out of sincere conviction and was thus a result of interpersonal communication, the relaxed atmosphere, and entertainment, rather than a product of mass propaganda.

World War II Memorials as Heritage: Problematic Places of the "Friendship of Nations"

Another special category of heritage objects—World War II monuments, memorials, and burial places—provided particular possibilities for debate. There were several reasons for including World War II memorials and burial places on the itineraries for foreign tourists. First, these places were the focal points of the "friendship of nations" cult, where the unity of all the Soviet nations in the common struggle against fascism was constructed. Second, these were places that manifested the solidarity of the working people and "all the progressive elements of the humankind" in the struggle against revanchism and militarism. As one of the reports from 1961 optimistically states, in Leningrad the common wreath-laying ceremony united the representatives of the German Democratic Republic and the Federal Republic of Germany who were previously estranged.[76] Meanwhile, as a Czech tourist observed after visiting a World War II monument in Odesa: "How easily the working people [representatives of different nations] understand each other."[77]

Third, the shortcomings of everyday life in the Soviet Union could be justified by reference to the victory over Nazism.[78] Some tourist guides even criticized the visitors for being "obsessed" with comfort and consumerism; thus, visiting "sacred" places related to World War II could bring a sublime dimension into their experience. The idea was that participating in these rituals would strengthen the unity between the hosts and guests. Visitors' positive reactions were proudly cited in the guides' reports.

Finally, the topic of the Soviet victory was a way of legitimizing Soviet dominance in Eastern Europe. The Inturist guides proudly quoted many positive reactions from foreign tourists after visiting memorial sites. A Bulgarian visitor to Odesa offered a typical comment: "We will never forget the story of the heroic city defense and glorious partisan deeds. The friendship between our peoples became stronger after these excursions."[79]

The friendship of the Ukrainian and Russian peoples in the war served as an additional argument for Ukraine being a part of the USSR. In official accounts of the war, the role of the "great Russian nation [*velikii russkii narod*] and other nations of the USSR" in the liberation of Ukraine and the Great Victory over fascism was highlighted, especially between the 1960s and 1980s.[80] Rituals expressing "gratitude" for fraternal assistance were supposed to offer confirmation of this unity. This was particularly the case in relation to places such as the burial site of outstanding Russian military leaders in Ukraine, including the grave of the anti-Nazi spy Kuznetsov in Lviv and general Vatutin in Kyiv. Similarly, foreign tourists in Ternopil were told that the city was liberated by representatives of all the nations of the USSR,[81] something for which the residents should be grateful.

Some visitors from capitalist countries seemed to be enthusiastic about World War II commemoration as well, at least according to the guides' reports. Particular significance was ascribed to the war during anniversary celebrations of the victory. The festivities were especially grand and impressive in those years. An American tourist to Odesa in 1970 was reported to have said, "I would like all Americans to visit the USSR and see the places related to the Great Patriotic War. It would have an impact on the admirers of war, and especially on American youth."[82] A French tourist, a veteran of the Resistance, meanwhile, noted that "the Soviet Union is the only country where heroes are remembered and honored."[83]

The key role of the wartime experience in people's biographies, its formative role in the postwar order, and its emotional power were instrumental in encouraging visitors to share personal memories. This was a good way to make the tourist experience more engaging and personalized in the view of Soviet managers. In Kharkiv, starting from 1966, meetings of East German tourists with members of the local German language club took place. Several representatives of the Kharkiv intelligentsia, some of them former inmates of the Buchenwald concentration camp, played a prominent role in the club.[84] According to the guide's report at least, the positive and welcoming atmosphere of meetings over a cup of coffee provoked frank testimonies and discussions (in German), with the visitors revealing that some of them had been Wehrmacht soldiers in the war. One female tourist cried, overwhelmed by the memories of her lost brother who was killed in action. The German visitors then condemned the fascist past and promised to struggle for peace, while Ukrainian songs and dances capped the friendly evening atmosphere. Obviously, such performances of folk culture were not inherent to the usual leisure activities of the Kharkiv intelligentsia, but rather something specifically performed for the foreigners. The German language club in Kharkiv figures prominently in the documents and reports as one of the best experiences for German tourists who were impressed by the locals' cultural knowledge, including familiarity with German high culture, and by the local flavors at the same time.

Visiting World War II sites was to serve as a tool of control, both political and emotional. One of the qualified guides generalized her many years' experience in her report and recommendations for the Kyiv–Moscow–Leningrad route in the early 1970s: "It is inadmissible to let the tourists visiting the [World War II Piskarevo] cemetery to march briskly through the rows of collective graves and to ask arrogant questions. After the guide presented a deeply thought-through narrative near the monument, the tourists leave the cemetery shocked, with a sense of the tragedy of Leningrad in the days of blockade."[85] The facts, she recommended, are to be given on the way to the cemetery, while on the spot the guide has to "generalize in artistic and literary form." However, such instrumentalization of the Soviet victory did meet with resistance from tourists in some cases. Unwillingness to honor the victims of World War II was expressed, for example, by a group of tourists from West Germany in Donetsk as only several people left the bus and went to lay the flowers at the Eternal Flame in 1968.[86]

In other cases, tourists initiated discussions about the meaning of World War II memorial sites. The Livadia Palace in Yalta, where the Yalta agreement was signed in 1945, was an obligatory destination for all foreign tourists coming to Crimea. In 1966, some Americans were reported to have engaged in a dispute with the guide.[87] Meanwhile, some statements uttered in 1971 that were deemed typical of West German tourists, included: "This is the place where our fate was foreclosed"; "partisan warfare is a violation of the rules of war as such"; "we feel guilty before the Jews, that is why we support Israel"; "threat from the East"; "fear of Russians." The report noted other "manifestations of the German character," but the competent guide managed to repulse these "ideological attacks" with a clear explanation of the Soviet position.[88] Another guide complained in 1986 that some youths from the Federal Republic of Germany were unwilling to visit Livadia at all, noting that "it is time to forget the past," "we have nothing in common with fascism," and "almost all the German soldiers did nothing bad yet you tell us about some horrors."[89]

Jewish tourists also caused their supervisors some difficulties. The Party bureaucrats and functionaries from the departments for religious affairs in 1960 considered international tourism a factor contributing to the dissemination of "dangerous" ideas, such as the special fate of the Jews in the war and dissatisfaction with the absence of special monuments commemorating the genocide of European Jews.[90] The tour guides had to be prepared to react properly to such statements. When a Jewish tourist from the United States, a certain Mermelshtein, asked why there was no single monument to the Jewish victims of fascism, the reply was that "we do not put monuments to particular ethnic groups, but to the victims of fascism in general. Soviet people not only liberated many peoples in Europe, but also rescued Jews and helped them to escape fascist persecution. But the Zionists gave up other Jews to Germans in order to save their own skin."[91] Generally, tour guides working with Jewish groups did not highlight any specifically Jewish places, except for synagogues, but propaganda meetings of tourists with Soviet Jews who enjoyed successful lives did take place. There were thus encounters with, for example, Jewish representatives of the artistic elite or managers of enterprises, such as a certain Kaplan who was the chief engineer at a factory in Odesa but not a Party member,[92] or the poet Riva Baliasna in Kyiv.[93] Indeed, considerations relating to the USSR's international reputation were one of the most important reasons behind the official decision to finally erect the monument in Babyn Yar in Kyiv (opened 1976), the largest Holocaust killing site on Soviet territory.[94] While many international visitors complained before the opening of the monument that they were not allowed to visit Babyn Yar, after 1976, it became something of a legitimate site for international visitors, at least for those who were specifically interested in it and requested this opportunity from their tour guides.[95] Still, many of the visitors continued to criticize the lack of recognition of the Jewish identity of the victims of Babyn Yar and persisted in asking "uncomfortable questions." They thus pushed the Soviet authorities to claim Babyn Yar as part of the Soviet heritage canon of World War II in order to dismantle competing (dissident and international) narratives relating to this site.[96]

Conclusion

As my research shows, examining international tourism more closely can be quite revealing for the understanding of the making and remaking of the national heritage canon under socialism. Even though international tourism to the USSR was relatively limited in scope, and exchanges between the visitors and locals were tightly controlled, communication on the grassroots level nevertheless impacted on both sides. Some of the perspectives of the foreign visitors, such as the demand for authentic Ukrainian national culture, resonated with existing Ukrainian patriotism on different levels, both institutional and personal, resulting in the greater presence of Ukrainian language and cultural assets in both tourist-related services and public spaces.

The result, the national (and in some cases transnational) heritage canon itself, was a dynamic and constantly renegotiated construct resulting from dialogue and exchanges involving tourists and experts. The latter include both tour guides and managers of the tourist industry, who themselves negotiated between ideological demands and commercial concerns on the central Soviet level, the republican level, and local levels. Indeed, the primary set of heritage sites and their respective narratives appeared to follow the official Soviet discourse quite closely, with its accents on both unity and particularism of the nations forming the USSR, its nativist understanding of the nation, and tendency to merge objects related to the pre-Soviet local history, imperial history, and Soviet modernizing efforts into a single narrative. Nevertheless, there was still space for divergent interpretations. In different contexts and communicative situations, the key elements of the heritage canon, such as Cossack history or national cuisine, were approached by the tourists and their guides in many ways, ranging from reducing Ukrainian nation to "low" culture, folklore, and tradition through making it part of modern leisure and entertainment practices to making it into a political statement in the struggle for self-determination. Even though the tour guides tried to maintain their position of authority and monopoly over interpretations of the sites visited by guiding and lecturing, the gradual shift to experiential and entertaining tourism, with more personalized and informal communication, were present in the USSR too, especially as the tourist industry became increasingly profit-oriented. It was under such circumstances, that the national coloring of the tourist infrastructure became more intensive, and historical and popular-cultural elements were increasingly included into the tours.

Obviously, any national coloring of the services and tours was a way to extract more hard currency and as such received support at the highest level from Party officials and Inturist managers, both on the union and republican levels. But the ways of introducing national and exotic styles, as well as the selection of items deemed representative of national heritage, was the subject of negotiations on different levels. It is also important to note that the nationalizing trend was not only a performance for the visitors' sake, but also part of a broader trend in the late-Soviet nation-building process.

Whether for groups from other socialist countries or from capitalist states, traveling to the USSR often came to mirror the experience of confirmation, renegotiation, and resistance to power relations imposed by the domination of USSR in the socialist camp and its role in Cold War competition. The visitors from abroad, especially those with family roots in the Ukrainian lands, followed different strategies, from polite dialogue to open confrontation. Tourists from the Ukrainian diaspora in Canada and the United States were viewed as ideologically suspect yet welcome guests and potential "friends of the USSR in the West" (and also the source of hard currency income), so the tourist service was oriented toward satisfying their needs and tastes. This in turn, though, also shaped the content of the heritage canon that was forming in Soviet Ukraine, as did encounters with tourists from neighboring states. They could provoke debates about the visions of the past and seek to claim the heritage in the border regions. The sites related to World War II were especially important in highlighting the processes of contestation, as they were both instruments for exerting emotional control and power, as well as an opportunity for personal witnessing, discussing, and sharing in the informal context.

After 1991, the Soviet national Ukrainian heritage canon largely survived, especially its nativist understanding of the nation, with accents on

Cossacks and folklore, together with Ukrainianized interpretations of the culture of its border regions. These have come to coexist with newly introduced ideas of multiculturalism, which are partly also staged for the sake of commercialized international tourism.[97] Though modernizing aspects of the Soviet era, such as industrial pride, technological progress, and internationalism, were largely disavowed in the 1990s, now they are once again coming to the fore, this time in the form of a fashion for socialist-era modernist architecture, including projects to adapt industrial buildings for cultural purposes, and the museumification of Soviet art. While these developments are in part inspired by Western trends and broader international fashions, they necessarily draw from the rich, native ground in which earlier cultural processes are rooted.

Iryna Sklokina is a research fellow at the Center for Urban History of East Central Europe in Lviv, Ukraine. She defended her Candidate of Sciences dissertation, "Official Soviet Politics of Memory of Nazi Occupation, case of Kharkiv, 1943–1985," in 2014. She recently coedited with Volodymyr Kulikov the volume *Pratsia, vysnazhennia ta uspikh: promyslovi monomista Donbasu* (Labor, Exhaustion, and Success: Company Towns of the Donbas; Lviv, 2018). She also coauthored the chapter "Regionalism Without Regions: Rethinking Ukraine's Heterogeneity" (O. Myshlovska and U. Schmid, eds., CEU Press, 2019). Her research interests include (post)Soviet memory politics, late-socialist consumer culture, and industrial heritage.

Notes

1. See, among others, Pitchford, "Introduction"; White and Frew, "Tourism and National Identities."
2. Park, "Heritage Tourism," 117.
3. Here I refer to the notion of tourism as national performance by Tim Edensor: Edensor, "Staging Tourism"; and idem, *National Identity*.
4. Anne Gorsuch and Diane Koenker describe Soviet tourism as an instrument of individuation and creation of more self-activating, improvising, mobile, and open-modern personality: Koenker, *Club Red*; Gorsuch and Koenker, *Turizm*, 1–14. Igor Orlov and Vardan Bagdasarian have studied foreign tourism to USSR, especially its organizational aspects, shortcomings, and propagandist role: Bagdasarian and Orlov, *Sovetskoe zazerkal'e*. Shawn Salmon showed that commercial interest was a part of the tourist industry in the USSR and how the black market played a role in it: Salmon, "Marketing Socialism." Olga Radchenko has analyzed the development of infrastructure, finances, and marketing, as well as propaganda aspects of Inturist specifically in the Ukrainian SSR: Radchenko, *"Inturist" v Ukraine*.
5. Wojnowski, *The Near Abroad*.
6. Zhuk, "*Popular National Culture* and *Advertising* in the *Soviet Travel Agencies*."

7. Rachel Applebaum has pointed to the symbolic meaning of visiting particular heritage sites in Czechoslovakia by Soviet visitors: namely, where the Soviet Army experienced glories in World War II as sites of Soviet imperial pride, and old castles and churches as sites of "resistance" to Soviet pressure and propaganda. Applebaum, "A Test of Friendship."
8. Donovan, *Chronicles in Stone*, see especially the chapter "*Zapovedniks* or Tourist Resorts: Marketing Heritage to National Audiences."
9. As the historiography of these issues is a booming field, I will only mention several recent works containing overviews: Kulick, "When Ukraine Ruled Russia"; Mitrokhin, *Russkaia partiia*; Ubiria, *Soviet Nation-Building in Central Asia*.
10. Primarily it is fund 4672 (the Department for Foreign Tourism at the Council of Ministers of Ukrainian SSR) of the Central State Archive of the Supreme Organs of Administration of Ukraine (TsDAVO); fund 1 (Central Committee of the Communist Party of Ukraine) of the Central State Archive of Public Organizations of Ukraine (TsDAGO). I am also grateful to Natalya Borys, who drew my attention to the documents of the Commission for Foreign Affairs (organ under the supervision of the Supreme Council of the Ukrainian SSR), at TsDAVO, f. 1. In the endnotes I use the abbreviation f. for *fund*, op. for *opis* (collection), spr. for *sprava* (file), and ark. for *arkush* (page).
11. Primarily this is the journal *Travel to the USSR*, published 1966–91 in English, French, German, and Russian specifically for advertising travel to the USSR among foreigners. I used the Russian-language version of this journal. I also refer to the Moscow-based journal *Turist* (published 1966–91) where it deals specifically with the international visitors to the Ukrainian SSR.
12. Fedorchenko and D'orova, *Istoriia turyzmu v Ukraini*, 84–85.
13. "Turistov stanovitsia vse bolshe..." In the 1960s, it was half of all the tourists to the USSR traveling to Ukraine: TsDAVO, f. 4672, op. 1, spr. 19, ark. 111. This decline of the share of Ukraine was due to the advancement of the tourism in the Caucasian and Central Asian republics.
14. See more on migration and shaping of diaspora identity in Satzevich, *The Ukrainian Diaspora*.
15. On Hungarians visiting Transcarpathia as their former native land, see TsDAVO, f. 4672, op. 1, spr. 173, ark. 11 (1973).
16. For example, in Odesa in 1970 there were sixteen objects of this kind: TsDAVO, op. 1, spr. 96, ark. 28–41.
17. TsDAVO, f. 4672, op. 1, spr. 60, ark. 29.
18. TsDAVO, f. 1, op. 22, spr. 19, ark. 11. In the summer season of 1972, in Yalta alone there were seven exclusively Ukrainian groups and many ethnic Ukrainians from abroad traveling in mixed groups and individually. TsDAVO, f. 4672, op. 1, spr. 140, ark. 82. Altogether, in 1972, more than 50,000 foreign tourists visited Crimea: TsDAVO, f. 1, op. 22, spr. 412, ark. 10.
19. Radchenko, *"Inturist" v Ukraine*, 159.
20. Ibid.
21. See especially the traveler's memoirs: Kushchak, *V obiimakh materiv*; Bohuslavets, *Na proshchu do ridnoi zemli*. See also the reports of tourist guides about visitors from the United States and Canada who tried to evade control and visit native vil-

lages in Rivne, Volyn, and Lviv regions: TsDAVO, f. 4672, op. 1, spr. 96, ark. 46–52; spr. 117, ark. 2–4; spr. 119, ark. 93; f. 1, op. 22, spr. 412, ark. 46. More on tourist visits to the villages by migrants, see Kaltenbrunner, *Das global vernetzte Dorf*, especially Chapter 9.1, "Tourismus und 'Kulturaustausch,'" 403–49; Radchenko, *"Inturist" v Ukraine*, 171–75.
22. See, for example, the critical remarks of Andrii Skaba, the chair of the Commission for Foreign Affairs, regarding the tour guides who "present only ancient Kyiv" to tourists, and the presentation of St. Andrew's Church on the new postal stamp. TsDAVO, f. 1, op. 22, spr. 18, ark. 74. See also the 1972 report of the tourist guide from Kyiv: TsDAVO, f. 4672, op. 1, spr. 140, ark. 32.
23. "Glavnyi interes—dostizheniia sovetskogo naroda," 2.
24. TsDAVO, f. 4672, op. 1, spr. 29, ark. 19–20.
25. See the lists of "uneasy" questions posed to the guides by the international visitors, from 1960–80s: TsDAVO, f. 4672, op. 1, spr. 174, ark. 4–5; spr. 95, ark. 37–39; spr. 96, ark. 86–92. On the activity of Ukrainian diaspora organizations with a focus on monitoring and advocating the use of Ukrainian language in the Ukrainian SSR, see: Tron'ko, *Na skryzhaliakh istorii*, especially 29–32, 221–23, 270–74, 304–15, 322–29; and Radchenko, *"Inturist" v Ukraine*, 163–71. The memoirs of the tourists of Ukrainian origin reveal their specific interest and criticism toward national policy in the Soviet Union: Kushchak, *V obiimakh materiv*; Bohuslavets, *Na proshchu do ridnoi zemli*; Lupul, *The Politics of Multiculturalism*, chapter III; Prokopiv, *Po 56 rokakh—na Ukraini*; Movchan, *Shcho varto b znaty*.
26. See more in Wojnowski, *The Near Abroad*.
27. TsDAVO, f. 1, op. 22, spr. 3, ark. 22, 55, 83–85; spr. 18, ark. 78. Especially telling is the suggestion of the member of the Commission for Foreign Affairs from 1973: "We should force people to use Ukrainian in these institutions [visited by foreigners]. Many people from Canada come to us, and in general foreigners would like to hear Ukrainian." TsDAVO, f. 1, op. 22, spr. 18, ark. 141.
28. TsDAVO, f. 4672, op. 1, spr. 19, ark. 31–32.
29. TsDAVO, f. 4672, op. 1, spr. 30, ark. 271.
30. "Ukrainskie kureni," (in Kyiv); Kirsanova, "V chertogakh Neptuna," (in Odesa); "Pobyvat v restorane," (in Zaporizhia).
31. TsDAVO, f. 4672, op. 1, spr. 170, ark. 28.
32. These notions, as well as "national coloring" (*natsionalnyi kolorit*), were used in the documents as self-evident and their meaning was not the subject of deliberate reflection.
33. One of most successful examples was the "Hut of Karas" ("Khata Karasia") restaurant in Kyiv, which was advertised on the international level. In *Travel to the USSR* it was described as a building with a traditional village architecture style, with embroidered decorative elements inside, wooden furniture, Ukrainian cuisine, and an ensemble of national instruments, but also as a place for "meeting characters from the opera" (alluding to "Zaporozhets za Dunaem"—the first opera in Ukrainian, written by Semen Gulak-Artemovsky in 1861, which later became a part of the Soviet canon of Ukrainian identity). This mix of low, kitsch-style folk culture and allusions to the high culture of opera formed a successful advertising strategy. See "Inturist predlagaet."

34. "Otkrytoe serdtse Sochi."
35. TsDAVO, f. 4672, op. 1, spr. 16, ark. 66.
36. TsDAVO, f. 4672, op. 1, spr. 30, ark. 142.
37. See, for example, on French tourists visiting the home of the head of the coal miners brigade Steblianko in Torez: TsDAVO, f. 4672, op. 1, spr. 29, ark. 139.
38. TsDAVO, f. 4672, op. 1, spr. 639.
39. See, for example, on Canadian Ukrainians in Kharkiv in 1961: DAKhO (State Archive of Kharkiv oblast), f. P2, op. 5, spr. 1095, ark. 78–79.
40. DAKhO, f.2, spr. 143, p. 51. Similar complaints from 1965: DAKhO, f. P2, op. 6, spr. 143, ark. 51.
41. TsDAVO, f. 4672, op. 1, spr. 118, ark. 91.
42. TsDAVO, f. 4672, op. 1, spr. 636, ark. 156 (on tourists taking the tour "Pensioneer" in 1987).
43. TsDAVO, f. 1, op. 22, spr. 166, ark. 112.
44. TsDAVO, f. 4672, op. 1, spr. 45, ark. 117.
45. TsDAVO, f. 4672, op. 1, spr. 140, ark. 117; Kirsanova, "V chertogakh Neptuna."
46. TsDAVO, f. 4672, op. 1, spr. 45, ark. 117.
47. TsDAVO, f. 4672, op. 1, spr. 173, ark. 15–16.
48. TsDAVO, f. 4672, op. 1, spr. 663, ark. 9.
49. TsDAVO, f. 4672, op. 1, spr. 636 (dated 1987).
50. The tourist guide should compare the pre-Soviet and Soviet periods to highlight the achievements of the latter. TsDAVO, f. 4672, op. 1, spr. 140, ark. 82.
51. "Krymskie vina," 29.
52. There are traces of this trend not only in the archival documents on international tourists, but also in some universal guidebooks and photobooks. See, for example, the imposing Ukrainian ethnic costume of the girl on the cover of Deliamure, *Krym* (in Russian and Ukrainian); inclusion of the memorial places of Ukrainian writers in Shcheglova, *Krym*, 112, and *Krym/The Crimea*, 72; children in Ukrainian ethnic costume dancing while in Artek children's camp in *Krym/The Crimea*, 42. However, in Crimea next to this pro-Ukrainian trend and homogenizing trends of Soviet melting pot culture, there were obvious signs of pro-Russian ethnicization. See, for example, the "poetic atlas" of Crimea that featured exclusively Russian poets in Rudiakov and Kazarin, *Krym*. One of the special cases of mixed representation of Russian and Ukrainian ethnic myths is "The Glade of Tales"—a children's amusement park constructed in 1970–80s in Yalta, with separate parts for "Ukrainian and Russian folk fairy tales' characters" and "Pushkin Glade."
53. TsDAVO, f. 4672, op. 1, spr. 119, ark. 60; spr. 636, ark. 5–7. The same statement on special attention to Ukrainian language skills in Transcarpathia can be found in TsDAVO, f. 4672, op. 1, spr. 95, ark. 39.
54. TsDAVO, f. 4672, op. 1, spr. 140, ark. 83.
55. TsDAVO, f. 4672, op. 1, spr. 636, ark. 6.
56. TsDAVO, f. 4672, op. 1, spr. 140, ark. 77.
57. See the detailed analysis of the case of the museum on Khortytsia island in Zaporizhia as a major effort of the Soviet Ukrainian patriots in Ganzer, *Sowjetisches Erbe und Ukrainische Nation*. An analysis of the longer history of the Cossack myth as one of the pillars of the Ukrainian nationalizing identity from the period of Russian Empire until the end of the Soviet Union is in Plokhy, *The Cossack Myth*.

58. "Na marshrute Dneprohes—Krym."
59. Bazhan, Shevchuk, and Ignatusha, *Zberezhemo tuiu slavu*.
60. Kharchiladze, "Pesnia Zaporozhskoi Sechi."
61. Thomas, "Gorod na dvukh moriakh."
62. In 1987, suggestions from local experts for organizing study tours for pensioners from abroad to Zaporizhia included topics on Scythian mounds, the history of Cossacks, Khortytsia, and Zaporizhia as a city created by the Dnipro water power plant. In the evening, the tasting of Ukrainian national dishes accompanied by Ukrainian national music were proposed. TsDAVO, f. 4672, op. 1, spr. 639, ark. 1–3 (1987).
63. TsDAVO, f. 4672, op. 1, spr. 16, ark. 47–48.
64. TsDAVO, f. 4672, op. 1, spr. 140, ark. 50 (1972).
65. The identification of Ukraine not only with more Sovietized cities of central and eastern Ukraine, but also with the cities of the western part is important here.
66. TsDAVO, f. 4672, op. 1, spr. 60, ark. 41–45.
67. See more on ethnic particularism and nativism as driving forces behind the making of the Soviet canon of the national Ukrainian history in the Stalinist period: Yekelchyk, *Stalin's Empire of Memory*.
68. In addition to this, Poles were described by many guides as being "arrogant and highly sensitive" and "highlighting their high social status." See more on the complications of the international exchange with the USSR around the turbulent moments of 1956, 1968, and 1980–81 in Wojnowski, *The Near Abroad*.
69. Even though the *Kresy* did not form the central pillar of Polish national memory under communism, the private memories and sentiments were preserved in the unofficial sphere; and starting from late 1970s, the loss of Lwów and Wilno were discussed in Polish *samizdat*. See Szacka and Sawisz, *Czas przeszły i pamięć społeczna*; Bakuła, "Kolonialne i postkolonialne aspekty"; idem, "Colonial and Postcolonial Aspects."
70. Spalle, *ZSRR*, 202.
71. Semionow, *Lwów*, 10.
72. TsDAVO, f. 4672, op. 1, spr. 663.
73. The neglect of the Jewish community, actually the second largest group in Lviv in 1939, should be noted here.
74. Anne Gorsuch and Diane Koenker have also paid attention to tourists' strategy in the USSR of maintaining good relations with the guides and supporting their ideological statements in order to exchange the loyalty for some benefits, such as more freedom, small additional help from guides, or positive depictions in the report.
75. TsDAVO, f. 4672, op. 1, spr. 640, ark. 37.
76. Afiani et al., *Apparat TsK KPSS i kultura*, 654.
77. TsDAVO, f. 4672, op. 1, spr. 96, ark. 31.
78. See, among others, TsDAVO, f. 4672, op. 1, spr. 29, ark. 27.
79. TsDAVO, f. 4672, op. 1, spr. 96, ark. 19.
80. See, among others, Koval, *Plechom k plechu v borbe protiv fashizma*, 5.
81. TsDAVO, f. 4672, op. 1, spr. 96, ark. 55.
82. TsDAVO. f. 4672, op. 1, spr. 95, ark. 5.
83. TsDAVO, f. 4672, op. 1, spr. 96, ark. 20. A similar comment from a French tourist from 1986 is found in TsDAVO, f. 4672, spr. 96, ark. 80.
84. TsDAVO, f. 4672, op. 1, spr. 30, ark. 26–27; spr. 96, ark. 97.

85. TsDAVO, f. 4672. spr. 95. ark. 138–39.
86. TsDAVO, f. 4672, op. 1, spr. 60, ark. 5.
87. TsDAVO, f. 4672, op. 1, spr. 29, ark. 26.
88. TsDAVO, f. 4672, op. 1, spr. 119, ark. 67.
89. TsDAVO, f. 4672, op. 1, spr. 638, ark. 87–88.
90. One of the clearest examples is the letter by Kostiantyn Polonnyk, the plenipotentiary for issues of religious cults in Soviet Ukraine, where he condemns tourists as "spies" and Zionists who seduce the Soviet citizens to tend to Jewish graves, found in TsDAGO, f. 1, op. 24, spr. 5106, ark. 65–70.
91. TsDAVO, f. 4672, op. 1, spr. 96, ark. 90.
92. TsDAVO, f. 4672, op. 1, spr. 96, ark. 31–32.
93. TsDAVO, f. 4672, op. 1, spr. 95, ark. 66.
94. For more evidence on international tourists visiting Babyn Yar, their discussions with tour guides, and criticisms of the Soviet government for its nonrecognition of victims' Jewish identity, see Mitsel, "Zapret na uvekovechenie." There are numerous works focused on the analysis of the post-Soviet development of the memorial landscape in Babyn Yar, with only a few discussing the Soviet period in more detail, such as Mankoff, "Babi Yar," and Khiterer, "Suppressed Memory."
95. Mitsel, "Zapret na uvekovechenie," 19–24.
96. Ibid., 24–29.
97. See more on multiculturalism as staged for the sake of international audiences in themed restaurants in Lviv and Chernivtsi (as well as in Kraków and Wrocław) in Narvselius, "Spicing up Memories."

Bibliography

Afiani, Vitalii, et al., eds. *Apparat TsK KPSS i kultura: 1958–1964. Dokumenty*. Moscow: ROSSPEN, 2005.

Applebaum, Rachel. "A Test of Friendship: Soviet-Czechoslovak Tourism and the Prague Spring." In *The Socialist Sixties: Crossing Borders in the Second World*, edited by Anne E. Gorsuch and Diane P. Koenker, 213–34. Bloomington: Indiana University Press, 2013.

Bagdasarian, Vardan, and Igor Orlov, eds. *Sovetskoe zazerkal'e: Inostrannyi turizm v SSSR v 1930-e—80-e gg*. Moscow: Forum, 2007.

Bakuła, Bogusław. "Colonial and Postcolonial Aspects of Polish Borderlands Studies: An Outline." *Teksty Drugie—Special Issue English Edition* 1 (2014): 96–123.

———. "Kolonialne i postkolonialne aspekty polskiego dyskursu kresoznawczego (zarys problematyki)." *Teksty Drugie* 6 (2006): 11–33.

Bazhan, Oleh, O. Shevchuk, and O. Ignatusha, eds. *Zberezhemo tuiu slavu: Hromaskyi rukh za uvichnennia istorii ukrainskoho kozatstva v druhii polovyni 50-h—80-h rr. XX st.: zbirnyk dokumentiv ta materialiv*. Kyiv: Ridnyi krai, 1997.

Bohuslavets, Lesia. *Na proshchu do ridnoi zemli: Vrazhennia z podorozhi*. Melbourne: Baida, 1984.

Deliamure, S. L., ed. *Krym: putevoditel*. Simferopol: Krym, 1968–69.

Donovan, Victoria. *Chronicles in Stone: Preservation, Patriotism, and Identity in Northwest Russia*. Ithaca: Northern Illinois University Press, 2019.

Edensor, Tim. *National Identity, Popular Culture and Everyday Life*. Oxford: Berg Publishers, 2002.

———. "Staging Tourism: Tourists as Performers." *Annals of Tourism Research* 27 (2000): 322–44.

Fedorchenko, Volodymyr, and Tetiana D'orova. *Istoriia turyzmu v Ukraini*. Kyiv: Vyscha shkola, 2002.

Ganzer, Christian. *Sowjetisches Erbe und Ukrainische Nation: Das Museum der Geschichte des Zaporoger Kosakentums auf der Insel Chortycja*. Stuttgart: Ibidem, 2005.

"Glavnyi interes—dostizheniia sovetskogo naroda." *Puteshestvie v SSSR* 5 (1977): 2.

Gorsuch, Anne E., and Diane P. Koenker, eds. *Turizm: The Russian and East European Tourist Under Socialism and Capitalism*. Ithaca: Cornell University Press, 2006.

"Inturist predlagaet." *Puteshestvie v SSSR* 1 (1985): 10.

Kaltenbrunner, Matthias. *Das global vernetzte Dorf: Eine Migrationsgeschichte*. Frankfurt am Main: Campus Verlag, 2017.

Kharchiladze, V. "Pesnia Zaporozhskoi Sechi . . ." *Turist* 3 (1968): 8.

Khiterer, Victoria. "Suppressed Memory: Memorialization of the Holocaust in Babi Yar (Kiev)." Unpublished paper, presented at the ASN World Convention, Columbia University, 23–25 April 2015.

Kirsanova, Genrietta. "V chertogakh Neptuna." *Puteshestvie v SSSR* 4 (1971): 34.

Koenker, Diane. *Club Red: Vacation Travel and the Soviet Dream*. Ithaca: Cornell University Press, 2013.

Koval, Mikhail Vasilievich. *Plechom k plechu v borbe protiv fashizma (Ratnoe i trudovoe sodruzhestvo ukrainskogo naroda s bratskimi narodami SSSR)*. Kyiv: Znanie, 1980.

Krym/The Crimea. Moscow: Planeta, 1971.

"Krymskie vina." *Puteshestvie v SSSR* 3 (1978): 29.

Kulick, Orysia Maria. "When Ukraine Ruled Russia: Regionalism and Nomenklatura Politics After Stalin, 1944–1990." PhD diss., Stanford University, 2017.

Kushchak, Andrii. *V obiimakh materiv*. New York: n.p., 1963.

Lupul, Manolii. *The Politics of Multiculturalism: A Ukrainian-Canadian Memoir*. Edmonton: Canadian Institute of Ukrainian Studies Press, 2005.

Mankoff, Jeff. "Babi Yar and the Struggle for Memory, 1944–2004." *Ab Imperio* 2 (2004): 393–415.

Mitrokhin, Nikolai. *Russkaia partiia: dvizhenie russkikh natsionalistov v SSSR, 1953–1985 gody*. Moscow: Novoe literaturnoe obozrenie, 2003.

Mitsel, Mikhail. "Zapret na uvekovechenie pamiati kak sposob zamalchivania Kholokosta: praktika KPU v otnoshenii Babiego Yara." *Holokost i suchasnist: studii v Ukraini i sviti* 1, no. 2 (2007): 9–30.

Movchan, Yulian. *Shcho varto b znaty: problemy ukrainskoho natsionalno-derzhavnoho vyzvolennia, podorozhni notatky, portrety, zustrichi ta kharakterystyky*. Toronto: Sribna surma, 1966.

"Na marshrute Dneprohes—Krym: Zametki o detskom turizme." *Na sushe i na more* 10 (1933).

Narvselius, Eleonora. "Spicing up Memories and Serving Nostalgias: Thematic Restaurants and Transnational Memories in East-Central European Borderland Cities." *Journal of Contemporary European Studies* 23, no. 3 (2015): 417–32.

"Otkrytoe serdtse Sochi." *Puteshestvie v SSSR* 1 (1973): 15–17.

Park, Hyung-yu. "Heritage Tourism: Emotional Journeys to the Nationhood." *Annals of Tourism Research* 37, no. 1 (2010): 116–35.
Pitchford, Susan. "Introduction." In *Identity Tourism: Imaging and Imagining the Nation*, edited by S. Pitchford and J. Jafari, 1–8. Bingley: Elsevier Science, 2008.
Plokhy, Serhii. *The Cossack Myth: History and Nationhood in the Age of Empires*. Cambridge, UK: Cambridge University Press, 2012.
"Pobyvat v restorane 'Kazachii dozor' v Zaporozhie." *Puteshestvie v SSSR* 1 (1975): 11.
Prokopiv, Mykhailo. *Po 56 rokakh—na Ukraini: Spohady z podorozhi*. New York: n.p., 1964.
Radchenko, Olga Nikolaevna. *"Inturist" v Ukraine 1960–80 godov: mezhdu krasnoi propagandoi i tverdoi valiutoi*. Cherkassy: Chabanenko Yu.A., 2013.
Rudiakov, Aleksandr, and Vladimir Kazarin. *Krym: Poeticheskii atlas*. Simferopol: Krym, 1989.
Salmon, Shawn. "Marketing Socialism: Inturist in the Late 1950s and Early 1960s." In *Turizm: The Russian and East European Tourist Under Socialism and Capitalism*, edited by Anne Gorsuch and Diane Koenker, 186–204. Ithaca: Cornell University Press, 2006.
Satzevich, Vic. *The Ukrainian Diaspora*. London: Routledge, 2002.
Semionow, Grigorij. *Lwów: przewodnik turystyczny*. Moscow: Novosti, 1970.
Shcheglova, A. S., ed. *Krym: marshruty vykhodnogo dnia*. Simferopol: Krym, 1980.
Spalle, Światosław. *ZSRR: Informator turystyczny*. Warsaw: Krajowa Agencja Wydawnicza, 1982.
Szacka, Barbara, and Anna Sawisz. *Czas przeszły i pamięć społeczna: przemiany świadomości historycznej inteligencji polskiej 1965–1988*. Warsaw: Uniwersytet Warszawski, 1990.
Thomas, Johannes. "Gorod na dvukh moriakh." *Puteshestvie v SSSR* 3 (1977): 15–16.
Tron'ko, Petro, ed. *Na skryzhaliakh istorii: Z istorii vzaemozv'iazkiv uriadovykh struktur i hromadskykh kil Ukrainy z ukrainsko-kanadskoiu hromadoiu v druhii polovyni 40-kh—1980-ti rr*. Kyiv: NANU, 2003.
"Turistov stanovitsia vse bolshe . . ." [interview with Victor Dobrotvor, the head of the Department for International Tourism at the Council of Ministers of the UkrSSR]. *Puteshestvie v SSSR* 3 (1979): 8.
Ubiria, Grigol. *Soviet Nation-Building in Central Asia: The Making of the Kazakh and Uzbek Nations*. London: Routledge, 2015.
"Ukrainskie kureni." *Puteshestvie v SSSR* 1 (1972): 33.
White, Leanne, and Elspeth Frew. "Tourism and National Identities: Connections and Conceptualizations." In *Tourism and National Identities: An International Perspective*, edited by Leanne White and Elspeth Frew, 1–10. New York: Routledge, 2011.
Wojnowski, Zbigniew. *The Near Abroad: Socialist Eastern Europe and Soviet Patriotism in Ukraine, 1956–1985*. Toronto: University of Toronto Press, 2017.
Yekelchyk, Serhy. *Stalin's Empire of Memory: Russian-Ukrainian Relations in the Soviet Historical Imagination*. Buffalo, NY: University of Toronto Press, 2004.
Zhuk, Sergei I. "Popular National Culture and Advertising in the Soviet Travel Agencies, 1964–1984." *Memoria y Civilización: Anuario de Historia* 14 (2011): 53–77.

CHAPTER 4

International Contacts and Cooperation in Heritage Preservation in Soviet Estonia, 1960–1990

Karin Hallas-Murula and Kaarel Truu

This chapter focuses on Estonian conservators' international contacts and cooperation from the early 1960s through to the end of the 1980s. During the Soviet period, Estonia and the rest of Baltic states were among the leading republics in heritage preservation in the USSR. The Estonian Heritage Law of 1961 was the first of its kind in the Soviet Union.[1] In 1966, legislation was passed to establish a conservation zone in medieval Old Tallinn, the first such endeavor in the Soviet Union. We argue that heritage experts' background, personal contacts, and opportunities to travel meant that despite the Iron Curtain, heritage preservation in Estonia remained connected to developments taking place in other countries, including both those in the West and in other socialist countries outside the USSR. This chapter thus positions Soviet-Estonian conservation practices and actors as inflected by processes, knowledge, and colleagues working outside national or republican borders, thus furthering the transnational turn in the study of heritage under socialism.

The first section of this chapter provides context by outlining different periods in heritage management in Soviet Estonia, pointing to both certain specificities of the Estonian case and the influence of the Soviet model of heritage protection and preservation in Estonia. The main focus here, however, are Estonian conservators' exchanges with colleagues from socialist and capitalist countries during the Soviet period. Estonian heritage experts' communication with their European colleagues is examined here in light of the emergence of international tourism in the USSR and in the context of the activities of ICOMOS. The travel reports of Estonian conservators preserved in the Estonian Heritage Board archive (Eesti Muinsuskaitseameti arhiiv) are particularly significant for this part of the study.

The second part of the analysis concentrates on one of the practical outcomes of contacts with other socialist bloc countries, namely the restoration work of the renowned Polish State Workshops for the Conservation of Cultural Heritage (Polskie Pracownie Konserwacji Zabytków, PKZ) that were active in Tallinn from 1978 to 1990. We argue that with Estonian experts continuing contacts with the rest of the world, they were not simply passive recipients of imported Polish conservation practices but became active partners in methodological discussions and decision-making relating to heritage objects conserved by Polish restorers in Estonia. In conclusion, we highlight that heritage practitioners' contacts abroad during the Soviet period played an important role in ensuring continuities that meant Estonian preservation practices and practitioners' professional development remained rooted in European ideas.

The Soviet period cannot be treated as a homogeneous period and a totalitarian paradigm should not be projected equally on all regions of the Soviet Union. Different levels of freedoms were tolerated in different periods. Stalin's totalitarian regime was replaced with Khrushchev's Thaw, while the years 1963–68 marked a relatively liberal period that has been termed the "golden sixties." In the context of our research, it is important to note that soon after Stalin's death in 1953 contacts with the West were allowed and even encouraged. The growth of Soviet tourism enabled people to travel not only to socialist countries but also to selected capitalist countries. It was especially so in Estonia where extensive communication with Finland was established.[2]

An important methodological consideration in research on the Soviet period involves decoding the ideological rhetoric of Soviet-era texts and thus reading "between the lines" and, where possible, comparing published materials with unpublished sources, such as the Estonian conservators' travel reports that were studied by Karin Hallas-Murula. All traveling was strictly controlled by the Committee for State Security (KGB) in the Ministry of Internal Affairs. Two personal files were opened on every person exiting the Soviet Union, one at OVIR (the Estonian acronym for the Department of Registration Foreign Travel in the Ministry of Internal Affairs) and another at the KGB special department.[3] After returning from abroad, it was obligatory to submit a report to the administrative bodies and the KGB. These reports are exceptional sources for historians today, even if they reproduced aspects of state ideology and complete openness was not possible in such texts. Nevertheless, most of the conservators' reports include sophisticated professional analyses, with recommendations for implementing innovations seen abroad into professional practice at home, often reflecting the shortcomings of heritage management in Soviet Estonia. Despite their status as official papers, plenty of the reports revealed genuine human emotions, such as the joy associated with being abroad again (for the older generation) or for the first time (for the younger generation), even if they were visiting another socialist country.

When researching the Soviet period, it is important to compare official records where possible with memoirs and interviews conducted more recently with the actors involved in these processes. Of course, such sources should also be read critically, as recent sources based on individual memories will also be subjective, selective, and shaped by public discourses. We have been able to apply the comparative reading of memoir sources from the time with recent oral history interviews (conducted by Kaarel Truu between 2016 and 2018) most effectively in the study of the exchanges with Polish restorers in Tallinn.

Heritage Preservation in Soviet Estonia

As a result of the specificities of the region's political and cultural history, heritage preservation in the Baltic states took on forms that differed from the other Soviet republics. In the interwar period, the Baltic states were independent republics and were incorporated into the Soviet Union only in 1940, much later than the majority of other Soviet republics. The Baltic region's medieval urban heritage, with its rich layer of Gothic architecture, was exceptional in the Soviet Union. The Baltic republics acquired a reputation as the "Soviet abroad," with the medieval urban heritage coming to represent European culture at large, something that was particularly evident in Soviet filmmakers' regular use of Riga and Tallinn's medieval urban Old Towns as the backdrop for scenes set in generic European cities.

In the prewar period, the education of art and architectural historians followed European cultural traditions. It was Swedish professor Sten Karling (1906–87) at Tartu University who introduced European knowledge into architectural history research in Estonia in the 1930s. Karling's students Helmi Üprus (1911–78) and Villem Raam (1910–96) became leading figures in postwar heritage protection and preservation in Estonia. They carried European cultural values through the Soviet period and taught them to the younger generations of historians. Soviet ideology manifested itself in loud rhetoric, but right after World War II it had limited influence on restoration practices because the key objective was repairing war damages. Already in 1944, following the end of the German occupation of the Baltic states, the Department for Protection of Ancient Monuments (later State Inspection of Architectural Monuments—Vabariiklik Arhitektuurimälestiste Kaitse

Inspektsioon) was created in Estonia, while in 1947 the first postwar Act of Protection of Monuments was passed.[4] In 1949, Tallinn with its medieval Old Town was included on the list of the twenty most valuable historical cities in the USSR that needed special protection and resources.[5] In 1950, the Scientific Workshop for Restoration (later KRPI and Eesti Ehitusmälestised that existed until 1992) was established. Such restoration workshops were established in most Soviet republics and served as the main institutions for design and practical works in heritage restoration and conservation.

The Sovietization of Estonian heritage management was similar to the Sovietization in all fields. State ownership of land and properties was established, central state planning was introduced, and Soviet ideology, which created new historical narratives, was enforced. Ultimately, all restored buildings had to become accessible to the Soviet population. Efforts to enforce Soviet ideology were powerfully expressed in the promotion in the immediate postwar period of new monuments that referred to the Soviet revolution and war memorials, which were subsequently inscribed into heritage lists. Several categories of previously listed architectural monuments—in particular, churches, manor houses, and palaces—were increasingly contested by socialist ideology, which propagated state atheism and class struggle.[6] In the Soviet Union, many churches were physically demolished or turned into secular objects (warehouses, sports-halls, etc.). There were some such cases in Estonia, too, including the conversion of Tartu Maarja Church into a gym. At the same time, Soviet authorities acknowledged the high historical value of Gothic churches in Estonia, as well as the importance of medieval city walls and domestic architecture in Estonia, as these objects were kept on the list of protected monuments. The same held true for some manor houses, despite their connection to the bourgeois lifestyle that the Soviet authorities condemned, as ten of these buildings were listed as monuments already in 1947.[7]

The more liberal period saw dozens of manors added to the list in 1964. Architecture produced during the independent Republic of Estonia (1918–40) was likewise not always compatible with the ideology promoted by the Soviet Union, with this period in particular rewritten into a Soviet narrative. Some buildings and monuments from this era were put into active use and turned into symbols of the new Soviet power, as was the case with the Estonian Parliament building from 1921 that became the seat of the Estonian SSR Supreme Council. In the exceptional cases where buildings from the 1920s and 1930s were included on lists of protected monuments, their initial functions and owners were omitted. The documentation and images of those buildings, as well as the majority of books and all newspapers from the period 1918–40, were put into special departments of archives and libraries that were accessible only with special permission from the KGB.

In the more liberal 1960s, Moscow authorities tolerated initiatives by individual republics and so the Law on Protection of Historic and Cultural Monuments was adopted in Estonia in 1961. As the first such case in the Soviet Union, it was significant that the legislation was drawn up by Estonian specialists, rather than being sent as a directive from Moscow enforcing Soviet standards. The Estonian law of 1961 has been evaluated as a progressive document that continued some ideas from the prewar period, such as cooperation with heritage enthusiasts and local amateur-historians and establishing expert-based advisory panels in the Building Ministry (architectural heritage) and Ministry of Culture (memorials, monuments of the history).[8]

The Soviet system also offered some advantages for heritage preservation. State-ownership of real estate meant that long-term planning and complex restoration works did not involve any complicated negotiations with the owners. In the 1950s already, Helmi Üprus started to propagate the idea of protecting Tallinn medieval Old Town as a representative historical ensemble, integrating its architectural and functional qualities. It led to the establishment of the Old Tallinn protected conservation zone in 1966, the first in the USSR. In Vilnius, the project for restoration of the Old Town as a complete entity was made earlier, in 1956, but it was not accompanied by legislation that would establish a protected zone with special status and statutes setting out the rules of conservation, restoration, and restrictions on new buildings. The Statute of the Tallinn Old Town as a Protection Area was a pioneering document as it expanded the concept of heritage from single buildings to encompass the entire area of the Old Town.[9] It became a recognized model that was followed in other cities of the Soviet Union. In 1969 a special meeting was organized in Moscow where protected zones in other Soviet cities were established.

There was active and regular communication between heritage actors and institutions across Soviet republics. Lithuania and Estonia, which offered progressive approaches to heritage management and conservation, frequently hosted study trips involving guests from other republics. As the Lithuanian researcher Vilte Janusauskaite observed in 2016, "when remembering the past, the architects and bureaucrats of that time still tend to stress the special Lithuanian position within USSR. Only Estonians were regarded as equals."[10] Lithuanian conservators were regularly invited as experts and consultants to other states within the USSR, including Russia and Ukraine.

In April 1955, the Central Committee of the Communist Party of the Soviet Union officially declared that Soviet citizens were allowed to travel abroad.[11] Soviet citizens' outbound travel rose significantly: from 486,000 trips in 1956 to 4.5 million in 1985.[12] The goal of allowing Soviet tourism abroad was to increase citizens' internationalist proletarian spirit, to promote a positive image of the USSR abroad, to strengthen friendship with peoples all over the world, and, most practically, to gain insight into foreign science and technology (in some cases this was blatant industrial espionage).[13] International contacts and traveling contributed to undermining the Soviet system more broadly.[14] In practice, it soon became evident that it was not possible to control the outcome of experiences of foreign countries. The strengthening of the influence of the capitalist "Western world" undermined the faith of Soviet ideals and engendered criticism toward the socialist system. This was replicated in the world of heritage experts.[15]

The emergence of international tourism in the Soviet Union in the 1950s mainly enabled visits to other socialist countries but also to selected nonsocialist states. The communication channels opened again soon after Stalin's death in 1953, with friendship societies and twinning agreements between Soviet and Finnish cities the favored forms of cooperation. The first of them were signed by Lahti and Zaporizhia in the Ukrainian SSR and Turku and Leningrad (today St. Petersburg). In 1955 Tallinn and Kotka became twin cities, which enabled Estonians to travel more easily to Finland and vice versa.

In 1959 a branch of the of All-Union travel agency Inturist opened in Tallinn. With regular ferry traffic between Tallinn and Helsinki established in 1965, communication between Estonia and Finland increased remarkably. In the period from 1956 to 1980 a total of 9,698 Estonian tourists visited Finland,[16] including many architects.[17] It was easier for some categories of Soviet people to travel than for the majority of others, thus architects and heritage specialists were among privileged groups.[18] In 1957 a group of the Architects' Union of the USSR included fourteen Estonian architects on a visit to Finland. Tourist groups of Estonian architects traveled to Finland in 1958, 1959, 1960, and 1963, while a group of thirty-six Finnish architects visited Tallinn in 1963. In 1966, an exhibition on the restoration of the Old Tallinn, made by the Estonian Architects' Union and the Scientific Restoration Workshop, was taken to the Finnish Architecture Museum in Helsinki, later also being shown in Turku, Hämeenlinna, and Oulu. The same year a seminar on heritage was organized for students from Tallinn and Helsinki, while special groups of heritage practitioners and restorers were formed, with a group of thirty-one Estonian restorers visiting Finland in 1969.[19]

By the mid-1960s hundreds of thousands of Soviet citizens each year crossed previously closed Soviet borders to travel abroad.[20] This was indicative of the integration of the Soviet Union into regional and indeed global processes of cultural exchange in many fields, both private and professional—including heritage protection and restoration.

Traveling and International Contacts Provided by ICOMOS-USSR

For many restorers, ICOMOS, founded in 1965 in Warsaw, offered opportunities to travel. The Soviet Union was actively involved in the international organizations UNESCO, ICOM, and ICOMOS. The activities of ICOMOS-USSR were some of the most important channels for exchanges of information, methodologies, and ideas relating to heritage conservations.[21] Soviet citizens were quickly promoted to leading positions in ICOMOS: Vladimir Ivanov, Vice President of the All-Union Heritage preservation organization (acronym VOOPIiK) became a Vice President of ICOMOS and was reelected for three terms.[22] In 1981, Jonas Glemža from Lithuania was elected as the Vice President of ICOMOS (acted until 1990), indicating the recognition that the country's highly developed heritage management enjoyed.

The ICOMOS-USSR Committee was a small and closed organization of around twenty-five people.[23] Fredi Tomps, the leader of Republican Inspectorate of the Protection of Architectural Monuments of the Estonian SSR, became a member of the ICOM USSR Committee as late as 1978. Already before that Estonians were involved in the activities of ICOMOS-USSR, using the possibilities for cooperation and travel. The first ICOMOS conference in which Estonian restorers and architects could participate was in Budapest in 1972.[24] No papers were presented by Estonians at this conference, but Jonas Glemža from Lithuania did give a talk.[25] The activity of Lithuanians within ICOMOS was recognized in September 1973 with the ICOMOS international symposium on the protection of historic town centers being held in Vilnius.[26] It focused on urban conservation issues in socialist countries, with representatives from countries including Poland, Czechoslovakia, Hungary, and the GDR, as well as the President of ICOMOS Pietro Gazzola, present at this successful event.[27] A group of seven Estonian conservators also attended this conference, including Helmi Üprus, Fredi Tomps, Dmitri Bruns, and others. In 1977 the Working Group of Socialist Countries for the Restoration of Monuments of History, Culture, and Museum Valuables was founded in Moscow. The participants of the first meeting in October 1978 included representatives from Bulgaria, Hungary, Vietnam, the GDR, Cuba, Mongolia, Poland, Czechoslovakia, and the Soviet Union. The Working Group was led by Poland, which was praised in particular for its restoration activity. The peak of the activities of the ICOMOS-USSR committee came with the ICOMOS Fifth general conference held in Suzdal', Russia, in 1978.[28] At this representative forum there was intensive communication between experts from Soviet republics and foreign countries.[29]

The cooperation generated through the abovementioned Working Group continued with an international heritage seminar held in Tallinn in November 1983. It was coordinated by the Ministry of Culture of the USSR along with local heritage authorities. The participants came from the GDR, Poland, Czechoslovakia, Hungary, Bulgaria, and the Soviet Union. Twenty papers addressed the conference theme: "Methodology and inventory of historical, cultural and museology heritage."[30] This was the first international heritage event of this level ever organized in Tallinn. It strengthened professional and personal contacts, serving as a test event for the Tallinn hosts ahead of the ICOMOS colloquium in the city in 1985.

The ICOMOS colloquium "Problems of the Protection and Present-Day Usage of Architectural Monuments" in Tallinn (4–7 June 1985) was the most important international heritage event in Estonia in the whole Soviet period. It was organized by ICOMOS-USSR in cooperation with the Estonian Building Committee. The venues of the international conferences were usually chosen according to the achievements in restoration that could be presented to foreign experts as examples of best practices in Soviet heritage protection. Being selected by the ICOMOS-USSR to host this international colloquium indicated the high regard in which restoration practices in Estonia were held.

The Soviet delegation from Moscow included twenty-seven participants. Among socialist countries, Poland had the biggest delegation, with eight persons. Capitalist countries were represented by Belgium, Denmark, Finland, Norway, France, and the United States, while Ethiopia and Vietnam also participated.[31] ICOMOS president Michel Parent was among those present in Tallinn. Altogether fifty-one papers were given at the conference where ICOMOS drew up a resolution[32] that declared that the adaptation of twentieth-century architectural monuments to contemporary functions should be conducted using the same scientific methods applied to older heritage.[33]

Hosting a representative international conference provided an important opportunity to demonstrate the achievements of Estonian restorers. A big exhibition was put on in the Niguliste (St. Nicholas) Church that had proved a very problematic case in terms of restoration and contemporary use. The initial idea was to turn the church into a Museum of the Great Socialist October Revolution, but this idea was abandoned and Niguliste became a museum of medieval art and a concert hall.

The ICOMOS colloquium was followed by the seminar of Nordic heritage professionals in 1987 in Tallinn. It was around this time that contacts with the International Centre for the Study of the Preservation and Restoration of Cultural Property (ICCROM) were established. Art historian Juhan Maiste was the first Estonian who attended the ICCROM restoration school in Rome in 1987. While always having to negotiate the controls exerted by the Ministry of Culture and the USSR-ICOMOS committee, Estonian heritage experts nevertheless established themselves in the international heritage community.

Estonian Conservators' Travels Abroad

Traveling abroad in special groups and individually, likewise for study trips, seminars, and conferences, enabled Estonian conservators to obtain knowledge and expertise from colleagues from socialist countries and the wider world. Their travel reports are an important source, describing their experiences abroad. In the Heritage Department archive there are almost fifty individual and group reports from sixty-five trips involving more than one hundred heritage specialists between 1969 and 1989.[34] Among the sixty-five trips, fifty-four were to socialist countries and eleven to capitalist ones (frequent working trips within the USSR to Russia and other Soviet republics are not included). The German Democratic Republic and Poland were the most frequent destinations (twenty-two reports from the GDR and twenty-one from Poland), while there were six reports each on visits to Hungary and Czechoslovakia. Among capitalist countries, Finland was the top destination. Five conservators also visited Yugoslavia.

The obligatory structure of the reports included a list of destinations and institutions visited and the people met during the trip. In the case of group visits, the reports featured a list of the members of the group alongside an outline of the visit, what was learned, and what could be implemented into practices at home. Some of the reports offer comprehensive analyses comparable to scholarly articles. The reports by Villem Raam and Helmi Üprus, the leading figures in Estonian heritage conservation, are particularly analytical and insightful, while also revealing their emotional responses to their experiences. Their professional status enabled them to be critical of the state while also making demands of the authorities.

In 1965, Villem Raam was appointed to the post of the chief specialist of the Restoration Workshops. Having faced repression under the Stalinist regime,[35] Raam started to travel abroad in the mid-1960s, and, perhaps surprisingly, his first visits were to capitalist countries. Raam traveled to Finland with a group of architects to observe the organization and heritage management system there. In 1967, he presented a seminal paper about the Finnish heritage protection system and principles at the heritage conservation seminar in Tallinn organized by the Estonian Architects' Association.[36] He became a member of the Finnish Heritage Society (Suomen Muinaismuistoyhdistys) in 1970—thus at a time when belonging to a foreign society was rare in the USSR. Raam also received personal invitations to travel. After returning from exile in Siberia, he reestablished contacts with his professor Sten Karling and fellow-student Armin Tuulse in Sweden. Karling invited him to lecture at Uppsala University in Sweden in 1973.[37] This trip lasted almost a month; but according to Raam's report, the necessary prolongation of the Soviet visa to Sweden for a whole month was not a problem at all.[38] In Sweden Raam visited many medieval churches and sites, worked in a Stockholm archive, and participated in a heritage conference in Visby.[39]

Helmi Üprus was also repressed by the Stalinist regime but avoided deportation to Siberia. She lost her academic job in 1950, her degree was annulled, and, for a while, she had to work in a factory. After Stalin's death in 1953, Üprus got a job at the Scientific Restoration Workshop, and in the late 1950s she was promoted to the position of leading specialist on architectural history. Üprus was permitted to travel abroad again,[40] in 1969 when she visited the GDR, and the following year she participated in an excursion to Italy organized by the Estonian Architects' Association.[41] In 1971, Estonian restorers were invited to the Heritage Days held in the Federal Republic of Germany that were dedicated to the history and restorations of the historical cities of the Hanseatic League, which included Tallinn. Helmi Üprus' visit to the FRG, which included a visit to Denmark after the conference, was included in the ICOMOS-USSR travel plans.

As recognized architectural historians, Raam and Üprus were excellent guides for international specialists' groups visiting Estonia. This role also increased their international contacts. Both of them also published scientific articles in foreign countries,[42] which was something of a significant exception in the Soviet period in the field of heritage conservation. Helmi Üprus repeatedly wrote about the need to increase communication with foreign colleagues. After returning from the GDR in 1969, she was convinced that historic city centers had to be kept free from traffic, while building big hotels should be prevented to avoid their touristification.[43] She encouraged establishing small restaurants and cafés in old towns instead, as she paid attention to the needs of local people.

Raam's list of suggestions after visiting the GDR in 1970 included establishing a library of Gothic heritage. He also emphasized the need for applied research and longer periods of working in foreign archives. While Helmi Üprus was proud that West German colleagues appreciated Estonian restoration practices, the knowledge of the field in the country, and Estonian colleagues' methodological competence,[44] Villem Raam claimed that Estonian heritage research and possibilities for international cooperation were far behind those of the socialist countries Czechoslovakia, the GDR, Hungary, Poland, and Romania.[45]

Foreign conservation practices, ideas, and methodology were continuously compared to those at home. In his report from 1973, architect Teddy Böckler noted that Hungarian restorers enjoyed good working conditions with well-equipped workshops and excellent organization of work.[46] He listed several things that could be learned from Hungarian restorers and implemented back home—namely, improving restorers' working conditions and communication within divisions of restorers, and also collecting architectural findings on site and preserving them for use in research.[47] After the trip to East Germany in 1974, Böckler included a separate list of suggestions for the restoration and new use of the Niguliste Church based on examples he observed there.[48] Böckler's reports were always richly illustrated with hand-drawn sketches.

When a report that was intended for local authorities also had to be presented to Moscow (as a rule to the Soviet Ministry of Culture), it had to be written into prepared forms that also included political questions. Besides listing all persons spoken to during the trip, it was also obligatory to indicate their attitude toward possible cooperation with the USSR.[49] The report by the heritage specialists Hain Toss and Jaan Vali on their study trip to the Federal Republic of Germany in 1979 indicated that German heritage specialists' attitudes toward the USSR were generally positive, with only one person among those they encountered listed as unclear.[50] Among the ideas suggested for implementation in the USSR, Toss and Vali mentioned the need for improving professional skills of restorers of historical paintings; the need to establish a chemical lab for the research of historical colors (this was ultimately implemented); the idea of creating pedestrian streets in historical town centers (the idea was quite new at that time); and the need for inventories of Estonian industrial heritage.[51]

A lot of professional literature was obtained during travels, as were tools used in restoration, adhesives, and colors, which were generally much better quality than those produced in the USSR. Having returned home, contacts continued through professional correspondence. Villem Raam and Helmi Üprus had wide-reaching professional correspondence with colleagues in Sweden, Finland, both German states, and the UK. The archives contain letters to the British Museum, the Victoria and Albert Museum, and others, concerning various art historical matters.[52] Yevgeny Kaljundi corresponded with René Sneyers, the Head of Belgium's Royal Institute for Cultural Heritage (Koninklijk Instituut voor het Kunstpatrimonium, KIK-IRPA—Institut Royal du Patrimoine Artistique), whom he had met in Zagreb in 1974. Educated as a chemist, René Sneyers was a recognized expert, serving as a UNESCO expert for restoration works. One of Yevgeny Kaljundi's letters concerned the problems with the restoration of the early fourteenth-century Church of St. John in Tartu. The letter was in French and contained rich documentation and drawings of the church.[53] Such correspondence typically addressed a particular problem in a restoration project, although the letters also contained personal details, offering fascinating insight into restorers' lives and attitudes. However, the limited space means we cannot go into more detail here. Still, the extent of professional correspondence, as well as the hosting of international events, demonstrates that Estonian heritage experts and practitioners were connected with colleagues within the USSR, across the socialist bloc, and over the other side of the Iron Curtain.

The PKZ Polish Restoration Company in Tallinn, 1978–90

Any study of international exchange between Soviet-Estonian and foreign heritage specialists would not be complete without reference to Polish restorers' practices in Estonia. The Soviet system allocated substantial finances to restoration, especially in the 1970s and 1980s. According to sources from the time, restoration was one of the fastest growing sectors of the Soviet economy in the late 1970s, with ninety-seven special organizations employing 19,000 people in the field in the USSR.[54] Restoration was well-financed in Estonia, too, particularly during preparations for the Tallinn Olympic Regatta as a part of the 1980 Moscow Olympic Games. For the period between 1976 and 1980, the budget for restoration grew to 28.7 million rubles, rising to 40 million rubles for the years 1981–85.[55] The field was prioritized with higher tariffs and favorable allocation of building materials and technologies.

It quickly became clear that the local restoration institutions—poorly equipped, undermanned, and underfunded—would not be able to do the job in time. Fearing that the Soviet Ministry of Culture would appoint Russian conservation companies to the task, Fredi Tomps, the Estonian member of ICOMOS-USSR, promptly presented the Moscow authorities with the idea of inviting the Polish State Workshops for the Conservation of Cultural Heritage PKZ to help.[56] Thus international contacts were put into practice, bringing Polish restoration companies to work in Tallinn between 1978 and 1990. PKZ, the leading company, was known for its effectiveness and had a globally expanding portfolio. Estonian specialists were well acquainted with and impressed by PKZ's capabilities. Significant expectations were attached to the importing of Polish expertise as it was recognized as the flagship of Eastern European conservation.

Arranging for PKZ to work in Tallinn was the result of an Estonian initiative and lobbying in Moscow and Warsaw. Fredi Tomps frequently had assignments to the Soviet Ministry of Culture in Moscow. His task was to convince the authorities in Moscow of the need to include restoration works in preparations for the Olympic Games to the greatest possible extent. At the same time, Tomps and Dmitri Bruns, city architect of Tallinn, both used their vacations and official journeys to Poland to meet PKZ executives and get them interested in the prospective works in Tallinn.[57]

Working contracts were drawn up between Soiuzvneshstroiimport (from the USSR) and Budimex (from Poland, representing PKZ). Both companies were building contractors operating in import and export markets (in the USSR it was not possible for republics to conclude contracts with foreign countries directly). This was PKZ's first commission in the USSR, and although there were plans to use the company in Leningrad and other cities, PKZ's work did not reach beyond the Estonian SSR until later in the 1980s. PKZ was given responsibility for three medieval sites: a dwelling house that was to serve in a new function as a restaurant; the Fat Margaret artillery tower, which was to become a Maritime museum; and a former prison that was being turned into a new Museum of Photography. For two of the sites, the preliminary designs had already been drawn up and delivered to PKZ. Polish specialists elaborated (and in some cases changed) the design, carried out field research, and created final architectural projects.

The Polish methodological approach was similar to that practiced in Estonian restoration institutions at the time. In general, everything postmedieval was to be eliminated in order to emphasize the medieval appearance of a building. However, Polish restorers liberally added new constructions and finishing details—decorative metalwork, door handles, and window elements—that were unfamiliar to Tallinn's medieval architecture and therefore looked like artistic falsifications to Estonian conservators. Thus, the Polish restorers' work was often seen as excessive or over-restoration. The finished sites proved that they preferred bold new colors to patina and often relied on educated guesses rather than actual research material. Some celebrated the results and the level of Polish craftsmanship; yet for some critics, their restored sites seemed monotonous and soulless, lacking historical layers and the sense of continuity expected of five-hundred-year-old buildings.[58]

Jaan Tamm, an experienced heritage management official, noted that each site the Polish company worked on featured architectural details that were copies of those that could be found in the Polish cities where the workers were from. The problems with the first objects restored by PKZ resulted in Estonians taking control of the restoration projects and working processes from 1980 onward. It was agreed that the projects were to be prepared by Estonian architects relying on local research. The actual restoration works on sites were left to the Poles. Thus, what was initially imagined as export of expertise turned into cooperation between Polish and Estonian restorers.

PKZ's renowned efficiency resulted in nearly thirty restored sites being completed in a rather short period. Altogether three-hundred Polish restorers were working in Tallinn on seven or eight objects every year throughout the 1980s.[59] Estonian restorers had never had the capacity to work in such volumes. The physical "Polish layer" of restoration is still evident in Tallinn Old Town today, thus it could be argued that PKZ exerted significant influence on the field of conservation in the Estonian SSR in the 1980s. However, the works after 1980 were organized in a way that the Estonian side held significant sway, contributing design and research elements, leaving only the execution of the projects to PKZ. Estonian conservation practices of the time were thus similar to those of their Polish colleagues, which made this arrangement possible. However, it seems that the Polish contribution was largely limited to the work of PKZ's skilled craftspeople. When conservation for the upcoming period between 1983 and 1990 was planned,[60] Estonian conservators remained unconvinced by Polish methodology and guidance. Instead, they were inclined to draw on experiences from objects restored in Riga and Vilnius. Consequently, while PKZ certainly left a mark on Estonian heritage conservation, the company did not have a serious methodological impact on its development. Polish restoration practices in Estonia revealed similarities as well as differences in thinking, as became evident in discussions over methodological questions on a very concrete, practical level. This led to occasionally heated disputes over the ideology and methodology of contemporary restoration.

The abundant list of sites restored by PKZ during the 1980s continued the established Soviet-Estonian practices that had been around since the 1960s but were already being questioned and deemed outdated by some professionals in the field. This in return encouraged local heritage professionals to move away from these practices and instead open up to Scandinavian and other Western influences.

Conclusion

Soviet-Estonian restorers' international travel demonstrates the active exchanges that they enjoyed with colleagues from both socialist and capitalist countries (Finland, Sweden, and West Germany, in particular). Estonian conservators were in contact with ICOMOS through its USSR Committee in Moscow and benefitted from opportunities to travel through ICOMOS, while also making the most of its channels of knowledge, such as participating in the conferences, accessing literature, and building new personal contacts.

External communication upheld and strengthened levels of professionalism. Seeing advanced restoration techniques and materials abroad contributed to the growing self-confidence of Estonian restorers in demanding the implementation of innovations and general improvement of Estonian conservation practice. This is why the activity of Polish conservators in Tallinn between 1978 and 1990 proved to be a somewhat controversial chapter in Estonian conservation history. Polish colleagues employed their restoration traditions in Estonia, with their methods differing slightly from what had become common practice in Estonia, namely an approach that was firmly rooted in historical and archeological research. Practical cooperation revealed differences in attitudes, which spared the discussions on the methodology of contemporary conservation. As a result, Estonia was not the passive receiver of Polish restoration works but established itself as a partner.

The Soviet-era intellectual leaders of Estonian heritage protection and practice were Helmi Üprus and Villem Raam. They were educated in the prewar period and enabled the continuation of Western European and Scandinavian know-how in the field of conservation. Having been oppressed by the Stalinist regime, they were opposed to Soviet rule. Nevertheless, after the end of Stalinism, they were able to maintain personal contacts with colleagues abroad and were allowed to travel to other parts of Europe again. Üprus and Raam remained recognized authorities for subsequent generations of conservators and historians in Soviet Estonia and in newly independent Estonia.

With its generous financing of heritage restoration in the republics of the Soviet Union and its support for intellectuals' international contacts, the Soviet regime, somewhat paradoxically, actually strengthened Estonian national identity. Heritage became one of the basic platforms of constructing a national collective memory that drew on the prewar period. In the late 1980s people became widely involved in the patriotic heritage movement, with the Estonian Heritage Society, established in 1987, quickly growing into a mass organization. Promoting knowledge of local heritage, initiating campaigns of collecting oral histories in order to reveal unwritten history, and organizing manifestations and numerous events all contributed enormously to the restoration of the independent Republic of Estonia in 1991.[61] The first Estonian government was labeled "the government of historians,"[62] with the historian Mart Laar, who contributed to the work of the opposition while head of the National Heritage Department of the Ministry of Culture of the Estonian SSR, becoming the first Prime Minister of newly independent Estonia.

Karin Hallas-Murula is an Estonian architectural historian. A graduate of Repin Institute of Arts, St. Petersburg (Russia) and CEU in Prague, she was awarded a doctorate from the Institute of Art Studies, Moscow, in 1992. In 1991 she founded the Museum of Estonian Architecture, serving twenty years as director. From 2012 to 2019 she was Professor of Architectural Theory and History at Tallinn University of Technology. She has published extensively on nineteenth and twentieth-century architecture and planning. She currently runs a private company and is involved in the EU COST project Dynamics of Placemaking and Digitization in Europe's Cities.

Kaarel Truu is a PhD candidate at the Estonian Academy of Arts. His academic research is focused on the restoration works carried out in Tallinn Old Town during the soviet period. He has worked in various positions in the field of cultural heritage since 2008, including as a conservation specialist in Tallinn City Cultural Heritage Department. He currently serves as an advisor on the Estonian National Heritage Board.

Notes

1. In the Lithuanian SSR, a republican heritage law was adopted in 1967; in Uzbekistan in 1968; in Armenia, Moldavia, and Belarus in 1969; and in Kazakhstan in 1971.
2. For more on this see: Pagel, "Eesti NSV turistid," 89.
3. Ibid.
4. In the prewar period there were two heritage laws, one adopted in 1925, the other in 1936.
5. J. Tamm, *Restauraatorid vanas Tallinnas*, 9.
6. See also: Jokilehto, *Arhitektuuri konserveerimise ajalugu*, 321–330.
7. Alatalu, "Muinsuskaitse siirdeühiskonnas," 222.
8. Ibid., 42.
9. J. Tamm, "Tallinna vanalinn," 106.
10. Janusauskaite, "Lithuania—the Standard Setter," 29–33, 32.
11. Gorsuch, *All This Is Your World*, 13; quoted in Pagel, "Eesti NSV turistid," 80.
12. Assipova and Minnaert, "Tourists of the World, Unite!"
13. Pagel, "Eesti NSV turistid," 83.
14. See Koenker, *Club Red*.
15. See Nikonova, "Gosudarstvennaia politika."
16. Ibid., 83–84.
17. For more on Estonian architects traveling to Finland, see Hallas-Murula, *Soome-Eesti*, 129–31.
18. Pagel, "Eesti NSV turistid," 80.
19. Soome sõidu aruanne, typescript, ERA T-67, 1, 1047 (P-1182), Estonian Heritage Board Archive, Tallinn.
20. Gorsuch, *All This Is Your World*.
21. Dushkina, "IKOMOS i otechestvennaia praktika," 68–72.
22. Ibid.

23. Ibid.
24. Materials of ICOMOS Budapest 1972, Helmi Üprus' files, 4, 261, not paginated, Estonian Heritage Board Archive, Tallinn.
25. Helmi Üprus' files, 4.261 in Heritage Board Archive. Not paginated.
26. Hansar, "Helmi Üprus and the Old Town of Tallinn."
27. Janusauskaite, "Lithuania—the Standard Setter," 32.
28. Dushkina, "IKOMOS i otechestvennaia praktika." For more information on these international committees and meetings, see also the conclusion of this edited volume.
29. Dushkina, "IKOMOS i otechestvennaia praktika."
30. Uuetalu, "Arhitektuuripärandi uurimine ja projekteerimine aastail," 8.
31. *Problems of the Protection and Present-Day Usage.*
32. Ibid., 203.
33. Ibid., 204.
34. Travel reports 1969–89, ERA T-76, 1. Estonian Heritage Board Archive, Tallinn.
35. Raam spent fifteen years in Siberia as political prisoner (1941–56). As a rule, after rehabilitation and returning back from Siberia repressed, such people were put under KGB surveillance. In general they were not allowed to travel abroad and their careers were subject to controls. Villem Raam and Helmi Üprus were exceptions in this case, perhaps due to their professional positions and the fact that they were well-known abroad.
36. Soiuz arkhitektorov Estonskoi SSR, *Seminar po voprosam okhrany i restavratsii*, 153–58.
37. Villem Raam, Aruanne ametisõidust Rootsi 4.09.–9.10.1973, typescript, ERA T-76, 1, 1729 (P-1892), 1, Estonian Heritage Board Archive, Tallinn.
38. Raam, Report, 1973.ERA T-76,1,1729 (P-1892), Estonian Heritage Board Archive, Tallinn.
39. Ibid.
40. In the 1930s, she had traveled in Great Britain, the Netherlands, Germany, Austria, and Hungary. Helmi Üprus' files, Estonian Heritage Board Archive.
41. Helmi Üprus, Itaalia reisi päevikud, manuscript, Helmi Üprus' files, 4, 271, 1, Estonian Heritage Board Archive, Tallinn.
42. Üprus, "Zur Regenerierung der Altstadt Tallinn/Reval"; idem, "The Old Town of Tallinn and Its Future"; idem, "Architektur der Altstadt Tallinns"; and others. Villem Raam published a dozen academic articles abroad, for example: Raam, "Die Domkirche zu Tallinn"; idem, "Das Birgitta-Kloster in Tallinn/Reval."
43. Üprus, Aruanne, 1969, ERA T-76, 1, 985, (P-1108), 15. Estonian Heritage Board Archive, Tallinn. At that time the high rise Inturist hotel Viru was under construction in the vicinity of Tallinn Old Town.
44. Üprus, Aruanne, 1969, ERA T-76, 1, 985, (P-1108), 55. Estonian Heritage Board Archive, Tallinn.
45. Villem Raam, Aruanne õppereis-seminarist Saksa DV-sse 1.–20. 09.1970, typescript, ERA T-76, 1,1158 (P-1303), 13, Estonian Heritage Board Archive, Tallinn.
46. Teddy Böckler, Spetsialiseeritud õppereis Ungari Rahvavabariiki, 19.09.–02.10.1973, typescript, ERA T-76,1,1730, (P-1893), 14-15, Estonian Heritage Board Archive, Tallinn.
47. Böckler, Spetsialiseeritud õppereis, 14.

48. Teddy Böckler and Leonhard Lapin, Aruanne Saksa Demokraatlikus Vabariigis toimunud sümpoosioni "Monumentaalsete arhitektuurimälestiste kasutamine tänapäeval" kohta 5.–11. maini 1974 (Tallinn, 1975) manuscript, ERA T-76, 1, 2203, 86–91.
49. Hain Toss and Jaan Vali, Otchet o rezul'tatakh komandirovaniia v GDR v mezhdunarodnom seminare po restavratsii pamiatnikov arkhitektury, Tallinn 1979, typescript, ERA T-76, 1, 10553 (A-347), 3, Estonian Heritage Board Archive, Tallinn.
50. Ibid., 3.
51. Ibid., 7–8.
52. Helmi Üprus' files. 3.3.2, 125, 3.3.4, 218, and others. Heritage Board Archive. Not paginated.
53. Toss and Vali, Otchet, 7–8.
54. Yevgeni Kaljundi, Üleliiduline restautraatorite konverents Moskvas 11.–16.12.1978, typescript, Tallinn, 1980, ERA T-76, 1, 10615, 4, Estonian Heritage Board Archive, Tallinn.
55. According to Rasmus Kangropool in 1977–80, Tallinn Old Town investments were 25 million rubles. Kangropool, "Tallinna vanalinna regenereerimisest," 13.
56. Interview with Fredi Tomps on 2 September 2016, notes in Kaarel Truu's possession.
57. Interview with Fredi Tomps on 2 September 2016 and Dmitri Bruns on 10 January 2017, notes in Kaarel Truu's possession.
58. Interview with Ülo Puustak on 1 December 2016, notes in Kaarel Truu's possession. A similar critique can be found in writings by Jaan Tamm and were also expressed by Boris Dubovik. Also Rasmus Kangropool has mentioned one of the first sites restored by PKZ as a bad example, Kangropool, "Tallinna vanalinna regenereerimisest," 19.
59. Seidla and Alatalu, Boris Dubovik, 120.
60. Tallinn Heritage Protection Division, 8, 102, 8, Tallinn Heritage Protection Division Archives, Tallinn.
61. M. Tamm, "Mälupoliitika," 147.
62. M. Tamm "The Republic of Historians."

Bibliography

Alatalu, Riin. "Muinsuskaitse siirdeühiskonnas 1986–2002: rahvuslikust südametunnistusest Eesti NSV-s omaniku ahistajaks Eesti Vabariigis." PhD diss., Tallinn: Estonian Art Academy, 2012.

Assipova, Zhanna, and Lynn Minnaert. "Tourists of the World, Unite! The Interpretation and Facilitation of Tourism Towards the End of the Soviet Union (1962–1990)." *Journal of Policy Research in Tourism, Leisure and Events* 6, no. 3 (2014): 215–30.

Dushkina, Natal'ia. "IKOMOS i otechestvennaia praktika sokhraneniia kulturnogo naslediia." *Observatoriia kultury* 6 (2005). Retrieved 13 November 2018. http://infoculture.rsl.ru/?news-jok.

Gorsuch, Anne E. *All This Is Your World: Soviet Tourism at Home and Abroad after Stalin*. Oxford: Oxford University Press, 2011.

Hallas-Murula, Karin. *Soome-Eesti: sajand arhitektuurisuhteid*. Tallinn: Eesti Arhitektuurimuuseum, 2005.

Hansar, Lilian. "Helmi Üprus and the Old Town of Tallinn." *Baltic Journal of Art History* 3 (2011): 57–76.
Janusauskaite, Vilte. "Lithuania—the Standard Setter for Urban Heritage Protection in the Former USSR?" In *Historical Perspective of Heritage Legislation: Balance between Laws and Values. International conference October 12–13, 2016, Tallinn. Conference proceedings*, 29–33. Tallinn: ICOMOS Estonia NC; ICLAFI; Estonian Academy of Arts, 2017.
Jokilehto, Jukka. *Arhitektuuri konserveerimise ajalugu*. Tallinn: Eesti Kunstiakadeemia, 2010.
Kangropool, Rasmus. "Tallinna vanalinna regenereerimisest." In *Eesti ehitusmälestised*, edited by Tiit Masso, 10–20. Tallinn: Valgus, 1990.
Koenker, Diane P. *Club Red: Vacation Travel and the Soviet Dream*. Ithaca: Cornell University Press, 2013.
Nikonova, Svetlana. "Gosudarstvennaia politika v oblasti ideologii i kultury v kontekste sovetskoi deistvitel'nosti (seredina 60kh—seredina 80kh godov XX veka)." PhD diss., Kazan State University of Architecture and Engineering, 2009. Retrieved 7 October 2018. http://www.dissercat.com/content/gosudarstvennaya-politika-v-oblasti-ideologii-i-kultury-v-kontekste-sovetskoi-deistvitelnost#ixzz5TFWI2SH4.
Pagel, Oliver. "Eesti NSV turistid Soomes aastail 1955–1980." *Tuna* 3 (2016): 79–94.
Problems of the Protection and Present-Day Usage of Architectural Monuments. ICOMOS International Colloquy, ESSR Tallinn, June 4–7, 1985. Tallinn: Valgus, 1987.
Raam, Villem. "Das Birgitta-Kloster in Tallinn/Reval: Empore und Altäre." *Nordost-Archiv* 75 (1984): 63–84.
———. "Die Domkirche zu Tallinn und ihre baugeschichtliche Bedeutung." *Konsthistorisk Tidskrift* 36, no. 4/4 (1967): 73–91.
Seidla, Anu, and Riin Alatalu. *Boris Dubovik: "Vanalinn—minu lemmmik."* Tallinn: MTÜ Eesti ICOMOS ja Ajakool OÜ, 2017.
Soiuz arkhitektorov Estonskoi SSR, eds. *Seminar po voprosam okhrany i restavratsii pamiatnikov arkhitektury: materialy*. Tallinn: Eesti Raamat, 1968.
Tamm, Jaan. *Restauraatorid vanas Tallinnas*. Tallinn: Perioodika, 1984.
———. "Tallinna vanalinn—40 aastat muinsuskaitseala, 10 aastat UNESCO maailmapärandis." In *Muinsuskaitse aastaraamat 2006*, 106–7. Tallinn: Muinsuskaitseamet, Tallinna Kultuuriväärtuste Amet, and Eesti Kunstiakadeemia, 2007.
Tamm, Marek. "Mälupoliitika." In *Eesti poliitika ja valitsemine 1991–2011*. Tallinn: TLÜ kirjastus, 2012.
———. "The Republic of Historians: Historians as Nation-Builders in Estonia (late 1980s–early 1990s)." *Rethinking History* 2 (2016): 1–18.
Üprus, Helmi. "Architektur der Altstadt Tallinns und ihre Abhängigkeit von der mittelalterlichen sozialen Struktur." In *Bürgertum. Handelskapital. Städtebünde*, edited by Konrad Fritze, 252–64. Weimar: Böhlau, 1975.
———. "The Old Town of Tallinn and Its Future." *Monumentum* 8, no. 4 (1972): 71–97.
———. "Zur Regenerierung der Altstadt Tallinn/Reval." *Deutsche Kunst und Denkmalpflege* 29, no. 2 (1971): 104–20.
Uuetalu, Heino. "Arhitektuuripärandi uurimine ja projekteerimine aastail 1978–88." In *Eesti ehitusmälestised*, edited by Tiit Masso, 3–9. Tallinn: Valgus, 1990.

PART II

Canonizing and Contesting the Past

Heritage, Place, and Belonging under Socialism

CHAPTER 5

Socialist Royalty?
The Ambiguities of the Reconstruction of the Royal Residence in Budapest in the 1950s

Eszter Gantner[1]

The Castle Hill and Royal Palace in Budapest, the most powerful symbol of Hungarian statehood, has been a continuous locus of public debate in light of discontinuities in state borders, political orders, and aesthetic and architectural trends, together with wartime destruction. A March 2016 *New York Times* article, "Hungarian Leader's 'Edifice Complex' Has Some in Budapest Rattled,"[2] commented on Hungarian Prime Minister Viktor Orbán's plans for the reconstruction of the well-known heritage site Castle Hill, which includes the former royal residence and the medieval quarter around the palace.[3] It was first designed as part of a project developed by Empress Maria Theresia in the eighteenth century. Since then, the castle and the area around it have been one of the most symbolic places in the country. It is worth noting that Orbán's office itself is to be found in the area around the Royal Palace. His plans for reconstruction were part of broader symbolic and political placemaking in relation to one of the most canonical and significant sites of Hungarian national history. The current efforts to transform it are just one case in a long line of such contested efforts. The socialist period was no exception, and it is on this period that I will focus in this chapter.

One of the major transformations of the Castle Hill area began in the 1950s, as the reconstruction of the royal residence was initiated by the Stalinist Rákosi government. This project was understood as a part of the Stalinist Communist transformation of Hungarian society, which at the same time served to strengthen national identity. Part of these endeavors involved the symbolic use of presocialist palaces and heritage sites under socialism as the seat of Communist government, as was the case in Moscow (the Kremlin) and Prague (the Royal Castle at Hradčany). In the

Hungarian case, reconstruction was necessary following the wartime destruction of much of the Castle Hill complex. As in Poland, with the Royal Castle in Warsaw, or in the USSR, with the tsarist palaces in Petergof and Tsarskoe Selo, significant sites of national history that formed part of the imperial and interwar heritage canons were reconstructed under socialism. This chapter thus seeks to offer insight into the ambiguous political and aesthetic aspects of the reconstruction of the royal residency, focusing on the 1950s and 1960s. It also considers how the debates surrounding the canonical symbol of Hungarian statehood related to international trends and which forms of concrete exchange took place regarding this case between reconstruction experts from various socialist countries.

In this contribution, I explore how the ambitious approach to reconstruction fits into the broader international landscape of reconstruction projects across the socialist bloc, while at the same time being a way of fulfilling goals within domestic politics by drawing on national tradition. While the specific measures taken during the reconstruction of Buda Castle have been explored elsewhere,[4] I approach the question by focusing on practices and knowledge transfer between heritage experts in socialist countries. This chapter examines the role of ideology and political power in the representation of the past. As in other socialist bloc countries, the socialist nation-building project in Hungary was shaped by transnational cultural transfers and the politics of socialist internationalism. In his work on the cult leader Mátyás Rákosi, Balázs Apor argues that even if the cult of Rákosi was arguably one of the most pervasive examples of orchestrated adulation in the Soviet bloc, it was nevertheless integrated into the transnational ritual culture of Sovietized Eastern Europe. This replica of the cult of Stalin was necessarily adjusted to local social and cultural contexts and shaped by national traditions of state-building.[5] The reconstruction and repurposing of the Castle Hill was embroiled in a similar network of tensions, as its existing canonical status as a site of national significance could not prove entirely malleable to ideological and aesthetic projects that were introduced by the socialist regime after World War II.

The Royal Palace as the Product of Both Past and Present

How heritage protection had been—and remained—part of a socialist revolution that was coupled with efforts toward nation-building was highlighted in the second volume of the yearbook *Magyar Műemlékvédelem* (Hungarian Historic Preservation). Published in 1964 by the Magyar Országos Műemléki Felügyelőség (Hungarian National Heritage Office),[6] three articles in the volume analyzed the impact of socialist legislation on heritage protection and preservation. Further papers outlined heritage protection practices in the Soviet Union and in other socialist countries, including Romania, the GDR, and Poland. The remaining articles presented case studies of restoration and preservation at particular sites in Hungary, with each of these contributions reflecting on the most crucial change in the field of heritage protection and preservation compared to the period before World War II—namely, the *nationalization* of heritage sites, museum objects, and public and private collections. This process was enabled by decree No. 13 issued by the Council of Ministers in 1949.[7] Simply put, it meant that the state was allowed to expropriate sites (including churches, castles, and synagogues) and private collections on the pretext of heritage protection. This shift toward the possibility of an overall nationalization of cultural heritage also entailed centralizing heritage protection and subjecting it to ideological guidelines at all institutional levels.

Besides establishing legal frameworks that aimed at exerting political control over heritage sites and reconstruction initiatives, the ruling Hungarian Working People's Party (MDP)[8] also embedded the fate of the sites into the regime's ideological framework of memory and history politics. This was straightforward in the case of the nationalization of the property of some minorities, such as that of the expelled Germans or murdered Jews. The selection of sites for protection relied on the expertise of preservationists, mainly art historians and archeologists, who carried out the registration, description, and restoration of the heritage sites. However, the final decision lay with the Communist Party; and the transformation of the sites into heritage, as a "product of the present," as G. J. Ashworth formulated it in 1994,[9] was an expression of the Party's ideological and political power.

This chapter explores how this shift in the function of heritage was realized in the context of the key symbolic site in Hungary: the Royal Palace in Buda. This case is particularly significant, as the Royal Palace constituted something of an ideological contradiction in Stalinist Hungary. On the one hand, it represented the delegitimized feudal and bourgeois past of the country; on the other hand, it stood as a symbol of the sovereign and great Kingdom of Hungary from medieval times to the recent past. Searching for historical legitimacy, the Stalinist Rákosi government had to incorporate the site's ambivalent symbolic and historic legacy into the newly created "socialist" narrative of the country's history. Two such examples were the centenary celebrations of the 1848–49 Revolution and the War of Independence that followed it. These created a unique opportunity to achieve the goal of legitimizing the new political system and the Party and its leaders.[10] They employed a highly selective and thus instrumental approach to historical periods and their architectural legacies in the search of a "usable past."

The architecture of bygone eras functions, according to Arnold Bartetzky,[11] as a powerful visual marker of the preferred version of national history and legitimation of state sovereignty. A letter from 1952 requesting guidance from the Hungarian government regarding the palace's reconstruction by the Architectural Planning Company KÖZTI (Középülettervező Vállalat) demonstrates this approach clearly, with the architects asking "for help and guidance for the proper representation of the intangible content of the palace in terms of quantity and proportion of different historical epochs."[12]

Over the course of almost ten centuries, the functions of the Buda Castle complex have shifted between different uses, ranging from royal residence, military fortress, and seat of government to university and library location. Thus, the socialist-era reconstruction also created its own historical narrative for the palace by selecting specific elements from the Royal Castle complex's history. It was necessary to identify those periods that would serve the ideological aim of emphasizing the legitimacy of the new regime in power.[13]

The history of the palace of the Hungarian kings in Buda goes back to the thirteenth century. It was first completed in 1265. The oldest surviving part of the present-day palace was built in the fourteenth century, while the Gothic palace of King Louis I of Anjou has also survived in part. In the fifteenth century, under the reign of King Matthias Corvinus, the Royal Castle became the first center of early Renaissance culture, arts, and learning north of the Alps. Matthias Corvinus rebuilt the palace in an early Renaissance style and invited mostly Italian humanists, artists, and craftsmen to the court. The palace also housed the famous library of the king, the Bibliotheca Corviniana. However, after the Battle of Mohács[14] in 1541, the Ottoman Turks occupied the town and the Royal Castle, and fortified the previous residence of Hungarian kings. After the siege of Buda in 1686 that ended with the conquest of the complex by Habsburg troops, the former palace was beyond repair following the destruction during the siege, so in 1715, King Charles III ordered the demolition of the ruins.

During the reign of Empress Maria Theresia of Habsburg, crowned queen of Hungary in 1741, the newly erected Baroque Royal Palace became the symbol of the good relations between the Hungarian estates and the Habsburg dynasty, as the Hungarian counties and cities, together with the Hungarian nobility, not only supported the reconstruction of the palace but also lent support to the queen in the War of the Austrian Succession.[15] Nevertheless, how the building would be used remained uncertain as the queen had no intention of leaving Vienna. So, in 1777 the queen decided that the University of Nagyszombat should move into the Royal Castle complex. The university remained there until 1783, when the faculties moved to the rapidly developing district of Pest on the other side of the Danube. In 1791, the palace became the residence of the new Habsburg palatine of the Kingdom of Hungary, Archduke Alexander Leopold of Austria. The palatinal court in Buda Castle became the center of Hungarian cultural life and high society at the beginning of the nineteenth century. After a relatively long peaceful period, the Revolution and the War of Independence in 1848–49 saw the Hungarian army lay siege to the Royal Palace on 4 May 1849, which endured heavy artillery fighting. The palace subsequently became one of the major iconic sites of memory associated with the resistance against the Habsburg dynasty.

The palace was rebuilt between 1850 and 1856 by Josef Weiss and Carl Neuwirth. Emperor Franz Joseph I of Austria visited Buda Castle in 1856 and 1857, and after the Austro-Hungarian Compromise of 1867, the palace played an important part in the crowning ceremony of Franz Joseph, who was crowned king of Hungary. It remained a symbol of the peace between the Hungarian people and the ruling dynasty after a decade of resistance and conflicts.

In the last third of the nineteenth century, Budapest experienced rapid development. Ambitious urban planning projects expressed the growing wealth and status of the Hungarian capital. The reconstruction of the Royal Palace became one of the major projects as the Hungarian government intended to create a Royal Palace that would be a match for other famous European royal residences.[16] The rebuilding lasted forty years, from 1875 to 1912, with the palace given the neo-Baroque appearance that it retains today by the lead architects Alajos Hauszmann and Miklós Ybl. After the collapse of the Habsburg Empire and removal of the dynasty in 1918, the Royal Palace became the seat of the new regent of the Kingdom of Hungary (a kingdom without a king), Miklós Horthy. He lived there from 1920 to 1944, a period when the palace was the center of the country's political and social life. In 1944–45 heavy fighting and artillery fire destroyed the entire building, thus raising the question of what shape the reconstructed Royal Palace would assume. The rich history of the building meant that it featured stylistic elements ranging across the Middle Ages and the Renaissance to Classicism and neo-Baroque. This eclecticism had to be negotiated as the Palace assumed new cultural functions by housing several museums and, from 1985, the National Széchényi Library.

With the establishment of the Stalinist system in Hungary in 1948, the palace would still retain its place as an object of national historical significance. However, the framing of its place in Hungarian national identity constructions changed completely. As my brief outline of the history of the site demonstrates, the Royal Palace stood for the long and independent history of the country and, after the political compromise of 1867, also for the vision of a strong Hungarian kingdom and less for the multiethnic Dual Monarchy.

Figure 5.1. Royal Palace, 1948. Source: Széchenyi Lánchíd újjáépítése, szemben a budai Vár / Reconstruction of Széchenyi Chain Bridge, opposite the Buda Castle (1948). Reproduced from Fortepan, Creative Commons CC-BY-SA 3.0.

After 1948, a significant challenge facing the authorities was how to include this story in the new socialist historical narrative and how to deal with the ruins of such a powerful site of Hungarian national history. The key for answering this question can be found in what was known as the Cultural Revolution (*kulturális forradalom*), which comprised of a set of cultural policies propagated by the new Communist government in similar fashion to other socialist countries.[17] The consequences of these policies for the Royal Palace were far-reaching. In her account on the Hungarian National Gallery, which was relocated to Buda Castle in 1957, the art historian Katalin Sinkó described how the historical layers were rearranged after the socialist revolution: "On the one hand, the exhibitions took into account those events and memories that could be associated with the present according to the ideology—that is, 'advanced traditions'—and, on the other hand, they have put them into a negative, 'retrograde' context, meaning that these events and memories had to be forgotten. This 'sentencing' to collective amnesia was an important tool for stigmatizing people."[18]

This also entailed increasing control over the field of the culture and memory politics. As the historian Tibor Huszár emphasized in his research on the cultural politics of the Hungarian Communist government,[19] the ideological influencing and attacking of former autonomous cultural bodies such as museums or expert organizations had been conducted through informal (conspiratorial) communicational channels, which allowed the growing destruction of the autonomy of various academic and expert institutions in the cultural sector. The goal was to establish a system of "socialist re-education," including rewriting and reinterpreting the past. The most important figure in the field of cultural politics, József Révai, Hungarian Minister of Education between 1949 and 1953, described this in a 1949 speech as follows: "What does a Cultural Revolution mean? . . . It means that we must put all means at the service of the socialist education of our people: school, agitation and propaganda, art, film, literature, all forms of cultural movement of the masses."[20] He also emphasized that the main coordinates of this revolution were marked out by the Soviet model that was applied in this field. "The new Hungarian culture not only considers Soviet culture as a model, but also becomes increasingly connected with it while preserving and developing its own national characteristics."[21]

This clearly signaled that the Soviet model was to be followed on every level of the Cultural Revolution. At the same time, Révai emphasized the importance of preserving the national character. This fusion of seemingly dichotomous elements—national culture and socialist internationalism, as manifested in the implementation of the Soviet model, as one example, and the multifaceted Hungarian past and the intervention of a socialist interpretation of it, as another—characterized the reconstruction of the Royal Castle as well.

Reconstruction and Transfer of Know-How between 1949 and 1953

The Stalinist leader of Hungary, Mátyás Rákosi, had a clear vision of the fate and reconstruction of the Royal Castle. According to a document from 8 April 1952, he not only had his own interpretation of the history of the site but also made recommendations for how it should be reappropriated and the forms its reconstruction should take.

> The building of the castle was a representative building, representing a monarchy. The emperor and the king wanted to show the richness of the people. . . . For us, the parliament is enough for representation. . . . We want to restore the castle building so that its exterior remains in its old form, and inside becomes modern, suitable for work. . . . I asked Comrade Orlov, whether it was

technically possible to have a modern design inside the traditional exterior. He said that the same happened in the Kremlin. I would like us to agree on this principle right now.[22]

As stated in this document, the redefinition of the building was guided from the autumn of 1949 by the idea of establishing the working headquarters of the ruling party there, providing a seat for its ministries, committees, and many other offices. This would have been the center of the political apparatus, while the parliament would have served a representative function. Besides having a working or practical function, Rákosi pointed out that the building would also serve a symbolic function, with the Kremlin deemed a model for the redefinition and reconstruction in Budapest. It, too, was to combine the historic architecture, and thus the glorious past, with more functionalist approaches. The architects István Janáky and Iván Kotsis were therefore invited to thoroughly modernize the interior and exterior of the palace.[23] Their proposed solution also followed architectural trends and gave expression to modernist architects' reservations toward the Baroque and any kind of Historicism as being "too ornate." This applied to the Hauszmann style,[24] the neo-Baroque reconstruction practiced by Alajos Hauszmann at the turn of the century.

Parallel to the political discussions about the role of the building, experts drew on archeological research and excavations that focused on the medieval period and were conducted at the site of the destroyed Royal Palace immediately after the war. Although the Rákosi government later lost interest in the medieval history of the site and the Castle Hill, the experts, led by the archeologist and art historian László Gerevich, began unearthing the remains of the medieval buildings and the excavation was one of the largest-scale castle excavations in Europe. The documentation and research on the medieval sites were organized and conducted by the architectural historian László Gerő from 1946 to 1966. The first reconstruction plan of the medieval remains was also conceptualized by Gerő in 1950 already and finalized in 1952. He viewed the reconstruction of buildings destroyed in World War II as a shared issue among heritage experts in socialist countries. He recalled his exchanges with colleagues from other countries in an article titled "Experiences in Monument Protection in Socialist Countries" (Műemlékvédelmi tapasztalatok szocialista országokban). In this particular article, László Gerő and his coauthor, the art historian Géza Entz, provided a short overview of the main characteristics of heritage protection and preservation in socialist countries, including some countries they had visited: "It is clear that our short study trips, discussions and occasional exchanges, and the limited knowledge of the relevant literature in these countries allow us to record only impressions. While in Czechoslovakia,

Poland, and the German Democratic Republic, we acquired personal experiences, from Romania we have significantly less information, and from Bulgaria and Albania no direct data are available."[25]

Gerő and Entz reported on a broad spectrum of practices and forms of knowledge transfers in the field of heritage preservation in those countries. They remarked on the large number of monographs on particular sites or site groups in Poland and Czechoslovakia, noting that such books were also designed for the public in the latter, aiding the popularization of such locations and their history. Gerő and Entz suggested developing similar publications for Hungarian readers. They also praised the variety and quality of the Czechoslovakian heritage journals, including *Zprávy Památkové Péče* (Bulletin of Monument Preservation) and *Pamiatky a Múzeá* (Monuments and Museums), while highlighting the relatively poor output in this field in Poland and Hungary.

After discussing their overall impressions, the authors offered more in-depth descriptions of specific approaches to conservation and protection, while also presenting extensive descriptions of technical practices in the GDR and Poland. They concentrated in particular on the work of the restoration workshops in Warsaw and in various places in the GDR, emphasizing the high quality of their work when compared to the very poor conditions in Hungary in this field.[26] In conclusion, Gerő and Entz highlighted the importance of foreign examples to the development of Hungarian heritage protection, conservation, and restoration, with a special focus on Polish, German, and Czechoslovak expertise. They recommended implementing transfers of know-how and practices through international exchanges of experience by organizing conferences and visits, among other measures.

The article drew on a book about the reconstruction of the Royal Palace that Gerő had published in 1951 already.[27] Designed for a broad readership, the book outlined the history of the palace and the Castle Hill, emphasizing their significance in national history. In the second part of the book, Gerő discussed the need for the excavations in the area, underlining the relevance of the medieval finds. One chapter even offered a broad panoramic overview of the contemporary European landscape of heritage protection.[28] Although the book was published at the peak of Stalinism in Hungary, Gerő cited and presented practices and developments from capitalist countries as well. He argued for reconstruction instead of conservation, emphasizing that the war and the degree of the destruction it had wrought meant the conservation of sites was impossible when not much remained of them.

Drawing on the example of Warsaw, where Polish citizens had demanded the reconstruction of the Old Town, he asked how a partly demolished but still "living" heritage site, which has special cultural or historic value, should

Figure 5.2. Construction works at the Royal Palace. Aerial image made by the Hungarian National Defense Association (MHSZ) (1963). Source: Légifotó a Budavári Palotáról (korábban Királyi Palota) / aerial photo of the Buda Castle (formerly the Royal Palace). Reproduced from Fortepan, Creative Commons CC-BY-SA 3.0.

be dealt with. To answer this question Gerő introduced some examples of restoration practices from the Soviet Union, explaining that selected sites, including the Kremlin, had been in a far better condition than the Hungarian sites and so in their case it was right to practice restoration. He continued with an analysis of the Polish reconstruction works, presenting them as a possible role model for the Hungarian case, referring to the lectures that Franciszek Ksawery Piwocki and his colleague Kazimierz Malinowski (or "Malinovszky" as he was named in Hungary) gave in Budapest in 1950. His information about the reconstruction works in Poland obviously came from this lecture, which not only introduced the institutes and system of heritage protection in Poland but also presented expert knowledge on various case studies from Wrocław, Gdańsk, and Warsaw. Gerő then turned to reconstruction practices in France, Italy, and Britain, praising the French government's efforts in reconstructing selected sites, such as Reims Cathedral, while also criticizing them for a more conservative approach in the field of heritage preservation and reconstruction. In conclusion, Gerő emphasized the modern and progressive tendencies in Hungarian heritage preservation and reconstruction, which provided the basis for the "role model" of the Royal Palace's reconstruction.[29]

As mentioned above, this knowledge and information were acquired partly through visits and meetings, and partly thanks to the fact that some Hungarian experts had access to foreign scholarly journals. Although it has not yet been established to what extent such transfers of knowledge and know-how influenced particular reconstructions during the early 1950s, in the case of the Royal Palace, the visit of the Polish experts had been documented and widely discussed by the Party members.

In 1952 the Rákosi government invited Polish experts, among them Jan Zachwatowicz who was instrumental in postwar reconstruction projects in Poland, to examine the reconstruction plans and excavations, and to compose a technical and best practice report about the reconstruction plans and development of the building and its area. Their document stated, "[T]he task of the Polish delegation was to examine the sculpting effect of the socialist center of Hungary's capital," referring to the castle's use as seat of the socialist government. The Polish experts further noted which internal compositional problems had to be solved in this context in order for the material shape of the Buda Castle to be adapted to the ideological content properly.[30] The Polish experts stayed between 4 and 10 September 1952, with their delegation including not only Professor Zachwatowicz but also Professor Zdzisław Mączeński from the Polish Academy of Sciences and three more architects (appearing in the original texts under the names of Stenynski, Ryshlowski, and Dziwulski).

Zachwatowicz, codirector of the Warsaw Reconstruction Office since 1945, proposed a concept for the integration of the "remains of the past" in the reconstruction of the palace. This diverged vastly from the approach employed by the Hungarian state, which had shown little interest in the medieval archeological material of the excavations. It was thus evident that the Polish experts favored material concepts over ideological concerns.[31] In their report, they emphasized that:

> The cultural history of Buda Castle is of particular importance for Hungary. Here in the center of the political power such architectural works had been created that had they not been demolished under Ottoman rule they would have come to represent such an invaluable cultural treasure to Hungary as the Cracow castle [Wawel] does for Poles. The elements of the Gothic fortress and the ruins and fragments of the impressive Renaissance castle built by King Matthias Corvinus bear witness to this value. Ongoing excavations in the castle are therefore very important in terms of Hungarian national cultural history. . . . All remnants are to be kept and incorporated in the future palace building, which will serve a new function. Given that in the socialist state, the nation's cultural values and care are integral to the new socialist culture, we have concluded after careful examination of the archeological finds that these remains and elements have not been sufficiently incorporated into the reconstruction plans.[32]

This quote gives an impression of the different perspectives that political authorities and experts had regarding the reinterpretation of the past. Although the Polish experts referred repeatedly to the socialist concept of culture and history in the text, it was nevertheless clear that their opinions on which periods were to be integrated in the reconstruction and how were closely linked to the understanding of the factuality of the material heritage depending on the outcomes of the excavations. This factuality gave them and their Hungarian colleagues limited but effective potential to argue against some political–ideological decisions, such as excluding medieval heritage, and to implement some of their ideas in the palace's reconstruction. Rákosi and his circle wanted a reconstruction that would remain faithful to the Neoclassicist architecture that was linked to the so-called Hungarian Reform Era,[33] which in the Party's view was one of the more politically and ideologically "progressive" periods of Hungarian history. The jury of the Ministry of Construction accepted a final reconstruction plan on 11 June 1953, even though it was impossible to realize given the catastrophic economic situation in the country in 1953. This difficulty was compounded by the death of Stalin, which weakened Rákosi's position in the Party, meaning that work at Castle Hill had to be stopped.

In the spring of 1955, under the Imre Nagy government, the Architectural Planning Council rejected the Socialist Realist elements of the former reconstruction plan, and instead supported what was known as the Janáky plan, which was interpreted as evidence that it was not possible to deviate from the Hauszmann style that had given the castle its appearance before the war. However, Rákosi's political position strengthened again as the year progressed, with one consequence being that the Architectural Planning Council was abolished on 29 September. Three months later, on 12 December, the Minister of Construction submitted the Janáky plan to the government for approval. However, the twentieth Congress of the Communist Party of the Soviet Union (14–25 February 1956) decided to dismantle the cult of personality associated with Stalin, the former First Secretary of the CPSU, paving the way for reforms and de-Stalinization, likewise beyond the USSR. This also affected the future function and so the reconstruction of the Royal Palace.

New Plans during a Period of Upheaval, 1956–59

On 14 June 1956, the Hungarian Political Committee decided to turn the palace into a public institution serving scientific and cultural purposes. The only restriction was that it should be kept suitable for purposes of the Party and state leadership if necessary. However, the revolution in the autumn of 1956 shifted the course of the palace's reconstruction. The Hungarian Socialist Workers' Party, which was formed in the aftermath of the Soviet invasion on 4 November 1956, developed a plan that would transform the palace into the "center of Hungarian cultural life," this time reflecting the post-Stalinist political agenda.[34] Ernő Mihályfi, a leading politician in the new government and editor-in-chief of the daily newspaper *Magyar Nemzet* (Hungarian Nation), noted in an article on the palace that the former authorities had planned to use the palace as an office space for the Party.[35] The new government, however, pursued the idea of opening it up to the people by providing access to the newly established cultural institutions housed therein, including museums and libraries. Ernő Mihályfi drew a parallel between this plan and the court under the reign of Matthias Corvinus, hoping that the palace and the new cultural center "would be the center of the Hungarian cultural life and would be perhaps so famous as it had been in the age of Rex Matthias."[36]

In parallel to the redefinition of its function from the "representative" to the "cultural," a new historic period—the Hungarian Renaissance—began to provide a source of reference and legitimacy for the Kádár government, symbolizing a new start after nearly a decade of Stalinist dictatorship in the country. In line with this shift, the architect Janáky had to reconfigure his plan for the reconstruction. However, in the summer of 1959, he was replaced in the planning office by Lajos Hidasi, who moved away from the initial plan to reconstruct the neo-Baroque style dome. This led to much debate, with the ensuing "dome discussion" elaborating on the arguments for and against its reconstruction, with some of those contesting the project because they believed that the dome represented Hungary's bourgeois imperial past. The debate dominated both the expert and public discourses about the palace for a long time.

Still, the new concept of turning the palace into a cultural center remained the focus of efforts over subsequent decades, beginning with the opening of the Hungarian National Gallery in the Palace in 1957 and culminating in the relocation of the Széchényi National Library to the same premises in 1985. The question of authenticity in the reconstruction of palace's former Baroque dome faded into the background.[37] The issue of the impact on the cityscape and the coherence of historic style had been discussed publicly from the 1960s in the newspapers *Népszabadság* (Liberty of the People) and *Magyar Nemzet*, demonstrating a more liberal and open atmosphere than had been characteristic in the 1950s. Interestingly, though, no foreign examples, whether from other socialist countries or elsewhere, featured in the debate. The exception to the rule was Pál Granasztói's publication "A budai palota a városképben" (The Buda Palace in the Cityscape) of 1964 that briefly mentioned the public celebration of the reconstruction of the Staatsoper (opera house) in Vienna and asked why there was a lack of enthusiasm toward the palace's reconstruction in Hungary.

The final decision on turning the building and the Castle Hill into a national cultural center was announced by the Economic Committee on 30 December 1959. Their decree named the institutions that would be incorporated into this center, including the National Gallery, the Budapest Historic Museum, the Széchenyi Library, and various institutes of the Hungarian Academy of Science. The plan was to be realized and finished by 1968.[38]

Conclusion

Taking Ashworth's concept of architectural heritage as a product of the present as its point of departure, this chapter has addressed the changes of the concept of heritage that occurred in the context of a highly centralized and authoritarian state structure. As the case study of the Royal Palace in Budapest demonstrates, the Communist Party provided the framework for determining what was to be considered heritage or not. It ultimately shaped the historical interpretation and contextualization of sites according to ideological criteria in order to stage them for purposes of political agitation.[39] However, this process was characterized by a certain ambiguity, as new socialist values were projected onto the building, while a curated version of national history had to be preserved at the same time. The Buda Castle thus corresponds with other reconstruction practices in Eastern Europe where, especially in times of political upheaval, the reconstruction of symbolic historic buildings often served as means of staging a long national tradition.[40] The political and social turbulence of 1950s Hungary shows that the state was not always effective in harnessing national heritage according to its own plans, with canonical sites providing the basis not only for popular contestation but also for a broad range of intellectual debates over the meaning of the past in the present.

Thus, beyond the state's ideological framing, heritage protection and reconstruction also required concrete expertise. It was also the case in Hungary that certain know-how and expertise were missing in this field, including workshops of the sort that were present in Poland as well as particular know-how for restoring certain artifacts. However, this expertise was secured through close exchanges with foreign experts, especially from Czechoslovakia and Poland. There was thus evidence of a gradual increase in internationalization involving other socialist states during the 1950s at the level of heritage practices. These exchanges within the socialist bloc reveal the changing international dynamics of new socialist regimes and refute the widely held assumption of absolute control of cultural issues by the Soviet Union in the region, although Soviet practices and models of course also influenced what took place in Hungary. As a consequence, a tension existed between the desire to impose an ideologized vision of heritage and practical realities. Thus, by reflecting economic constraints as well as (grudgingly) accepting Polish and others' expert advice, the ideological model of the castle building could never be realized. The elements of the past that survived into the present were so diverse in art–historical, architectural, and ideological terms that this site could not be framed according to a singular national narrative. The Royal Palace complex might be the symbolic embodiment of the nation-state, but it also reflects how complex and prone to contestation symbolic constructions of the nation can be.

The debates on the historical layers and the present-day use of the Royal Palace are ongoing today. Indeed, there is a degree of continuity with the symbolic revamping under socialism in Orbán's efforts to displace the National Gallery and install his office on a site from which "as many vestiges of Communist rule as possible" should be removed "to create a concrete expression of the nationalism his governing party espouses."[41] The National Gallery was brought to the site as part of the socialist Cultural Revolution, to open up, symbolically and practically, the seat of power to the people and to provide a broad overview of the art–historical canon. The debates at the time over the form the restored Royal Palace should take were also the subject of public, political, and expert discussions. They resulted in the selection of some historical layers in restoration work, whereas others were disregarded. The Hungarian government's National Hauszmann Program, a campaign launched in 2019 and involving extensive restoration work on the site, puts the spotlight on destroyed parts of the castle complex from around 1900 that were overlooked in the reconstruction work after World War II. While this program reconsiders some of the decisions taken by the socialist authorities, what remains central both in the socialist past and the postsocialist present, however, is the emphasis on the nation in the efforts to refurbish the Royal Palace in Budapest.

Eszter Gantner (1971–2019) was a research fellow and project coordinator at the Herder Institute for Historical Research on East Central Europe from 2013 to 2019. She studied Law, History, and Political Sciences in Budapest, Jerusalem, and Berlin, and obtained her PhD in History from the Humboldt University of Berlin in 2010. In 2015 and 2016, she was visiting scholar at the Harriman Institute, Columbia University. She published widely on Jewish culture and history, heritage, and the urban history of East Central Europe.

Notes

1. This chapter is a revised version of an original draft that Eszter Gantner wrote before she passed away in summer 2019. Since then, the chapter has been revised by the coeditors of this volume, Corinne Geering and Paul Vickers. We wish to extend our warmest thanks to Eszter's family, her colleagues at the Herder Institute for Historical Research on East Central Europe in Marburg, Peter Haslinger and Heidi Hein-Kircher, as well as Gáspár Salamon and Orsolya Heinrich-Tamáska at the Leibniz Institute for the History and Culture of Eastern Europe (GWZO) in Leipzig for their much-appreciated help in clarifying the Hungarian source material.
2. Lyman, "Hungarian Leader's 'Edifice Complex.'"
3. Marosi, "Die restaurierte Geschichte."
4. Harrach, "The Reconstruction of the Buda Castle Hill."
5. Apor, *The Invisible Shining*, 15, 24.
6. Derczényi, Gólya, and Entz, *Magyar Műemlékvédelem 1959–1960*.
7. "1949. évi 13."
8. The Hungarian Working People's Party (Magyar Dolgozók Pártja, MDP) was the ruling Communist Party of Hungary from 1948 to 1956. Its leader was Mátyás Rákosi until 1956. During the Hungarian Revolution of 1956, the Party was reorganized into the Hungarian Socialist Workers' Party (MSZMP) by a circle of Communists around János Kádár and Imre Nagy.
9. Tunbridge and Ashworth, *Dissonant Heritage*, 6.
10. Apor, *The Invisible Shining*, 64.
11. Bartetzky, "Einführung," 10.
12. Response by Lajos Gádoros to the instruction of Minister Lajos Szíjártó on the reconstruction of the wings of Buda Castle in 1952, cited in Kókay, "Dokumentumok," 325.
13. For an overview, see Száboby and Száraz, *Die Burg Buda*.
14. The Battle of Mohács was one of the most significant battles in Central European history. It was fought on 29 August 1526 between the forces of the Kingdom of Hungary, led by Louis II, and those of the Ottoman Empire, led by Suleiman the Magnificent. The Ottoman victory led to the partition of Hungary for several centuries between the Ottoman Empire, the Habsburg Monarchy, and the Principality of Transylvania. The Battle of Mohács marked the end of the Middle Ages in Hungary.
15. Niederhauser, *Mária Terézia*, 150–63.
16. For a comparative perspective on the reconstruction of the Buda Castle between the Compromise and World War II in the European context, see the chapters by Péter Farbaky and Péter Rostás in Telesko, Kudriovsky, and Nierhaus, *Die Wiener Hofburg und der Residenzbau in Mitteleuropa*.
17. On the role of revolutionary cultural policies in other socialist countries, see Alonso González, *Cuban Cultural Heritage*; Alonso González, Comer, Viejo Rose, and Crowley, "Introduction."
18. Sinkó, *Nemzeti képtár*, 52.
19. Huszár, *A hatalom rejtett dimenziói*, 22.
20. Révai, *Kultúrális forradalmunk kérdései*, 5–6.
21. Ibid., 34.

22. "... A Vár épülete egy nagyhatalomnak, nem akármilyennek, egy monarchiának volt a reprezentatív épülete. A császár és király meg akarta mutatni a népnek a gazdagságát.... Nemcsak a császárok száma, de a királyoké is alaposan megfogyatkozott és hamarosan el fog fogyni. Nekünk elég a Parlament reprezentációs célra.... A Vár épületét ugy szeretnénk helyreállítani, hogy a külseje megmaradjon a régi formában, belül modern, munkára alkamas helyiségek legyenek.... Megkérdeztem Orlov elvtársat, hogy technikailag lehetséges-e a külső falak megtartása mellett belül modern elrendezés. Azt mondotta, ennek semi akadálya nincs. Ugyanez történt a Kreml-ben. Szeretném, ha mi most elsősorban elvben ebben egyeznénk meg. Nem a regi királyi palotának reprezentáció céljára való helyreállítása.... Ott lenne a központi pártvezetőség, meghatározandó minisztériumok, esetleg a miniszterelnökség, olyan hivatalok, ahol kicsi a forgalom...." Mátyás Rákosi cited in Kókay, "Dokumentumok," 329.
23. Majtényi, "Folt a kék díványon."
24. Ibid.
25. Entz and Gerő, "Műemlékvédelmi tapasztalatok szocialista országokban," 13.
26. Ibid., 17.
27. Gerő, *A budai vár helyreállítása*.
28. Ibid., especially the chapter "A Műemlékvédelem alakulása: Az elvek módosulása 1945 után Magyarországon és külföldön," 17–34.
29. Ibid., 33.
30. Polish experts' report 1952, reprinted in Kókay, "Dokumentumok," 337.
31. On material culture, see Ludwig, "Materielle Kultur."
32. Polish experts' report 1952, reprinted in Kókay, "Dokumentumok," 339.
33. The Hungarian Reform Era was a period in the first half of the nineteenth century, which led to an awakening of Hungarian national identity claims. The beginning of this period also saw the foundation of the Hungarian Academy of Sciences, while the era culminated in the 1848 revolution.
34. "A Gazdasági Bizottság 10.327/19S9.sz. határozata a budai volt királyi Palota rendeltetéséről," reprinted in Kókay, "Dokumentumok," 341.
35. Mihályfi, "Legyen a vár a kultúra vára," 7.
36. Ibid.
37. Granasztói, "A budai palota a városképben," 10.
38. "A Gazdasági Bizottság 10.327/19S9.sz. határozata a budai volt királyi Palota rendeltetéséről," reprinted in Kókay, "Dokumentumok," 341–42.
39. Bartetzky, "Einführung," 28–32, 19.
40. Ibid., 28–32, 18.
41. Lyman, "Hungarian Leader's 'Edifice Complex.'"

Bibliography

"1949. évi 13. törvényerejű rendelet a múzeumokról és műemlékckről." Retrieved 11 December 2018. http://www.jogiportal.hu/index.php?id=9z3lryh41d5xwfhb6&state=19600501&menu=view.

Alonso González, Pablo. *Cuban Cultural Heritage: A Rebel Past for a Revolutionary Nation*. Gainesville: University of Florida Press, 2018.

Alonso González, Pablo, Margaret Comer, Dacia Viejo Rose, and Tom Crowley, eds. "Introduction: Heritage and Revolution—First as Tragedy, Then as Farce?" *International Journal of Heritage Studies* 25, no. 5 (2019): 469–77.
Apor, Balázs. *The Invisible Shining: The Cult of Mátyás Rákosi in Stalinist Hungary, 1945–1956*. Budapest: Central European University Press, 2017.
Bartetzky, Arnold. "Einführung." In *Geschichte bauen: Architektonische Rekonstruktion und Nationenbildung vom 19. Jahrhundert bis heute*, edited by Arnold Bartetzky, 7–38. Cologne: Böhlau, 2017.
Derczényi, Dezső, József Gólya, and Géza Entz, eds. *Magyar Műemlékvédelem 1959–1960. Az Országos Műemléki Felügyelőség Kiadványai 2*. Budapest: Akadémiai Kiadó, 1964.
Entz, Géza, and László Gerő. "Műemlékvédelmi tapasztalatok szocialista országokban." In, *Magyar Műemlékvédelem 1959–1960. Az Országos Műemléki Felügyelőség Kiadványai 2*, edited by Dezső Derczényi, József Gólya, and Géza Entz, 13–19. Budapest: Akadémiai Kiadó, 1964.
Gerő, László. *A budai vár helyreállítása*. Budapest: Panorama, 1951.
Granasztói, Pál. "A budai palota a városképben." *Népszabadság*, 1 November 1964.
Harrach, Erzsebet C. "The Reconstruction of the Buda Castle Hill after 1945." In *Rebuilding Europe's Bombed Cities*, edited by Jeffry M. Diefendorf, 155–69. London: Palgrave Macmillan, 1990.
Huszár, Tibor. *A hatalom rejtett dimenziói: Magyar Tudományos Tanács, 1948–1949*. Budapest: Akadémiai kiadó, 1995.
Kókay, György. "Dokumentumok—a volt királyi palota háborús veszteségeiről és újjáépítésének előzményeiről." *Tanulmányok Budapest múltjából* 29 (2001): 293–343.
Ludwig, Andreas. "Materielle Kultur, Version: 1.0." *Docupedia-Zeitgeschichte*, 30 May 2011. Retrieved 27 March 2020. https://docupedia.de/zg/Materielle_Kultur.
Lyman, Rick. "Hungarian Leader's 'Edifice Complex' Has Some in Budapest Rattled." *New York Times*, 9 March 2016. Retrieved 27 March 2020. https://www.nytimes.com/2016/03/10/world/europe/hungarian-leaders-edifice-complex-has-some-in-budapest-rattled.html.
Majtényi, György. "Folt a kék díványon: Az uralmi elit életformája Magyarországon az 1950-es, 1960-as években II. rész." *Beszélő* 12, no. 10 (2007). Retrieved 27 March 2020. http://beszelo.c3.hu/cikkek/folt-a-kek-divanyon-0.
Marosi, Ernő. "Die restaurierte Geschichte: Denkmalpflege, Museumstätigkeit, und Rekonstruktion in Ungarn seit 1990." In *Geschichte bauen: Architektonische Rekonstruktion und Nationenbildung vom 19. Jahrhundert bis heute*, edited by Arnold Bartetzky, 291–323. Cologne: Böhlau, 2017.
Mihályfi, Ernő. "Legyen a vár a kultúra vára." *Magyar Nemzet*, 27 November 1957.
Niederhauser, Emil. *Mária Terézia*. Budapest: Pannonica, 2000.
Révai, József. *Kultúrális forradalmunk kérdései*. Budapest: Szikra, 1952.
Sinkó, Katalin. *Nemzeti képtár: "Emlékezet és Történelem között."* Budapest: Magyar Nemzeti Galéria, 2009.
Szabóby, Zsolt, and György Száraz. *Die Burg Buda*. Budapest: Corvina, 1990.
Telesko, Werner, Richard Kudriovsky, and Andreas Nierhaus, eds. *Die Wiener Hofburg und der Residenzbau in Mitteleuropa im 19. Jahrhundert*. Vienna: Böhlau, 2010.
Tunbridge, J. E., and G. J. Ashworth. *Dissonant Heritage: The Management of the Past as a Resource in Conflict*. London: John Wiley & Sons, 1994.

CHAPTER 6

Justifying Demolition, Questioning Value

Urban Typologies and the Concept of the "Historic Town" in 1960s Romania

Liliana Iuga

Heritage policies in socialist Romania are usually associated with narratives of extensive destruction. Particularly well known is the story of Ceaușescu's grandiose projects, such as the People's House in Bucharest, for which an area of seven square kilometers was cleared of previous construction. The plans for reconstructing Bucharest also led to the brutal demolition of numerous historical monuments, including many churches. Similar projects were implemented in other Romanian cities, too.[1] While acknowledging the traumatic impact of these interventions on collective memory, this contribution argues, however, for a more complex understanding of the topic. It highlights the debates on built heritage in socialist Romania and their connection to urban planning strategies.

In this chapter, I look at the conceptualization of the "historic city" in the work of architectural historian Gheorghe Curinschi to analyze some of the problems embedded in the construction of the preservationist discourse. I frame this case study from a historical perspective that emphasizes the tensions brought in by modernization, while also discussing alternative proposals advanced by some other architects. Curinschi's ideas are particularly relevant as he was a politically engaged professional who tried to reconcile the discourse on the value of historic towns in Romania with the Communist authorities' radical plans for urban reconstruction and modernization. Given the particularities of what could be considered an "old district" in the cities and towns of socialist Romania, I argue that this discourse was simultaneously canonizing and contesting built heritage.

In 1967, Gheorghe Curinschi,[2] at that time working for the Bucharest-based Department for Historic Monuments, published a volume titled *Centrele istorice ale orașelor* (Historic City Centers). This event could be interpreted as a logical outcome of the growing interest in built heritage following the signing of the Venice Charter in 1964, especially since Curinschi himself had attended the event, officially known as the Second International Congress of Architects and Specialists of Historic Buildings, together with two other Romanian architects.[3] Moreover, when the book was published, radical interventions in centrally located historic districts were under way in several Romanian towns. There was little evidence of concern about the potential loss of these areas' heritage value, nor were there any preliminary professional discussions regarding the conceptualization of the city centers.[4] Areas for redevelopment had been chosen rather pragmatically, determined by the need to raise new representative architectural ensembles, while investment costs were thus limited by exploiting plots with existing modern infrastructure.

In light of this, one would have expected Curinschi's book to address this shortcoming by emphasizing the need to preserve the historic built environment in rapidly changing towns and by showing how it could contribute to enhancing a city center's attractiveness. However, instead of taking a critical stance against these interventions, Curinschi assumed most demolition had been legitimate.[5] While sharing an opinion that was widespread among socialist planners regarding the obsolescence of old buildings,[6] Curinschi also seemed to agree that the demolished structures had lacked historic and aesthetic value. As he put it, quite broadly, "every town has a historic past, yet not every historic past is valuable."[7]

Why would an architectural historian working for Romania's most important institution of monument preservation make such a bold statement, particularly since he was familiar with the latest international debates in the field? Certainly, the resolutions adopted as part of the Venice Charter extended the definition of historic monuments beyond individual buildings to encompass entire areas of historic and architectural significance while emphasizing that safeguarding the monuments' authenticity was a shared responsibility.[8] And yet, Curinschi's statement suggests little concern for the reevaluation of built heritage values in Romanian cities and towns. So, what does his position tell us about the conceptualization of the historic city in the Romanian context? In the 1950s, Curinschi established his reputation as a politically engaged professional after publishing a series of articles on monument protection, in which he emphasized the Russian influence on the development of Romanian architecture.[9] While his publicly expressed position could be seen as merely paying lip service to the government's agenda of radical urban reconstruction, I suggest that there is something more to his claims.

Curinschi's dissatisfaction was directed particularly toward the small-scale commercial and residential buildings occupying much of the historic area in many Romanian towns. He deemed them aesthetically irrelevant and even detrimental to a positive urban image. Furthermore, he suggested that major monuments would be of greater value when surrounded by new architecture rather than "swimming in a sea of decrepit buildings."[10] As an exception, he praised the value of fortified Transylvanian towns,[11] which he considered worthy of preservation. In this contribution, I aim to place these ideas and statements in the broader context of intellectual debates regarding the value of the historic built environment in Romanian towns. I position these debates in the broader international context, both within and outside the socialist bloc, on the significance of historic towns. I thus point to the intersections of national discourses with international trends and debates over heritage preservation—and destruction. I argue that rather than reexamining the heritage value of the built urban fabric in light of the discussions in Venice, professionals such as Curinschi continued to promote ideas that had been advanced in interwar debates regarding Romania's developmental path between modernism and traditionalism. Still, while the interwar modernists based their arguments for radical reconstruction on aesthetics and the need to bring visual order in towns with a "chaotic" development, the Communists privileged social and economic concerns, emphasizing the necessity of increasing living standards even in historic districts.

By publishing a book destined to be read by generations of young architects studying at university under his guidance, as well as by other practitioners in the field, Curinschi brought a key contribution to the conceptualization of the historic town in Romania and institutionalized, within the socialist context, ideas regarding heritage values in urban areas. Yet his views also called into question, for example, the fact that historic areas in Romanian towns equally deserved protected status.

The Historic Town in the Eastern Bloc

From the mid-nineteenth century, interest in "historic towns" developed in response to the destructive effects of industrialization and modern urban planning. As the conservation ethos expanded, it was not only individual monuments, but entire districts consisting of buildings of architectural and historic interest that were considered worthy of preservation.[12] While the approaches to historic towns differed in various national contexts owing to a variety of factors from cultural traditions to the timing and pace of industrialization, the definition of what constituted urban built heritage prioritized aesthetics over social or functional concerns until the late 1970s.[13]

The literature on historic towns in the Eastern Bloc has focused so far on a few case studies, emphasizing either state-led initiatives of "manufacturing" urban heritage sites as expressions of national pride, or, quite the opposite, modernizing projects that transformed old districts into contested urban spaces. Heritage policies in different socialist countries carried the imprint of national or local legacies in the field. Poland and Czechoslovakia displayed particularly strong traditions in this regard. The reconstruction of Warsaw's historical core in the aftermath of World War II is often described as an expression of patriotism and of a desire to overcome war traumas by reestablishing a sense of continuity through the built fabric,[14] although the focus on the city's historic center and its reconstruction often overlooks just how radically much of the rest of the urban fabric was reworked. The reconstruction of heavily damaged structures, however, would not have been possible without the long-term engagement of Polish preservationists. Historic districts had been included in the definition of historic monuments in the interwar period already as they were surveyed as part of a nation-wide scientific initiative to document the built heritage.[15] Similar initiatives appeared in Czechoslovakia as well, where thirty-five towns had received protected status during the interwar period already. Spared from major destruction during the war, they benefitted afterward from further legislative and institutional conservation measures that also sought to ensure their sensitive integration within urban planning schemes.[16] Experts in Prague not only developed a historical–materialist theory of heritage, drawing on the dialectic of tradition and innovation,[17] but also insisted on the importance of integrating historic districts into plans for the socialist reconstruction of cities. In addition, the government endorsed initiatives to establish "urban historical reserves" in areas that had preserved to a large extent their medieval layout. Architects argued that the modernization of infrastructure and facilities would make such areas attractive living quarters for the people. They deemed it the right of citizens "to enjoy the historical interiors and the old streets, in which their ancestors have lived."[18]

Nevertheless, the relation between old and new built fabric tended to be full of tensions rather than concessions. As soon as the nostalgic waves of postwar reconstruction faded, and modernism stepped in with ever greater confidence, historic districts were increasingly targeted by urban redevelopment projects during the 1960s. Especially when these neighborhoods carried strong cultural and emotional meanings for the local community, they became spaces for contesting state-endorsed visions of urban modernization. The case of the Arbat district in central Moscow, analyzed by Stephen Bittner in his well-known book *The Many Lives of Khrushchev's Thaw*, demonstrates that such disputes generated broader public support for and engagement with preservation.[19]

The 1970s brought a significant shift in preservationist attitudes, as the definition of urban heritage broadened to include previously neglected nineteenth-century tenement districts.[20] Florian Urban has documented the gradual "rediscovery" of such districts in East Berlin, which resulted in several state-endorsed urban design projects that aimed at rehabilitating old buildings and recreating an "old town atmosphere." These initiatives culminated with the "invention" of the city's medieval nucleus, Nikolaiviertel, which was (re)constructed to a large extent from prefabricated elements in a historicizing style in celebration of Berlin's 750th anniversary. Urban locates the significance of this gesture in the field of symbolic politics. He argues that the making of built heritage and its appropriation as a form of usable past was intended to assert political legitimacy for the East German regime in the context of economic crisis and rivalries with the West.[21] Nevertheless, many inner-city districts with turn-of-the-century architecture, such as Prenzlauer Berg, remained in a state of neglect. These sites became attractive for marginal groups and countercultural movements.[22]

Historic Legacies and Heritage-Making in Socialist Romania

When compared to other countries in the region, the historic city rarely constituted a topic on the preservationist agenda in Romania. The interwar Commission for Historic Monuments had few members (between five and nine), with its activities focused mostly on the restoration of medieval and/or religious monuments.[23] Although legislation was passed relating to this issue in 1892, 1913, and 1919,[24] the first comprehensive nation-wide inventory was carried out only in the 1950s.[25]

The conceptualization of what constituted built heritage in the country reflected local patterns of urban development, largely following the regional divisions existing until World War I. In 1918, Romania emerged as a state incorporating regions with different urban traditions. Moldova and Wallachia had long been under Ottoman control, while Transylvania had been part of the Habsburg Empire.[26] Transylvanian towns, with a historical core planned and delimited by medieval walls,[27] displayed a variety of buildings in various architectural styles, from Gothic to Baroque and Neoclassicism. The region had enjoyed stronger professional interest in building preservation, particularly during the Austro-Hungarian period. During the interwar years, separate commissions for monument protection functioned in the new regions incorporated into Romania. The members of the Transylvanian one, regardless of nationality, had been trained in Vienna and Budapest, and continued to work with inventories and instruments elaborated during the Austro-Hungarian period.[28]

The towns in Moldova and Wallachia, known as *târguri* (market towns), had developed organically without the constraints of fortifications, as they had been explicitly forbidden by the Ottomans. Their historical core consisted mainly of churches, palaces, and houses in a style mixing the local vernacular with Neoclassicist influences, as well as low-rise late nineteenth-century buildings with ground-floor commercial spaces, all arranged in an irregular street network. The historicity of the old town was obscured not only by the relative newness of the built fabric, but also by the scarcity of visual and written sources documenting the appearance of the premodern town. Moreover, stereotypical views describing these towns as "large villages" were commonplace in historical scholarship even as late as the 1960s.[29] Both politicians and planners alike believed that such cityscapes embodied "the difficult legacy of the past" and had to be reshaped, since the small scale of the buildings, the "ill-regulated" street network, and the precarious condition of most of the housing stock were deemed incompatible with the modernizing goals of the regime.[30]

Although the legislation on historic monuments promulgated in Romania in 1955 conferred protected status to individual buildings only, the existence of historic towns in Transylvania was implied in that almost all houses in old towns were listed individually. Sighișoara, the only town that had preserved its fortification system almost intact, was listed as a single unit, namely as a citadel[31] "with the surrounding walls, towers, and bastions, including all civil and religious buildings,"[32] constituting a medieval relic of undisputed architectural and historical value.

In October 1966, one year before the publication of Curinschi's book, the Architects Union organized a debate regarding the "systematization"[33] of historic centers in Romania, which were largely divided into two typological categories. The first one included the "towns with very valuable monuments, framed into a housing stock and amenities in an established architectural style, and in a relatively good state of maintenance."[34] This category referred to the Transylvanian towns founded by German colonists in the Middle Ages (e.g., Brașov [Kronstadt/ Brassó], Mediaș [Mediasch/ Medgyes], Sighișoara [Schäßburg/ Segesvár], and Bistrița [Bistritz/ Beszterce]). Enclosed by fortifications, these towns had preserved their original street networks together with a significant part of their medieval structures. The second category regarded "towns in which historic monuments, very valuable in themselves, are enclosed into a more recently constituted built

Figure 6.1. Historic Center of Brașov. The compact form of the medieval town is clearly evident. The town hall is located in the middle of the square, in the vicinity of the Gothic-style church. Source: Virgil Bilciurescu, "Studii pentru sistematizarea centelor istorice ale orașelor Brașov, Sibiu, Sebeș-Alba, Târgoviște," *Arhitectura* 14, no. 6 (1966): 53. Used with permission.

environment, which does not display any particular interest from the point of view of architecture or built value." The towns listed in this category included Târgoviște, Iași, Suceava, some of the oldest towns from Moldavia and Wallachia, and former capitals of the corresponding medieval states.[35]

The Legacy of Interwar Debates

This classification was not simply a product of the postwar context but instead reflected the perceived cultural and historical differences between the regions that became part of Greater Romania. The long-time president of the Commission for Historic Monuments, the historian Nicolae Iorga, wrote that "Between Bucharest [on the one hand] and Brașov, and especially

Sibiu (Hermannstadt/ Nagyszeben) and Sighișoara [on the other hand], there is an essential distinction that we will never be able to remove."[36] He referred, for example, to different types of urban development reflected in the streetscape: while in Bucharest houses were usually detached and surrounded by lots of greenery, Transylvanian towns appeared more compact, with buildings in continuous fronts displayed along the streets. As a traditionalist, Iorga praised the rural character of Romanian towns and their organic development as an element of national authenticity while criticizing nineteenth-century Western influences as tasteless and chaotic.[37] Writer G. Călinescu similarly stated that the historic character of Romanian towns had been lost during the nineteenth century as the bourgeoisie imported Western architectural models and disregarded national specificity.[38] Both Iorga and Călinescu praised an idealized image of the picturesque traditional town, yet they also avoided any references to the concrete social or economic aspects of the urban life.

More technocratic-oriented figures such as Cincinat Sfințescu,[39] an engineer and urban theorist who wrote extensively on the need to redevelop Bucharest according to the principles of the garden town movement,[40] similarly differentiated between "compact towns enclosed within defensive walls, currently constituting the central part of the contemporary city" (e.g., Brașov, Sibiu, Timișoara), and somewhat ambiguously defined "towns with an irregular and diffuse development up to the present."[41] Sfințescu's approach connected built heritage to functionalist planning. In the case of Transylvanian towns, he recommended the separation of the old town from the more recent outlying districts by a ring road, the demolition of decrepit buildings lacking historical and architectural value, and the rehabilitation of the valuable ones. In towns without a fortified medieval nucleus, traffic could be rationalized through the opening of new streets cutting through land with lower construction densities.[42] This solution would spare potentially valuable buildings situated on the old streets from demolition, while also being more cost-effective, as it implied the expropriation of poorer and less densely built-up areas.[43]

Interwar modernists perceived the old town as an obstacle to progress and openly demanded its immediate erasure. Avantgarde painter and architect Marcel Iancu stressed the need to radically reconstruct Bucharest according to a revolutionary, geometric plan, taking into consideration transportation and public health concerns.[44] Not even streets famous for their picturesque appearance, such as Bucharest's Lipscani, could be spared from demolition.[45] Every single part of the city was to be made anew. The postwar context continued to be shaped by this intellectual framework, despite the ideological rupture caused by the Communists' coming to power.

"Historic City Centers"

Despite the Cold War divide, the Romanian professionals' approaches to monument protection and restoration continued to be significantly informed by international discourses and practices. Curinschi's work draws mostly on specialized literature from Italy, France, and some Eastern Bloc countries (the USSR, Hungary, Czechoslovakia, and Poland). From today's perspective, the number of books and articles consulted looks quite modest, but it was still a substantial body of literature for the time.[46] Particularly relevant seems to have been the experience of postwar reconstruction of historic towns, especially as implemented in Poland and Germany, which legitimized an understanding of the concept as a conscious, state- and expert-led plan of urban modernization that restored a sanitized version of the old town. As John Pendlebury has similarly argued in the case of Britain, the postwar historic city was strongly influenced by functionalist principles and implied high degrees of intervention in a historic built fabric that had often come to be perceived as redundant.[47] In the case of socialist countries, ideology also played a role, as the principles of historical materialism structured and legitimized heritage values. From this perspective, the material remains of the Middle Ages (i.e., feudalism) were perceived by default as heritage and remained part of the canon of heritage under socialism or were indeed added to it. Using historical materialism as an analytical frame resulted in an almost technocratic approach to the built heritage, with scarce references to culture, ethnicity, or questions of agency. The history of cities was therefore perceived as the transformation of the urban form during various historical periods, each of them being characterized by specific aesthetic taste and functionality. Essentially, this narrative described the built fabric as the result of a dynamic process of constant transformation and alteration. In this context, further interventions under socialism would therefore appear perfectly justified.

This intellectual framework is reflected extensively in Curinschi's work. *Historic City Centers* was published in 1967, during the most liberal period in the history of socialist Romania. The book was intended as a methodological guide for approaching the "preservation versus modernization" dilemma in Romanian towns subjected to a rapid process of socialist industrialization. While acknowledging the imperative of change that manifested itself as an "extensive process of socialist transformation," Curinschi rightly observed that the destruction of heritage could result from an oversimplified view on this sensitive issue.[48] He argued that the revitalization of historic districts should be approached through a process of "dialectical negation" consisting of the removal of the negative traits, the selection and preservation of the positive ones, and the introduction of the new elements without significantly altering identified historical values.[49] The concept of "reconstruction," very popular among urban planners in socialist countries at the time, was considered appropriate to the Romanian context, since "the largest part of the built fabric has a reduced economic, functional, constructive and aesthetic value."[50] As an alternative concept, the author proposed "the socialist transformation of cities" (i.e., the selective replacement of the existing built fabric instead of the complete erasure implied by the process of reconstruction).[51]

The list of heritage values considered in Curinschi's analysis clearly reflected the Western art history canon, emphasizing recognized architectural styles, monumentality, and historical significance. Central to his perspective was "selectivity," a principle borrowed from the theory and practice of restoration. As he wrote elsewhere, "the approach of the restorer does not have to be the one of an archivist, who is obliged to equally preserve the tiniest piece of paper and a valuable document...."[52] The principle has been in fact central to the postwar conceptualization of the historic town[53] and had been applied in the reconstruction of historic towns in Poland and Germany heavily damaged during the war.

The urban typologies discussed in the book place the seven Transylvanian towns founded by German colonists in a separate category.[54] Their compact form organized around a central square represents "the classical type of feudal town developed in Western and Central Europe, as well as in the Baltic countries. The largest part of the specialized literature refers to this type of town."[55] The appreciation of Transylvanian medieval towns combines the Marxist historical vision of where feudalism was essential in the historical development toward the socialist society with traditional views on heritage, where medieval monuments in particular are treasured.[56] Curinschi, balancing these viewpoints, agreed therefore that the "feudal" historic towns should be preserved in their entirety, with "all the components of the urban space."[57]

However, the value of historic centers with more recent architecture (i.e., buildings from the nineteenth and twentieth centuries) should not "be understood in a territorial sense," he argued, but rather with reference to "some valuable urban characteristics."[58] Thus, "positive characteristics of the street network," such as its historical value and the ability to define urban spaces with a specific character, should be maintained and integrated within the new urban planning schemes.[59] Questions of scale should also be taken into consideration by finding the "right" relation between the old and the new structures.[60] The answers seemed quite straightforward in the case of fortified towns, where international experience provided consistent evidence regarding the appropriate interventions: the maintenance of the medieval street network, housing rehabilitation, demolition of invaluable buildings and their replacement with infillings, restoration of major monuments, while preserving the skyline of the historic center and the proportion of built volumes.[61] More problematic was providing precise solutions for towns that developed without fortifications, which were predominant in Romania. In such cases, the street system was identified as the only element of undisputed value, as the last remnant of the "feudal past."[62] While the old building stock would be gradually replaced,[63] a case for preservation could be made for selected portions of the old town based on their "picturesque qualities."[64]

For the socialist urban planners in Romania, it was essential to avoid transforming historic centers into relics of the past and instead ensure that they remained the functional center of the city. Curinschi challenged this claim and advocated the modernization of infrastructure,[65] as well as the construction of new buildings serving contemporary functions, such as sociocultural, administrative, commercial constructions, surrounded by large squares for mass gatherings. Conversely, spaces for socialization and leisure (e.g., restaurants, pubs, coffeehouses, small cinemas and theatres, parks), which had made the city center into an attractive place in the past, were largely disregarded by the new planning schemes. Rather than adhering to specific "socialist values" or agendas, in which consumption was disregarded in favor of factory production, this narrow understanding of functionalist principles could be more correctly related to the modernizing, and indeed modernist, ethos. The cases of Brasilia and Toulouse discussed in the literature are similarly illustrative of the rejection of old forms of production, sociability, leisure, and consumption associated with street life, the small store, and workshop in favor of motorized traffic, mass consumption, and bureaucracy.[66]

Nonetheless, functionalism was not by default detrimental to preservation. According to Curinschi, buildings of a more problematic ideological nature (e.g., religious or feudal structures) could be preserved as long as they received new functions.[67] In other words, the contradiction between old and new could be also solved in favor of the former; the new should not be understood only as a new material form, but also as the refunctionalization or repurposing of the old.[68] Although Curinschi seemed to bow before the imperatives of modernization throughout his book, stating that "the new has to express itself and become dominant,"[69] in this case he tried to find a workaround by suggesting that it was mostly a question of how the new was framed. What is quite notably missing from his argument is the "classical" socialist position, according to which the value of historical buildings was located in their aesthetic qualities, reflecting the craftsmanship of artisans, as William Morris famously argued.[70] In fact, the people—those from the past, as well as those from the present—whether users or creators of the built environment, were altogether absent from the discussion.

Redefining the Concept of Historic City

As Curinschi's book demonstrated, theory alone could not provide alternatives to the traditional views on the concept of historic city in Romania. In the following years, long-held stereotypes were contested precisely by those practitioners who engaged in research, such as the architect Virgil Bilciurescu. In a detailed project for the historic town of Brașov presented at the meeting of the Architects Union in 1966, Bilciurescu, who was also a member of the Department for Historic Monuments, discussed practical solutions to be implemented in urban preservation. Concentrating on the area delimited by the medieval fortifications, the project proposed the revitalization of the built environment and the introduction of amenities, the preservation of the street network, as well as the revitalization of the economic function through the reorganization of the commercial network. Emphasis was put on the notion of local specificity, identified with the characteristic townscape, in particular the sinuous streets, the characteristic facades, and the medieval city walls. Interventions would be preceded by surveys investigating the different layers of the built structures with the aim of identifying particularly valuable architectural elements that could be emphasized during restoration works. The authors of the project hoped that the elaboration of detailed studies demonstrating the advantages of housing rehabilitation would "prevent local authorities from taking inappropriate measures in what regards the buildings belonging to the old center."[71] Arguably, implementing such a project would not only improve the city's image and benefit tourism but would also be cost-effective. Contrary to what was argued at the time in the GDR, namely that the construction of prefabricated blocks would cost less than the restoration of old tenements,[72] Bilciurescu's calculations indicated the revitalization of the building stock would be two to three times less expensive.

Modernist architects attending the meeting fully disregarded such solutions and advocated comprehensive redevelopment. Cezar Lăzărescu, Romania's leading modernist architect, presented a planning proposal for the city center of Pitești in southern Romania that suggested the erasure of all existing buildings, with the exception of one church, and their replacement by new representative constructions, such as the Party headquarters, the House of Culture, and office and commercial spaces.[73] As Lăzărescu explained, the old town character could be implied by maintaining a low scale for the new constructions.[74] In such cases, preservationists typically

Figure 6.2. Historic Center of Pitești. In the foreground, the Orthodox church is surrounded by trees and an elongated green area. Most buildings are relatively small-scale, late nineteenth-century constructions. The recently built modernist apartment blocks replacing some of these buildings on one side of the street are integrated into the scale of the old town. Source: Cezar Lăzărescu, "Studiu pentru sistematizarea zonei centrale Pitești," *Arhitectura* 14, no. 6 (1966): 51. Used with permission.

agreed that the existing built fabric should be gradually replaced, yet recommended saving "characteristic" segments of old streets on account of their picturesque qualities.[75]

As a footnote to a discussion that clearly cut across regions and urban typologies, Bilciurescu also presented a project for the Old Court area in Târgoviște, the former medieval capital of Wallachia. Contrary to views that ascribed little value to the built fabric of towns outside of Transylvania, he stated following on-site examination that other areas apart from the medieval ruins would be worth of preserving, such as the nineteenth-century commercial center (*târg*) and a residential district remarkable because of its "garden city" character. More generally, Bilciurescu implied that research enabled a reevaluation of the value of historic areas, declaring that "the moments when we were surprised by unimagined beauties hidden in buildings that at the first sight looked totally uninteresting and even displeasing were not uncommon."[76] Despite this enthusiasm, further discussions showed that the architects in the audience were caught somewhere between functionalist concerns and a lack of clear direction, questioning, for example, whether old buildings were still adequate for modern living[77] and complaining that the concept of the city center itself had hardly been addressed in professional debates.[78]

From 1964 to 1977, projects for urban preservation were drawn up for approximately thirty cities and towns in Romania, while a similar number of conservation areas were delimited following negotiations with local administrations.[79] Although the projects focused initially on the medieval core of Transylvanian towns, they were further extended to towns in Wallachia and Moldova regions, which lacked visible markers of historicity, except for the rather obvious examples of religious architecture. It is important to mention that these initiatives were not coordinated at a national level, resulting rather from the fragmented efforts of individual experts. However, the stylistic extension of the concept of monument to include local vernacular and previously despised styles, such as eclecticism, allowed Romanian preservationists to claim heritage value for larger portions of the inherited built fabric.[80]

Although the concept of historic towns was slowly adapted to the Romanian context, the implementation of such projects was met with resistance by local authorities. Even well-documented projects for the revitalization of historic districts, such as the one for Brașov, enjoyed limited support from the local People's Council. In 1971, the local administration agreed to finance the restoration of only ten buildings considered "interesting from a historical and architectural point of view."[81] Most restoration financed from the local budget in fact concerned the medieval towers and, occasionally, buildings that could be put to public use.[82]

The planners' perspective remained anchored in a very narrow understanding of economic value, which also privileged the superiority of the new over the old. One UNESCO report highlights the weight of the economic argument in the struggles for preservation in developing countries such as Romania:

> Conservation takes a disproportionate amount of time, money, and administrative and political negotiation as compared with that normally demanded by administration, planning and building. It is quicker, politically more dramatic, and often cheaper to bulldoze, or build on open fields. Very clear justification is necessary, *particularly in developing countries where available resources are usually scarcer*, and the scramble for development on almost any terms tends to sweep all other considerations aside.[83]

In my opinion, the idea of urban restoration seemed unappealing to political decision makers in Romania not just because of the costs, but primarily because it would not bring any considerable benefits in terms of urban image or political capital. Certainly, fragments of a sanitized and adequately shaped historical landscape could be tolerated if they either contributed to the regime's sense of pride and legitimacy, or if they functioned as an element of urban beautification. However, demolition also offered comparative advantages, in that it allowed for the relocation of people and the creation of new social hierarchies alongside the creation of a modern urban image. Investing in restoration of old buildings just for the sake of improving the tenants' living standards made little sense in a system in which most resources were scarce and distributed according to a hierarchy of privileges.[84]

Conclusion

In this chapter, I have argued that the conceptualization of the "historic town" in 1960s Romania was influenced by perceived, long-standing regional differences in urban typologies, as well as by the persistence of an intellectual tradition inspired by Western models, which defined the historic town as having a compact form delimited by medieval walls, a well-articulated street network with continuous built facades, and monumental or at least solid buildings ideally displaying a coherent architectural style. The towns fitting this description could be conveniently preserved, while the others, despite containing picturesque and attractive elements, were generally not considered truly "historic." Moreover, following the logic of historical materialism, urban landscapes appeared to be in a permanent process of transformation, a premise that justified further intervention under socialism.

However, the reconsideration of architectural heritage values offered the opportunity to rethink long-held stereotypes. The project on Târgoviște demonstrated that attentive examination of the built fabric could offer alternative arguments for preservation. Nonetheless, as Lăzărescu's proposal clearly indicated, there was more at stake than just arguing for the value of the old town. The civic center,[85] a strongly politically endorsed project, was also intended to be located in the heart of the city. Although at that point it was still vaguely defined in terms of functionality and structure, the civic center was envisaged as a representative space for the regime, providing the planners with a legitimate argument for reshaping the old urban fabric in city centers. Ultimately, the decisions in favor of redevelopment or preservation depended on the use value of the built environment for the local administration and other prominent local actors.

Despite efforts toward reconceptualization, the historic town was never turned into an area protected by national-level legislation in Romania, in contrast to countries such as France, Italy, the United Kingdom, Poland, Hungary, or the Soviet Union, which during the 1950s and 1960s adopted various types of conservation laws for historic areas.[86] During the 1970s in particular, members of the Department for Historic Monuments often engaged in exhausting negotiations with local architects, planners, and politicians, while trying to expand the scope of their institutional power. However, these efforts were frustrated by the insufficient human, financial, and institutional resources at the Department's disposal.[87]

In the 1980s, Romania was internationally known for the large-scale destruction of built heritage, particularly in Bucharest.[88] Although the massive destruction wrought by the 1977 earthquake triggered the plans for radical reconstruction under Ceaușescu's close supervision, the preservation of historical districts in Romania's capital city was never taken seriously by local decision makers. Discussions between representatives of the Department for Historic Monuments and the heads of the urban planning institute in Bucharest in the 1970s reveal strong resistance on the part of the latter to approve even the completion of a study to identify areas of architectural and historical significance in Bucharest.[89]

It should be also emphasized that the historic city was a rather new concept on the preservationist agenda in postwar Romania. It was defined, discussed, and reconceptualized based on the legacy of interwar debates, international models, and the experiences of various heritage practitioners in a political context dominated by the ideology of reconstruction and the tremendous pressure exerted on the urban fabric by industrialization and urban modernization. In practical terms, the outcomes were highly diverse, ranging from restoration works, preservation, and the reappropriation of ideologically unsound buildings to neglect and large-scale demolition. My broader argument is that it is necessary to look beyond the supposed exceptionality of the Romanian case and instead investigate the deep-rooted mechanisms informing heritage conceptualizations and policies. By taking seriously the categories used by politicians, planners, and preservationists, it is possible to provide a better account of the motivations behind the urban redevelopment plans that radically transformed cityscapes in socialist Romania.

Liliana Iuga is an urban historian currently based in Cluj-Napoca, Romania. She received her PhD from the Central European University, Budapest, Hungary. Previously, she studied history and art history in Cluj-Napoca, Romania, and Perugia, Italy, and was a visiting fellow at the Center for Urban History at the University of Leicester, UK. Her research focuses on topics that connect the history of architecture, urban planning, and heritage preservation with nationalism and state building during the twentieth century.

Notes

1. At the end of the 1980s, historian Dinu Giurescu published a report, intended mostly for an international audience, on the demolition of built heritage under Ceaușescu. Raw numbers were used to emphasize the proportions of destruction: "At this writing the architectural urban fabric of at least 29 Romanian towns has been 85–90 percent demolished and replaced by apartment buildings with a completely different urban character. Large scale demolitions are underway in an additional 37 towns." Giurescu, *The Razing of Romania's Past*, Foreword.
2. Born in Bessarabia, Gheorghe Curinschi graduated in 1949 from the Institute of Architecture in Bucharest. He remained at the Institute to teach the history of architecture alongside Professor Grigore Ionescu, while also being a member of the Department for Historic Monuments. He even served as technical director of the institution between 1963 and 1968. In his autobiography, Curinschi mentions having attended training courses abroad (such as one in Italy, 1961), and traveling extensively throughout Italy, the Balkans, and Western Europe, and also to Asia. It is also interesting to mention that Curinschi signed his articles and books using three different spellings of his name. Initially, he appears as Kurinski, a spelling not characteristic of the Romanian language, where the letter "k" is rarely used. As he originated from Bessarabia, one can assume that this was either his original name, or a convenient choice reflecting his pro-Soviet attitude. Later on, when he moved to Bucharest, and Romania increasingly distanced itself from the Soviet Union, he spelled his name in a manner more specific to the Romanian language, namely "Curinschi" (similar to Italian). Toward the end of his career, he added "Vorona" to the original name, although the source of this choice is unclear. It could either reflect an affinity for Italian culture (it is similar to Verona), or it could be inspired by the medieval monastery Voroneț. In any case, until his death, he used "Gheorghe Curinschi-Vorona" to sign his writings. His autobiography dated July 1977 was published by Colesnic using the name Gheorghe Curinschi.
3. The other two participants were Grigore Ionescu, professor of architectural history at the Institute of Architecture in Bucharest and at that point director of the Department for Historic Monuments, and Richard Bordenache, who took over the position from 1967 until 1971. Interestingly, both architects had been adherents of interwar modernism, yet chose a career in monument preservation after the Communists seized power in Romania. The trio is represented in a picture published in Curinschi-Vorona, *Arhitectură, Urbanism, Restaurare*, 4.
4. Cocheci, "Problemele sistematizării orașului Craiova," 43.
5. Curinschi, *Centrele istorice*, 7.
6. On the concept of obsolescence in the socialist context, see Urban, *Neo-historical East Berlin*, 40.
7. Curinschi, *Centrele istorice*, 8.
8. Stubbs, *Time Honored*, 137–38.

9. G. Kurinski, "Lupta poporului pentru independență"; Curinschi, "Cu privire la originile arhitecturii monumentale românești." It should be also mentioned that Curinschi was actively involved in the reorganization of the Institute of Architecture, criticizing its previous "bourgeois" structures. Y. Kurinski, "Un an de muncă pe tărâmul reformei învățământului arhitecturii," 208.
10. Curinschi, *Centrele istorice*, 7, 136. In Curinschi's view, the only problem with this solution is that constructing higher buildings ensuring proper "urban" densities would obstruct the focus on the old monuments; therefore, one should find the "right" relations between new and old in terms of scale.
11. Ibid., 44–47. Following the percepts of historical materialism, he rejected the claim that these towns were founded by German colonists according to a preestablished plan, arguing instead for their organic development from agricultural settlements.
12. Lamprakos, "The Idea of Historic City," 17–20; Choay, *The Invention of the Historic Monument*, Chapter Five, "The Invention of An Urban Heritage," 117–37.
13. Rodwell, "Urban Conservation in the 1960s and 1970s," 3.
14. Glendinning, *The Conservation Movement*, 363–69. See also the chapter by Julia Röttjer in this volume.
15. Historic districts and urban ensembles were included within the category of historic monuments by the 1928 legislation and surveyed as part of a comprehensive effort. After the war, it was precisely the existence of these comprehensive building surveys that made possible the reconstruction of Warsaw's Old Town. Zachwatowicz, *Protection of Historical Monuments*, 17–18, 24.
16. Glendinning, *The Conservation Movement*, 374. The protection of historic towns in Czechoslovakia was supported through an adequate institutional and legal framework (i.e., the State Institute for the Reconstruction of Historic Towns and Monuments, organized in 1954, and the 1958 conservation law, which recognized the protected status of urban conservation areas).
17. Glendinning, *The Conservation Movement*, 360.
18. "Cinci ani de restaurare a orașelor istorice cehoslovace," 280–83.
19. The movement was institutionalized through the creation of the All-Russian Society for the Protection of Historical and Cultural Monuments. Bittner, *The Many Lives of Khrushchev's Thaw*, 141–73.
20. See, for example, the case of Kazimierz district in Kraków. A former Jewish district, Kazimierz had been the object of several nonimplemented urban redevelopment projects in the 1950s and 1960s. In the 1980s, architects reconsidered its historical value and drafted alternative plans for "revalorization," although as little as 10 percent of the buildings were considered to be in a good state of repair. Murzyn, *Kazimierz, The Central European Experience*, 120–36.
21. Urban, *Neo-historical East Berlin*.
22. A well-known example is Prenzlauer Berg in East Berlin. Ladd, *The Ghosts of Berlin*, 107–8.
23. Arhivele Naționale Istorice Centrale București, Fond Academia de Științe Sociale și Politice a RSR, Secția de istorie și arheologie, 1/1964, f. 51–52.
24. Grama, "Searching for Heritage, Building Politics," 63–64.
25. *Lista Monumentelor de Cultură de pe Teritoriul RPR*.
26. To some European travelers, Balkan cities appeared messy and dirty, ugly and incoherent, with a deficient infrastructure and anachronistic functions. See Jezernik,

"Western Perception of Turkish Towns." The towns in Wallachia and Moldavia were situated at the periphery of this space and constituted a slightly different case, since no mosques or other specific Ottoman buildings had been constructed on their territory. However, similar stereotypes were in evidence in their case, as well.
27. For an analysis of the built fabric of the medieval towns in Transylvania, see Băldescu, *Transilvania medievală*.
28. Opriș, *Protejarea mărturiilor cultural-artistice*.
29. Oțetea, Prodan, and Berza, *Istoria României*, 675–79.
30. These aspects were emphasized in articles on urban reconstruction in the 1960s. See, for example, *Arhitectura* 10, no. 2 (1959): 5, 16–17; *Arhitectura* 15, no. 6 (1964): 34–35, 47; *Arhitectura* 16, no. 1 (1965): 4. The "heavy legacy of the past" was a leitmotiv in every socialist country. For the case of East Berlin, see Urban, *Neo-historical East Berlin*, 39–40.
31. A comprehensive monograph of the town was published in 1957. Dobowy, *Sighișoara*.
32. *Lista Monumentelor de Cultură de pe Teritoriul RPR*, 121.
33. Urban and regional planning was referred to in the Romanian context as "systematization."
34. Bilciurescu, "Sistematizarea centrelor istorice ale vechilor noastre orașe," 46–48.
35. Ibid.
36. Iorga, "Cum au fost și cum trebuie să fie Bucureștii," 45.
37. Ibid., 45–50.
38. Călinescu, "București," 88–89.
39. Cincinat Sfințescu (1887–1955) was trained in Bucharest as an engineer and specialized in urban planning in Berlin. A recent project that investigates Sfințescu's legacy, largely ignored after World War II, is http://www.sfintescu.ro/en/cincinat-sfintescu/ (accessed 23 March 2020).
40. Sfințescu, "Studiu asupra planului general de sistematizare al capitalei"; idem, "Zonificarea urbanistică a municipiului București."
41. See Sfințescu, "Congresul Internațional pentru Locuințe și Amenajarea Orașelor."
42. This solution was adopted in late nineteenth-century Bucharest. See Lascu, *Bulevarde bucureștene până la al doilea război mondial*.
43. The drawing of the alignment plan for Bucharest was influenced by the Municipality's lack of financial resources for expropriation. This explains why most streets were never quite straightened, preserving instead their premodern pattern. Rădulescu, "Despre aplicarea servituților de retragere la sistematizarea orașelor," 16.
44. Iancu, "Utopia Bucureștilor," 307.
45. Ibid., 312.
46. Curinschi, *Centrele istorice*, 275–77. The prevailing influence of the Italian school of restoration is also openly stated in Curinschi, *Restaurarea monumentelor*, 7.
47. Pendlebury, "The Modern Historic City," 254–55.
48. Curinschi, *Centrele istorice*, 6.
49. Ibid., 26.
50. Ibid.
51. Reconstruction refers to an action of replacing old constructions with new ones. Other terms describe different types of interventions in the built fabric. For exam-

ple, "restructuring" relates to the modification of the street network and the organization of the building stock, and "remodeling" refers to moderate interventions in the built structure, while preserving the street network and most part of the built fabric. Ibid., 26–28.
52. Curinschi, "Restaurarea monumentelor în pas cu progresul arhitecturii," 12.
53. Pendlebury, "The Modern Historic City," 259.
54. Curinschi, *Centrele istorice*, 44–47.
55. Ibid., 51.
56. Ibid., 31–35.
57. Ibid., 57.
58. Ibid., 55.
59. Ibid., 57, 93.
60. Ibid., 74.
61. Ibid.
62. Ibid., 65.
63. Ibid., 94–95.
64. The old streets' picturesque quality would justify their preservation as "witnesses" of the old town. Ibid., 103.
65. Ibid., 6.
66. Wakeman, *Modernizing the Provincial City*; Holston, *The Modernist City*, Chapter Four: "The Death of the Street."
67. Curinschi, *Centrele istorice*, 158–60.
68. Ibid., 163.
69. Ibid., 162.
70. William Morris, "Westminster Abbey," June 1893, retrieved 23 March 2020, https://www.marxists.org/archive/morris/works/1893/west.htm. See also Miele, "The First Conservation Militants."
71. Project ISCAS nr. 3271/ 2-1966. This was a pioneering project in the Romanian context, establishing a methodology for the rehabilitation of historic districts that could be later applied nation-wide. The cost of works was estimated at almost 10 million lei, the equivalent of the Department for Historic Monuments budget for one year. Institutul Național al Patrimoniului-Direcția Monumentelor Istorice, Procese verbale vol. X, PV nr. 9/ May 17, 1967, f. 2–3.
72. This view was expressed by the architect Richard Paulick in Glendinning, *The Conservation Movement*, 379.
73. By contrast, the studies made by Bilciurescu's team proposed the construction of a new city center some distance away from the old one, which would remain essentially a tourist attraction.
74. Lăzărescu, "Studiu pentru sistematizarea zonei centrale a orasului Pitești," 50–51.
75. Bilciurescu, "Sistematizarea centrelor istorice ale vechilor noastre orașe," 46–49.
76. Idem, "Studii pentru sistematizarea centrelor istorice."
77. Ionescu, "Putem reda unor construcții vechi funcțiunea de locuire?," 68.
78. Vernescu, "Centrul să cuprindă în primul rând dotări," 70–71. The author criticized the tendency of using centrally located areas for housing rather than services and office space.
79. Greceanu, "Delimitarea zonelor protejate urbane."

80. The most comprehensive study was on the historical area of Bucharest and was conducted by the Institute of Architecture. Cristea, Sandu, Popescu-Criveanu, and Voiculescu, "Studiu de delimitare a zonei istorice a orașului București."
81. Institutul Național al Patrimoniului-Direcția Monumentelor Istorice, Procese verbale XIV 1971–73, PV nr. 7/ July 7, 1971, f. 1–2.
82. The medieval towers were restored in Brașov, Mediaș, Sighișoara, and Sibiu, and efforts were made to ensure proper conservation of the fortification walls. Greceanu, "Realizări privind protecția unor centre istorice din sudul Transilvaniei," 41–43.
83. UNESCO, *The Conservation of Cities*—emphasis mine.
84. The topic of inequality in housing redistribution has been explored in the literature on various socialist countries. Szelényi, *Urban Inequalities under State Socialism*; Le Normand, "The House that Socialism Built," 356–59; Fehérváry, *Politics in Color and Concrete*, 77, 99–100.
85. On the development of the civic center concept in Romania, see Răuță, "Civic Centers under Ceaușescu's Rule."
86. Glendinning, *The Conservation Movement*, 304–14, 372, 374. Other relevant case studies include some of the republics of the Soviet Union, with Estonia the first one to pass heritage legislation in 1961. Ibid., 376; see also the chapter by Hallas-Murula and Truu in this volume.
87. During the 1970s, its structure was weakened through successive reorganizations and internal conflicts. The legislation for national cultural heritage promulgated in 1974 contributed to the further neglect of built heritage by putting moveable cultural goods at the center of political interest. Finally, the Department for Historic Monuments' reorganization enforced at the end of 1977 led to the dismissal of most experts and specialized workers.
88. On the extent of the destruction, see Giurescu, *The Razing of Romania's Past*.
89. Institutul Național al Patrimoniului-Direcția Monumentelor Istorice, Procese verbale XIV, PV nr. 16/September 21, 1973, f. 1–3.

Bibliography

Băldescu, Irina. *Transilvania medievală: Topografie și norme juridice ale cetăților. Sibiu, Bistrița, Brașov, Cluj*. București: Simetria, 2012.
Bilciurescu, Virgil. "Sistematizarea centrelor istorice ale vechilor noastre orașe." *Arhitectura* 17, no .6 (1966): 46–49.
———. "Studii pentru sistematizarea centrelor istorice ale orașelor Brașov, Sibiu, Sebeș-Alba, Târgoviște." *Arhitectura* 17, no. 6 (1966): 52–63.
Bittner, Stephen. *The Many Lives of Khrushchev's Thaw: Experience and Memory in Moscow's Arbat*. Ithaca: Cornell University Press, 2008.
Călinescu, G. "București." In *București: Istorie și urbanism*, edited by Andrei Pippidi. Iași: Do-minoR, 2002.
Choay, Françoise. *The Invention of the Historic Monument*. Cambridge, UK: Cambridge University Press, 2001.
"Cinci ani de restaurare a orașelor istorice cehoslovace." *Monumente si muzee* 1, no.1 (1958): 280–83.

Cocheci, Teodor. "Problemele sistematizării orașului Craiova." *Arhitectura* 16, no. 1 (1965): 43.
Colesnic, Iurie, ed. "Gheorghe Curinschi-Vorona—un mare istoric al arhitecturii." In *Basarabeni în lume*. Volume 3, 12–31. Chișinău: Biblioteca Națională a Republicii Moldova, 2007.
Cristea, Doina, Alexandru Sandu, Șerban Popescu-Criveanu, and Sanda Voiculescu. "Studiu de delimitare a zonei istorice a orașului București." *Arhitectura* 28, no. 6 (1977): 38–47.
Curinschi, Gheorghe. *Centrele istorice ale orașelor*. Bucharest: Editura Tehnică, 1967.
———. "Cu privire la originile arhitecturii monumentale românești." *Arhitectura* 7, no. 9 (1956): 28–34.
———. *Restaurarea monumentelor*. Bucharest: Editura Tehnică, 1968.
———. "Restaurarea monumentelor în pas cu progresul arhitecturii!" *Arhitectura* 19, no.6 (1968): 6–14.
Curinschi-Vorona, Gheorghe. *Arhitectură, Urbanism, Restaurare*. Bucharest: Editura Tehnică, 1996.
Dobowy, Erich. *Sighișoara: Un oraș medieval*. Bucharest: Editura Tehnică, 1957.
Fehérváry, Krisztina. *Politics in Color and Concrete: Socialist Materialities and the Middle Class in Hungary*. Bloomington: Indiana University Press, 2013.
Giurescu, Dinu. *The Razing of Romania's Past*. Washington, DC: U.S. Committee, International Council on Monuments and Sites, 1989.
Glendinning, Miles. *The Conservation Movement: A History of Architectural Preservation; Antiquity to Modern*. London: Routledge, 2013.
Grama, Emanuela. "Searching for Heritage, Building Politics: Architecture, Archaeology, and Imageries of Social Order in Romania (1947–2007)." PhD diss., University of Michigan, 2010.
Greceanu, Eugenia. "Delimitarea zonelor protejate urbane în România în timpul regimului comunist." *Arhitext Design* 6, no. 5 (1998): 27–31.
———. "Realizări privind protecția unor centre istorice din sudul Transilvaniei (1960–1972)." *Buletinul Monumentelor Istorice* 17, no. 1 (1973): 41–48.
Holston, James. *The Modernist City: An Anthropological Critique of Brasilia*. Chicago: The University of Chicago Press, 1989.
Iancu, Marcel. "Utopia Bucureștilor." In *București: Istorie și urbanism*, edited by Andrei Pippidi, 302–13. Iași: Do-minoR, 2002.
Ionescu, P. H. "Putem reda unor construcții vechi funcțiunea de locuire?" *Arhitectura* 6 (1966): 68.
Iorga, Nicolae. "Cum au fost și cum trebuie să fie Bucureștii." In *București. Istorie și urbanism*, edited by Andrei Pippidi, 40–58. Iași: Do-minoR, 2002.
Jezernik, Bozidar. "Western Perception of Turkish Towns in the Balkans." *Urban History* 25, no. 2 (1998): 211–30.
Kurinski, Gheorghe. "Lupta poporului pentru independență împotriva robiei turcești, oglindită în arhitectura epocii lui Ștefan cel Mare și Petru Rareș." *Arhitectură și urbanism* 3, no. 4–5 (1952): 37–43.
Kurinski, Yura. "Un an de muncă pe tărâmul reformei învățământului arhitecturii." *Revistele Tehnice AGIR. S. Arhitectură și Construcții civile* 3, no. 4 (1949): 208.

Ladd, Brian. *The Ghosts of Berlin: Confronting German History in the Urban Landscape.* Chicago: University of Chicago Press, 1997.
Lamprakos, Michele. "The Idea of the Historic City." *Change over Time* 4, no. 1 (2014): 8–38.
Lascu, Nicolae. *Bulevarde bucureștene până la al doilea război mondial.* Bucharest: Simetria, 2011.
Lăzărescu, Cezar. "Studiu pentru sistematizarea zonei centrale a orasului Pitești." *Arhitectura* 17, no. 6 (1966): 50–51, 71.
Le Normand, Brigitte. "The House That Socialism Built: Reform, Consumption, and Inequality in Postwar Yugoslavia." In *Communism Unwrapped: Consumption in Cold War Eastern Europe*, edited by Paulina Bren and Mary Neuberger, 351–73. Oxford: Oxford University Press, 2012.
Lista Monumentelor de Cultură de pe Teritoriul RPR. Bucharest: Editura Academiei R.P.R., 1956.
Miele, Chris. "The First Conservation Militants: William Morris and the Society for the Protection of Ancient Buildings." In *Preserving the Past: The Rise of Heritage in Modern Britain*, edited by Michael Hunter, 17–37. Stroud: Alan Sutton Publishing Ltd., 1996.
Murzyn, Monika A. *Kazimierz, The Central European Experience of Urban Regeneration.* Kraków: International Cultural Center, 2006.
Opriș, Ioan. *Protejarea mărturiilor cultural-artistice din Transilvania și Banat după Marea Unire.* Bucharest: Editura Științifică și Enciclopedică, 1988.
Oțetea, Andrei, David Prodan, and M. Berza. *Istoria României.* Volume 3. Bucharest: Ed. Academiei R.S.R., 1964.
Pendlebury, John. "The Modern Historic City: Evolving Ideas in Mid-20th-century Britain." *Journal of Urban Design* 10, no. 2 (2005): 253–73.
Rădulescu, T.A. "Despre aplicarea servituților de retragere la sistematizarea orașelor." *Monitorul Uniunii Orașelor din România* 6, no. 3–6 (1929): 15–17.
Răuță, Alexandru. "Civic Centers under Ceaușescu's Rule: The Failure to Articulate a Professional Discourse." *Studii de Istoria și Teoria* 1 (2013): 105–19.
Rodwell, Dennis. "Urban Conservation in the 1960s and 1970s: A European Overview." *Architectural Heritage* 21, no. 1 (2010): 1–18.
Sfințescu, Cincinat. "Congresul Internațional pentru Locuințe și Amenajarea Orașelor." *Monitorul Uniunea Orașelor din România* 6, no. 9–10 (1929): 3–28.
———. "Studiu asupra planului general de sistematizare al capitalei." In *București: Istorie și urbanism*, edited by Andrei Pippidi, 102–146. Iași: Domino, 2002 [1919].
———. "Zonificarea urbanistică a municipiului București." In *București: Istorie și urbanism*, edited by Andrei Pippidi, 176–261. Iași: Domino, 2002.
Stubbs, John H. *Time Honored: A Global View of Architectural Conservation.* Hoboken, NJ: John Wiley and Sons, Inc., 2009.
Szelényi, Iván. *Urban Inequalities under State Socialism.* New York: Oxford University Press, 1983.
UNESCO. *The Conservation of Cities.* London: Croom Helm, 1975.
Urban, Florian. *Neo-historical East Berlin: Architecture and Urban Design in the German Democratic Republic 1970–1990.* Farnham, UK: Ashgate, 2009.

Vernescu, Dinu. "Centrul să cuprindă în primul rând dotări." *Arhitectura* 6 (1966): 70–71.
Wakeman, Rosemary. *Modernizing the Provincial City: Toulouse 1945–1975*. Cambridge, MA: Harvard University Press, 1998.
Zachwatowicz, Jan. *Protection of Historical Monuments in Poland*. Warsaw: Polonia Publishing House, 1965.

CHAPTER 7

Making Sense of Socialism through Heritage Preservation
Stories from Northwest Bohemia

Čeněk Pýcha

This chapter discusses the continuities and discontinuities of heritage preservation and the changing meanings of the concept of heritage itself through a regional lens, drawing on the case of Northwest Bohemia. It could be argued that given the radical changes of political and social systems in twentieth-century Central Europe (the creation of new states, forced migration, and the excesses involved in state-controlled industrialization), discontinuity should be the central characteristic. Upon closer examination, however, the story becomes more complex.

Broadly speaking, socialist ideology was radical and future-oriented in the late 1940s and early 1950s. An interesting variant of this ideology emerged in Czechoslovakia that explained historical events and phenomena through the perspective of class struggle, thus enabling some chapters of history to enter the prevalent revolutionary narrative.[1] Revolutionary discourse drew on the past, shaping how heritage was conceived and what emerged as socialist heritage. This could be considered a new category of heritage that was formed of a complex nexus of both continuities and discontinuities or disruptions in using the past to create visions of the future. Although the essence of the concept of heritage lies in the continuity of the relevant values from the past, the stories of the concrete heritage sites in Northwest Bohemia examined in this chapter very often invoke destruction and discontinuity.

Following World War II, the symbolic order in the region of Northwest Bohemia was completely reconstructed. Before the war, German communities inhabited the borderlands of Czechoslovakia, including Northwest Bohemia. Almost three million German inhabitants were expelled from their homes between 1945 and 1946. During the period from 1945 until the late 1950s, the region could be considered the center of what emerged as socialist heritage in Czechoslovakia. This space was to provide legitimation for the socialist government in Czechoslovakia. As Eagle Glassheim has noted, the Czechoslovak borderland was a laboratory for the state-socialist regime.[2] And, as I argue, heritage preservation in Northwest Bohemia was just one aspect of reality there that was subject to state-led experiments.

The vision of socialist heritage was both accepted and contested, as socialist heritage built on continuities as well as discontinuities, with the latter exacerbated in Northwest Bohemia by population transfers. Socialist heritage is used here to signify the shifts in the significance of the concept of heritage and the meanings attached to sites under the state socialist regime that came into existence in Czechoslovakia after 1948. This chapter is using the term "socialist heritage" to signify both the "authorized heritage discourse"[3] promoted by state authorities and the process of (re)appropriation of new heritage sites by society. I explore continuities and discontinuities of understandings and usages of heritage, both as a concept and as sites, in the wake of political and social changes. In this chapter, I focus on the local conditions of heritage preservation in a small region of Northwest Bohemia, with the case studies concentrating primarily on the town of Duchcov (German: Dux). During the state-socialist era in Czechoslovakia (1948–89), Duchcov became an important place in the official narrative that stressed traditions of class struggle, with a strike in the 1930s becoming a significant site in official claims. My approach focuses particularly on the dynamics of socialist conceptions of heritage and how they interacted and intersected with other, often older, layers in the local interpretation of heritage. As I argue, conceptions of socialist heritage did not align with historical and political caesurae familiar on the national and indeed bloc-wide scale. The expulsion of Czech Germans after World War II and the new political regime after 1948 did not necessarily mean discontinuities with previous concepts of heritage. As the case of Duchcov shows, the appropriation of authorized heritage discourse by local politicians enabled the protection of values that diverged in various ways, as I will explain, from the official state ideology that was associated with radical modernity and the utopian socialist future. In practice, the authorized heritage discourse that developed dynamically incorporated the new heritage sites pertaining to official ideology as well as older realms of heritage, including religious buildings and sites related to the nobility.

The Space of Northwest Bohemia

As the starting point for the analysis, Duchcov is not a random choice. This location offers a microcosm of many of the problems that I consider to be key issues in the specific approach to heritage preservation in socialist Czechoslovakia. Duchcov and the whole region of Northwest Bohemia underwent dynamic development in the twentieth century.[4] The region was first part of the Austro-Hungarian Empire; then after World War I it was included for a very short period in the Province of Deutschböhmen (declared part of Austria) before becoming part of the new Czechoslovak Republic. After the Munich Agreement of 1938, it was incorporated into the Third Reich. The end of World War II brought the restoration of the Czechoslovak state, and, finally, Northwest Bohemia became part of the Czech Republic after the dissolution of Czechoslovakia in 1993. These political changes went hand in hand with social changes, with the expulsion of the Sudeten Germans from the borderlands after World War II having the most significant social consequences. In Duchcov, for example, the number of citizens dropped from 19,000 in 1930 to 12,000 in 1950, a decline of over 36 percent, which was not as severe as in other areas and districts of Northwest Bohemia that lost more than 70 percent of their citizens. It is important to note that the Czech community in Duchcov was quite strong before World War II, forming one of the Czech isles in the predominantly German region. Thus, there was stronger continuity in the postwar development than in neighboring cities like Teplice (Teplitz) or Ústí nad Labem (Aussig). Nevertheless, the sense of belonging to this place was disrupted by population transfers and efforts to create a revised canon of artifacts from the past under socialism.

In this contribution, I do not work with a static concept of geographical region. Instead, I prefer to use a more dynamic and performative concept that defines space according to the relationships and networks that come into existence between particular sites. "Space" can be defined, following Michel de Certeau, as a practiced place: "The street geometrically defined by urban planning is transformed into a space by walkers. In the same way, an act of reading is the space produced by the practice of a particular place: a written text, i.e., a place constituted by a system of signs."[5] According to this concept, we can see heritage preservation as one of the practices that transforms places into space, just as speaking transforms words into sentences. While the sites that I am describing in this study are located in a concrete geographical region, they can be read as illustrations of the broader symbolic structures that form the focus of my analysis—namely, continuities and discontinuities with traditional forms of heritage (for example religious buildings); typical aesthetics of socialism; and their potential for (re)appropriation by historical agents. Thus, the position of heritage sites in the particular historical and geographical reality of the borderlands of Northern Bohemia following the expulsion of the significant German population and during the construction of state socialism is read in terms of symptomatic efforts to construct a broader "socialist heritage" that drew on the past in a way that would support the development of the state's vision of a socialist utopia. What I explore here are the entanglements of the material and narrative traces of the particular sites with the efforts to construct a universalist narrative of socialist progress, heritage, and modernity. These efforts illustrate the nexus of continuities and discontinuities in the way the authorized heritage discourse used the past in a region where the tension between the Romantic notion of the heritage landscape and industrialization has a longer history, such as with the Krušné hory (Erzgebirge, Ore Mountains) having been a location of mining since the Middle Ages that continues until this day.[6] Thus, the dynamics of historical development influenced not only the sociopolitical aspects of the area, but also the shape of the space and the physical conditions for people living here. This idea of a homeland with which inhabitants felt a sense of belonging was one of the veins of continuity that socialist heritage tapped into, but this was combined with socialism's future-oriented vision of society and politics.

The Concept of Heritage and the Authorized Heritage Discourse in Local Conditions

The main sources for my inquiry are lists of regional and state heritage sites, in particular the local lists of the heritage sites compiled in the 1940s and 1950s and the central legislation used for defining heritage sites from the late 1950s onward when the institutions of heritage preservation underwent centralization and professionalization in Czechoslovakia. I will focus on the changes made to these lists, exploring them not only in terms of the heritage sites themselves but also in terms of the structure of the classification employed that led to new types of sites being considered as heritage. These lists are important because they trace the pertinent discourse of the time and manifest the outcome of discussions and decisions that created a canon of approved heritage sites. My approach thus offers insight into the history of heritage discourse under socialism in Czechoslovakia, while also highlighting the significance of what was omitted from the lists and discussions.

Generally, I combine a structuralist approach to the lists of heritage sites, with selected case studies that are then read through a deeper microhistorical lens. Laurajane Smith defines heritage as a set of cultural and social practices.[7] Here I combine existing research into the concept of heritage and the shifts in heritage discourses with a local focus that is necessary for understanding how concrete historical agents adopted the concept of heritage.[8] On the one hand, there is a heritage discourse that has informed the general interpretation of the past, while, on the other hand, local agents adopted this discourse in their distinctive way. Both aspects are important for understanding heritage concepts under state socialism. Thus, this case study of often-overlooked local practices of and discourses on heritage preservation under state socialism in Czechoslovakia also contributes to the knowledge of structures of authority over decision-making more broadly.

This approach thus involves recognizing the regime's both totalitarian and authoritarian tendencies, particularly between 1945 and 1989. At the same time, the character of the state socialist regime was changing and developing. The focus on heritage preservation and interpretation could supplement the generally accepted periodization of socialist Czechoslovakia that is characterized by strong oppression in the 1950s, followed by an era of liberalization that led to the attempted revolution of 1968, which was thwarted thus interrupting this trend. Thereafter came the consolidation of the Communist Party's power in the period of Normalization, which was accompanied by general apathy until the late 1980s. The focus on specific aspects of social life (in this case heritage preservation) uncovers some practices that are more complex than this broad periodization might suggest. For example, some forms of resistance—conscious or not—could emerge from below and involve the appropriation of public discourse for individual, and community, goals. This is particularly relevant for the study of the Czechoslovak borderlands (including Northwest Bohemia), as the works of Eagle Glassheim and Matěj Spurný, for example, have shown.[9] This was a region where the transformation of the population and landscape after 1945 was particularly acute but did not always run according to state plans. This can also be shown to be the case in relation to approaches to heritage on the local level. While heritage studies approaches have been applied in research on Czech (and Czechoslovak) contemporary history, the focus generally has been on professionals working in heritage preservation[10] or on the legacies of art and architecture from the state-socialist era today.[11]

The archival sources I work with primarily illustrate the institutional level of heritage preservation, which was an important element in the process of modernization and the rise of power of the secular state.[12] Canonization of heritage sites can be interpreted as an act of power. It is not only in the context of state socialism that power and heritage have intersected. As Stuart Hall has noted, under colonialism there were attempts to create "timeless, true and inevitable" conceptions of heritage to reinscribe power.[13] Another postcolonial scholar, Laurajane Smith, coined the term "authorized heritage discourse" (AHD), which she defined as the discursive formation that creates prerequisites and conditions in society that lead to the protection of some objects as monuments of the past. A consequence of the AHD is, according to Smith, that "it defines who the legitimate spokespersons for the past are."[14] What these concepts have in common with my case study are the efforts to suggest a universal form of heritage for a subordinate population. What I seek to explore is how, on the local level, these universalizing claims were both implemented and contested. There were individuals with personal motivations, goals, and memories that enabled them to develop their own concepts of the past. These also applied to the local authorities responsible for implementing, or rather altering, the state's intentions. Thus in my approach, there are gaps for individual interpretations of heritage between the official versions expressed in the authorized heritage discourse as recorded in archival documents.

The multidimensionality of the socialist heritage preservation is also visible in the terminology used. The most valuable heritage sites were declared "national cultural monuments" (*Národní kulturní památka*). The national characterization linked heritage sites to the specific operationalization of the concept of the nation by the Communist Party of Czechoslovakia. In official interpretations of history, national character was still stressed, although particular sites became part of the approved canon of the authorized heritage discourse when the significance of social issues could be clearly demonstrated. The fifteenth-century Hussite movement, for example, was interpreted in this way. The idea was that the Czech character of the past should be seen to match present-day social, revolutionary, and progressive ideals, thus establishing a sense of continuity.[15]

There was a long tradition of keeping records of cultural monuments connected with reforms that started in the Enlightenment. For Northwest Bohemia, we find documents dated to the second half of the nineteenth century that are oriented specifically toward the reconstruction and preservation of sacral buildings, such as those relating to the Central-Commission zur Erforschung und Erhaltung der Baudenkmale (Central Commission for the Study and Conservation of Architectural Monuments) that was founded in Vienna in 1850. However, these documents do not resemble the complex lists under socialism.[16] During the period of the First Czechoslovak Republic, heritage protection was not centralized, and financial support was relatively low.[17] There was also no specific heritage law or legal interpretation of heritage that could coordinate actors involved in heritage protection from academia or state institutions.

After World War II, the state administration faced a huge challenge in Czechoslovakia. The state confiscated many heritage sites, including seats of noble families, while finding it difficult to fulfill its promise of protecting heritage. The National Cultural Commission (1947–51)[18] was charged with managing these objects and property, as visiting castles and chateaus remained an important cultural practice in postwar Czechoslovakia with such sites dominating conceptions of heritage. After 1948, state-backed cultural representatives demonstrated continuity with the popular tradition of visiting castles and chateaus by integrating them into the public reinterpretation of history.[19] Each former seat of the nobility, which American scholar Cathleen Giustino described as "estate museums,"[20] hosted exhibitions intended to illustrate the changing vision of political, art, and cultural history.

The popularity of visits to chateaus and castles grew throughout the era of state socialism. However, the authorities' plan to tell the story of class struggle enjoyed limited success. In the professional journals on heritage preservation, there were some criticisms of exhibitions that were intended to reveal the political context of the concrete historical building.[21] Some official documents pointed out the need to improve the quality of installations and guided tours of castles and chateaus, with many critiques challenging the positive image of nobility presented by some exhibitions and guides.[22] This kind of agenda shows that the techniques of persuasion had failed in the case of the estate museums.

Cathleen Giustino argues that the guided tours and their success at creating parallel worlds in the reality of the authoritative regime, as "[t]he opening of the gates of former aristocratic residences in Czechoslovakia, like Ratibořice, allowed possibilities for escapes from both the everyday routines of work, school, and home, and from socialist ideology."[23] My interpretation would be that the Romantic "touch of past time" was experienced by the majority of visitors to estates museums to the extent that it overshadowed the socialist narrative presented there. The popularity of this cultural practice remains strong even now in the Czech Republic.

Heritage preservation was part of the agenda of different institutions (the Státní památkový úřad—State Heritage Office; the Státní fotoměřický ústav—State Photometric Institute; and the Státní archeologický úřad—State Archeological Office) that were subordinate to the Ministry of Culture, which means that there were some guidelines for heritage preservation, but their use and applicability differed in each case because the rules and lists of the monuments were not centralized. In 1953, the Státní památková správa (State Heritage Administration) was founded with the aim of centralizing these offices. Indeed, the turning point for heritage preservation in Czechoslovakia was the law adopted in the year 1958 (22/1958) that included the establishment of a new central institution, the Státní ústav památkové péče a ochrany přírody (State Institute of Heritage Care and Nature Protection), with regional offices (including, for example, one based in Ústí nad Labem that was responsible for the region explored here).[24]

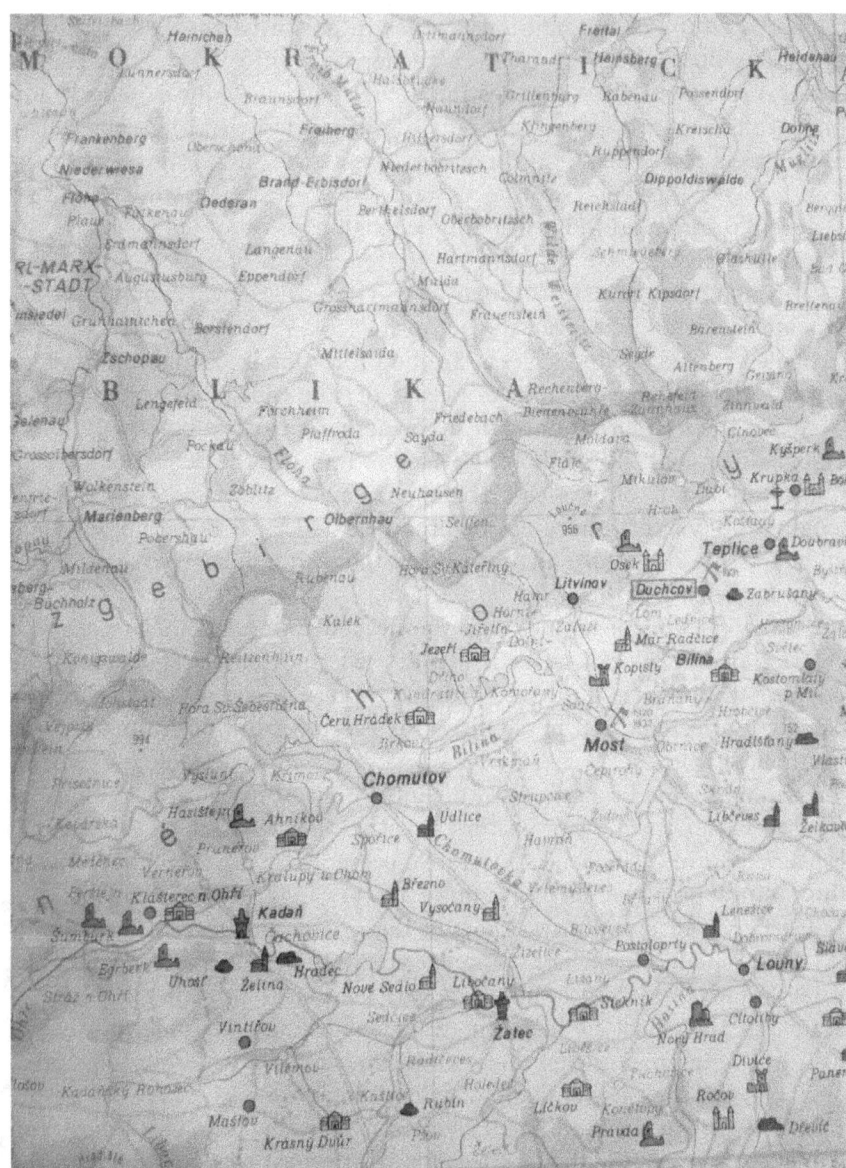

Map 7.1. Excerpt of the map of cultural monuments. The symbol near Duchcov refers to a "memorial of the struggles of the working class against capitalism." Reproduced from J. Hobzek, E. Šamánková, and V. Patera, *Mapa kulturních památek ČSSR: 1:500000*. Prague: Kartografické nakladatelství, 1968. Used with permission.

In the archival sources, the use of terminology relating to heritage preservation was unstable, especially before the legislative clarification of 1958,[25] as different historical agents used a variety of terms for describing heritage sites. The etymon of the word was usually the Czech word for memory (*pamět*) with different suffixes (*památnost, pomník, památník, pamětihodnost, památka*). In reading the sources, I trace how the terms used were significant indicators of the frictions produced by encounters of authorized, state-sanctioned heritage discourses and practices, on the one hand, and local administrators' practices, on the other. The fact that existing terminology remained in place before heritage preservation became the subject of legislation is evidence of a degree of localized autonomy over heritage practices and meanings showing that the sites were rooted in the active memory of society during this period.[26]

Heritage after World War II: Discontinuity or Continuity?

A list of "heritage sites" (*památnost*) in the district of Duchcov (*Soupis památností duchcovského okresu*)[27] was written up by a local politician and cultural official in 1949. The list formed part of the communication between the representatives of the district of Duchcov[28] and the regional government in Ústí nad Labem, offering a local perspective on heritage preservation in this era. In 1949, following the restructuring of local administration, regional governments also took up some responsibilities in heritage protection. It is reasonable to suppose that this local list was used to map the monuments for the new administration on the higher level.

We can see the list as a map of heritage sites of that period in Duchcov and its surroundings. Divided into eleven cities and villages, it contains a total of thirty-five heritage sites. A potential visitor would find the largest number in Duchcov (fourteen), with others in surrounding villages and smaller cities. The descriptions of the heritage sites are not of a technical or expert nature, but they do also include art objects. Thus, the perspective of what is considered a heritage site is not unified. There is no precise outline of categories or types of heritage sites on the list, but it is obvious that there are different sources and reasons for the understanding of what heritage site meant during this time.

The largest group (seventeen) of the Duchcov heritage sites is religious, with particular emphasis on churches—two of them Evangelical, the rest Catholic. Six of the heritage sites are industrial (a spinning mill, a porcelain factory, machine works, and three coal mine pits—two of which have a special category: memorial mine pits). The rest includes a chateau, various memorials, a city hall, a fountain, and some paintings. It is obvious that the most important source of heritage were buildings (the majority of them religious) and other pieces of art. We could mark these heritage sites as traditional because they fall under heritage protection as already defined in the beginning of twentieth century by the authorities in the Central European region.

However, there are some heritage sites on the list that cross different realms of heritage. For example, the author of the list mentioned the municipal cemetery in Duchcov, specifically the memorials to mining disasters located in the cemetery. These heritage sites thus combined the traditional religiosity of the cemetery with the solidarity and mutual belonging of the miners. This thesis is also confirmed with the special category of the memorial mine pits. These are the Döllinger (1879, 21 victims) and Nelson III (1934, 144 victims) mine pits, where mining disasters occurred. The memory of mining disasters was still alive and widespread in the community in the 1950s owing to what Jan Assmann called "communicative memory."[29] There were already some signs of official commemoration (i.e., cultural memory), though, which in the case of the cemetery also offered an indication of the first shifts toward a conception of socialist heritage. In this sense, socialist heritage incorporated some ideals and values of social solidarity beyond the forms in which authorized heritage discourse appropriated these concepts.

This was a time of negotiations over what the heritage of the new political regime and its ideology would be. With the help of the list from 1949, I would like to stress continuities and ruptures in the historical narratives associated with heritage preservation in the socialist present in the town and its surroundings. The development of heritage preservation in the area demonstrated connections to broader efforts in Czechoslovakia and the socialist bloc to develop an ideological conception of heritage, while at the same time being informed by the highly specific conditions of a region shaped by Germans and their subsequent expulsion. There was thus evident discontinuity in heritage preservation as Czech citizens removed some of the most visible traces of German character of the town in Duchcov, including the statue of the German minstrel Walther Von der Vogelweide, who was mistakenly believed to have been born in Duchcov, as well as the bust of Ludwig van Beethoven. This rewriting and cleansing of public space was a regular phenomenon.[30] Nevertheless, despite the population transfers and subsequent destruction of heritage traces, there are some evident continuities in how the past was approached, meaning a sense of belonging to the region strengthened.

In the archival holdings of the State Heritage Administration, there is a document called *Verzeichnis kulturhistorisch wertvoller Baudenkmäler im Landkreis Dux* (List of culturally and historically valuable buildings in

Duchcov district) written by an official of the local building authority in Duchcov in 1940, which by then was part of the Third Reich.[31] It was produced as part of fire protection measures. This list contains mostly religious heritage sites, with the majority of them also included on the list from 1949. We can assume that the author of the list of heritage sites from 1949 had this older list before his eyes.

The 1940 list is also arranged by location, but it contains just seventeen heritage sites here, all of them connected with the church. The sole exception is the thermal spring (Riesenquelle) in Lahošť (Loosch). There are also differences in the names (1949: *památnosti*, an older term for memory sites—1940: *kulturhistorisch wertvolle Baudenkmäler*, which are culturally and historically valuable buildings) and perhaps also in the goals of the lists. But it is clear that the traditional way of relating to the past through churches is supplemented by new sources of heritage in 1949, and not only those relating to the victims of World War II. This is evident in the case of the railway bridge in Duchcov (Duchcovský viadukt).

The first traces of socialist heritage preservation in the region were evident in 1949, although the town's most important socialist heritage site was not immediately granted official recognition, even on the local level. When the status of "national cultural monument" was introduced by a specific law in 1958[32] and the national cultural monuments were declared four years later, there were diverse heritage sites from different eras on the list of national heritage sites. Among such luminaries as Prague Castle, Karlštejn Castle, and the Czech national hill Říp there was also Duchcov viaduct, a small train bridge at the edge of the town.

Duchcov Viaduct:
A Case Study of the Authorized Heritage Discourse

The Duchcov viaduct was supposed to tell one of the last chapters in the narrative of the new socialist history, illustrating class struggle in the era of the First Czechoslovak Republic. This story was especially important as a source of legitimacy for the Communist government, along with the antifascist resistance during World War II.[33] There were some interesting outcomes produced by negotiations over heritage, with a sculptor from Prague being turned down in favor of a local author for the memorial. The archival documents indicate that the main reason could have been the high cost of the piece of art by the academic sculptor.[34] In 1954, local Communist elites unveiled the memorial at the site where a strike had been crushed and four workers killed in 1932. The memorial offered a place where the myth about the heroes of class struggle could be embodied and canonized. Other media also cocreated this myth, with a drama[35] and a book of reports[36] on the strike being produced. However, it was the memorial that served as the central place where commemoration and other festivities could take place.

It was not the monument that was considered for listing as a protected heritage site in 1962, but rather the bridge itself. A small train bridge (*viadukt*), the point where the path to the town was crossed by the gendarmes during the strike in 1932, was declared a national cultural monument. The memorial was supposed to underline the shift of the symbolic meaning of the event to a physical place. This shift is really important, and it is significant for socialist heritage preservation in the Czechoslovak context. The Duchcov viaduct was a new kind of heritage site. The architecturally insignificant bridge had the same value as the Prague Castle in the hierarchy of heritage preservation. In a way, this site resembled the commemoration of battlefields, with the fallen workers taking the place of fallen soldiers. However, such strong emphasis on a piece of infrastructure, as was the case in Duchcov, was quite unusual. The bridge itself became the symbol not only of the event, but also of the town in iconic communist-era representations, including diplomas for children and prizes for the winners of athletic competitions. The physical substance of the heritage site played an important role in negotiations over the heritage protection of this place. Commemorations of the event changed quite radically in the town during the 1960s. The representatives of Duchcov decided to move the monument in 1963 because continued coal mining had caused significant deterioration in the conditions around the area of the bridge. The monument thus found a new location in the town center, next to the castle park. The bridge (still under highest level of heritage protection) became an orphan in the emerging periphery on the edge of the mine pit. The monument in the town center acquired a new architectural form, namely the symbolic wall that was supposed to resemble the bridge. The new location was more appropriate for festivities and ceremonies, although the authenticity of the place was relatively weaker.

A significant moment in the negotiations over the future of the town was the mining company's request to remove the status of national cultural monument from Duchcov viaduct in 1968. The representatives of the town vigorously opposed the request. The reaction and argumentation of the local representatives represent a remarkable example of the appropriation of authorized heritage discourse to make it part of how local people created a sense of belonging and identification with their hometown. It is obvious from the argumentation that the Duchcov viaduct could have been seen as a workaround. The letter written by the municipality openly criticized environmental conditions in the town and surrounding areas, attributing the problems to coal mining. The representatives wrote that "the plenary

MAKING SENSE OF SOCIALISM THROUGH HERITAGE PRESERVATION *181*

Figure 7.1. Duchcovský viadukt, current state (2011). Photograph by Adam Pokorný.

Figure 7.2. Memorial to the killed workers, Duchcov (Duchcovský viadukt). Museum of Duchcov (sometime between 1954–63). © Museum Duchcov. Used with permission.

Figure 7.3. Transfer of the monument to the new site (1963). © Museum Duchcov. Used with permission.

Figure 7.4. A school class with the monument. Museum of Duchcov (after 1963). © Museum Duchcov. Used with permission.

meeting also noted that the mining activity disrupted the town on all sides, as evidenced by the chateau garden, watercourses, waterlogged areas in Křinec and Bažantnice. Also, the higher authorities did not pay attention to the overall environmental condition of the town."[37] Unlike in older and more recent documents recording negotiations over the Duchcov viaduct as an important heritage site, there is no mention of the importance of the train bridge as a memorial site of the workers' movement in this letter. Perhaps the atmosphere of the Prague Spring encouraged the local authorities to openly address the environmental situation in the town and surroundings, expressing their worries about the future of the town during negotiations over the status of this heritage site. The authors of the letter even declared that the request to remove its status as a national cultural monument was "in contradiction of state discipline." They were referring to the government resolution of 1963 that "had provided confidence in the existence of the town."

Indeed, the discourse used by the state mining concern in its request to remove the status of national cultural monument is itself an interesting case of appropriating heritage.[38] The document begins with a reference to the history of mining in the region, especially in Duchcov, which according to a record drawing on the town chronicles dates back to 1403. The author linked the tradition of mining to the tradition of miners' community that had been expressed by strikes and miners' struggle against national and social injustice. The 1931 event was seen in this sense as the most noticeable part of the tradition. Implicitly, the logic of the document suggested that the event was part of the mining tradition and heritage that could have been honored by the development of mining by the company concerned. Though the company representatives also used pragmatic arguments (the strike had been commemorated enough with the monument relocated to the town center, while the railways viaduct no longer served as a bridge), it was important for them to demonstrate their interpretation of mining tradition and heritage. The attitude of the local authorities proved more successful in the end; the representatives of the local heritage institute confirmed it and the status of national cultural monument of Duchcov viaduct remained until 1995.

The story of the bridge in Duchcov documents the operationalization of heritage preservation during the state socialist era. Beyond the use of the story of four martyrs to legitimize the regime in the region, there were other efforts to instrumentalize the heritage potential of this place. As the story of moving the monument indicates, the Duchcov viaduct was an important factor in negotiations over the future of the whole town that was threatened with disappearance due to the expansion of coal mining. The most important monument of class struggle in the region helped protect the town and varied heritage of different eras. What did not change, however, was the discursive framework evident in the archival sources, with the importance of heritage sites linked to the workers' movement given priority. The municipal authorities in particular adopted this type of argumentation and official language in their interpretations of the town's history from a socialist perspective. Consequently, the history of the town was connected to the future rather than the past, even if the same discourse could be used to protect different values—including, for example, Baroque heritage. In Duchcov, the local authorities appropriated the authorized heritage discourse in the struggle over the future of the town, which became embroiled in the politics of memory.

Following the definition of the power-related aspects of heritage preservation presented in the introduction, it is clear that this case offers quite a different perspective on the politics of memory, as it was not employed in the sense of rivalry over identity. Nevertheless, heritage was nevertheless political as it affected concrete decisions negotiated on the local level. The narratives and practices around heritage preservation cherished quite different values other than the story of four dead workers, which prevailed in the dominant narrative of authorized heritage discourse.

Socialist Heritage Sites

The characteristics of a socialist heritage site, as outlined in the case of the Duchcov viaduct, may also be found in other heritage sites on the list of national cultural monuments from 1962.[39] Two of them were buildings in Prague—the first being the U Kaštanu house, where some activist workers founded the Social Democratic Party in 1878. It was considered an important part of the history of the workers' movement and the Communist Party narrative. In 1953, the son of one of the founders of the Social Democratic Party and the Czechoslovak president, Antonín Zápotocký, opened a museum on the origins of the workers' movement in this building. Lidový dům (the People's House) was the seat of the Social Democratic Party during the First Czechoslovak republic. An important event in Communist mythology, the Congress of the Social Democratic Party of Russia of 1912 that was led by V. I. Lenin, took place in this building. The Lidový dům was also turned into the Museum of Lenin in 1953.

At the National Memorial on Vítkov Hill, the other national cultural monument located in Prague, was the mausoleum of Klement Gottwald, the first Czechoslovak Communist president. He was embalmed and exhibited in the mausoleum between 1954 and 1962. However, the building itself has its roots in the interwar First Republic. It was built as a memorial to the Czechoslovak legionaries of World War I, although it was not finished until the beginning of World War II. In this case, the socialist regime appropriated the building that should have served as the key site for the sacral mythology of the former regime, the First Czechoslovak Republic. The new ideology filled the site with new meaning and values, but there was a strong continuity with the interwar period in the form and language used. It thus constitutes an important moment in the interpretation of the construction of identity of the new regime in the 1950s.

The authority of authorized heritage discourse grew stronger in subsequent years in Czechoslovakia. The government declared a large number of national cultural monuments in 1978,[40] suggesting a change in the structure and typology of protected heritage sites. The professional journal of heritage preservation explained that the extension of the list of monuments involved the addition of heritage sites relating to the workers' movement, antifascist resistance, and liberation by the Red Army that were underrepresented in the earlier list. The author of the article mentioned the thirtieth anniversary of the *Vítězný únor* (Victorious February, the 1948 coup and the beginning of the state socialist era in Czechoslovakia) as an opportunity for declaring new national cultural monuments.[41] In 1962, there were only three heritage sites directly connected with the workers' movement and another three connected with a socialist interpretation of modern history among thirty-three heritage sites. In 1978, however, ten heritage sites relating to the workers' movement and eight heritage sites connected to the resistance movement during World War II were listed among a total of twenty-five new national cultural monuments. The map of the heritage sites had changed radically, particularly the proportion of the most important places and eras that could be commemorated here. It is clear that the concept of heritage protection was developing dynamically. Under the socialist interpretation, heritage protection shifted away from a stress on the historical value of the artifacts—as many of the new heritage sites were symbolic, there was nothing to preserve, to reconstruct, or to touch from the past in such cases.

It is possible to see the continuity between the heritage values that had been preserved in the case of Duchcov viaduct since 1962 and the new set of monuments declared in 1978. The new national cultural monuments related to contemporary history, with the typical structure of a monument marking the place of an event with an accompanying memorial offering an interpretation. However, there was one important shift: the physical materiality of a heritage site was not decisive in order for something to receive the highest status of heritage protection. An object such as a viaduct that could be really protected, reconstructed, restored, and would compress the historicity of the event was not more likely to acquire such status after

1978. Instead, it was the symbolic meaning of a monument that provided sufficient value justifying heritage protection.

It can thus be argued that heritage protection was losing the referential framework that had linked it to the conservation of material artifacts and their value. Relatively new statues and memorials, museums and birthplaces (with no traditional value of the material artifacts created in history) became heritage. Obviously, one of the more important goals of socialist heritage preservation in Czechoslovakia was to protect the present and the contemporary interpretation of the past. The majority of these national cultural monuments, including the Duchcov viaduct, were stripped of the highest rank in heritage protection after 1989 as their value was too closely bound to the socialist interpretation of history (although they did retain the status of cultural monuments). They were removed from the highest level of heritage protection, but they remained largely unscathed in the public space. Sometimes, smaller modifications were made by adding to the text or by removing some of the more obvious ideological elements from a monument. Thus in Duchcov, for example, statues of a worker woman and a militiaman were removed, leaving only the main memorial in the form of a relief. Today, these monuments are often in bad shape and the local authorities often struggle to develop a coherent plan for them.

Four new heritage sites were declared national cultural monuments in the region of Northwest Bohemia in 1978, three of them connected with the workers' movement or with contemporary history—Osek, Velké Hamry, and Rumburk. Osek is already familiar from the 1949 list produced in Duchcov, with the memorial of the 1934 mine disaster being included on that list, rather than the monastery. In Velké Hamry, there was a memorial to a strike that happened in the 1930s, while Rumburk was declared a national cultural monument because a rebel was executed there during World War I. There were two challenges for constructing heritage in Northwest Bohemia, both of them relating to coal mining. The landscapes of Duchcov, Most, and a number of other cities had the potential to tell a story about the suffering, the struggle, and the victory of the working class, especially through events like strikes and mine disasters. But the coal mines also led to the destruction of different layers of memory in the landscape; the majority of the heritage sites on the 1949 list were no longer in existence at the beginning of the new millennium.

Destruction under Socialism and after 1989

Coal mining, particularly opencast mines, developed quickly throughout the region. The mining plans threatened the existence of cities and villages. The story of the destruction of the old city of Most and subsequent construction of the new city (the demolition of Most began in 1965) is particularly well known.[42] The city of Most was sacrificed to enable the development of coal mining. Matěj Spurný, who elaborated on the story in his book,[43] interprets the discourse relating to the demolition of an existing city and the construction of a new utopian city for the inhabitants who should produce a higher yield in coal mining as part of the productivist ideology. The old was to make way for the new. However, this process did not unfold without contestation, as heritage preservation was one of the fields where criticism was expressed.[44] This led to the strange coexistence of heritage values with a landscape that was transforming significantly and even saw a whole city relocated. The greatest evidence of this coexistence is the famous action of moving the Church of the Assumption of the Virgin Mary in 1975. The church was moved, using a track and specialist technology, to a location more than eight hundred meters away, while the tower was disassembled and rebuilt at the new site. This expensive action shows that the socialist authorities were interested in protecting the past, even if they used methods that might be seen as problematic with regard to maintaining the authenticity of the site.

Before the decision to destroy Most was made, state institutions, the management of mining companies (owned by the state), and also some professionals and public initiatives (for example, the Club for the Old Prague—Klub za starou Prahu) had been involved in negotiations since the 1950s. Lists of heritage sites in areas where there was potential to develop coal mining played an important role in the negotiation. It seems from the documents that it was the preserved medieval urban structure rather than particular monuments and heritage sites that were deemed to have significant heritage value. The lists contained only heritage sites related to religiosity and some burgess houses.[45] In this case, heritage preservation professionals applied the conception of heritage, manifested in architectural and art monuments, that had been handed down from the interwar period.

This pattern played out in Duchcov, too, where the castle park was once home to a Baroque hospital with a chapel that important artists of the time worked on (Ottavio Broggio, Václav Vavřinec Reiner, Matyáš Bernard Braun, and Ferdinand Maximilian Brokoff; 1716–28). The church, which was in poor condition due to neglect and the decline of the Waldstein noble family, was demolished in 1958 along with part of the park.[46] The site was supposed to be engulfed by an opencast mine.[47] But extensive discussions over the fate of the Baroque hospital, which can be traced in the correspondence between the representatives of the Ministry of Culture, the Ministry of Fuels, the regional government, representatives of the city, and a heritage association (Club for the Old Prague, at this time a platform for professionals in heritage preservation), makes clear that there were differences of opinion among state representatives during the socialist era (likewise in the 1950s) and that there were significant debates and discussions in the realm of political decision making, especially at the local level of politics. What was remarkable in this case were the arguments employed by the defenders of the hospital. The chief argument rested on the art–historical value of the building and pieces of art. There were also arguments that stressed the complex value of the town as a whole, as its revolutionary significance had by then become clear in the narratives attached to the viaduct. The discussions even referred to the social importance of the building, as it was dedicated to the care of the elderly. In one document, the role of the monuments in the process of creating bonds among the incoming Czech citizens who arrived after 1945 to the new homeland was also stressed.[48]

The historical agents operationalized their argumentation in line with the general conditions and the general discourse that ascribed important value to the monuments relating to social and revolutionary movements. This suggests acceptance of the discourse, even if it proved contradictory on some levels. For the purposes of the preservation of the Baroque heritage site, it was nevertheless necessary to find some progressive arguments. In the case of the hospital, this strategy succeeded only partly; the building was demolished, but some pieces of art and even the fresco were preserved. They were even publicly displayed later and used to illustrate successes of Czechoslovak heritage preservation. This story of the destroyed hospital is significant because it renders clear an important paradox in socialist heritage preservation. While many monuments and heritage sites were destroyed during the socialist era, the role of heritage preservation was stressed heavily in the public sphere, especially from late 1960s onward.[49] The hospital was destroyed, but the highly valued fresco in the dome by V. V. Reiner was saved and removed in 1956 before the destruction and could thus be exhibited during the EXPO in Montréal eleven years later. Then, in 1983, it was displayed at a new pavilion built for the fresco in the chateau garden. Here the apparent success of heritage preservation was manifested in the fresco put on exhibition in the new frame of the pavilion. However, the story of the threatened fresco was not over as the architecture and construction of the pavilion did not prove entirely compatible with the fresco and it has been fading and vanishing continuously to this day.

Some other pieces of art and places from the 1949 list vanished definitively: three of the municipalities have so far been demolished: Fláje made way for a water reservoir, while Liptice and Libkovice were replaced by mine pits. Fláje and Liptice were destroyed during the state-socialist era, but the story of Libkovice is particularly interesting because it was the last village in the Czech Republic to be demolished because of mining. This happened in 1991–93, but the village church was not demolished until 2002. The decision to demolish the village was made before the Velvet Revolution of 1989. The inhabitants of Libkovice were not able to use the reestablished democratic mechanisms and institutions to save their homes after 1989. Libkovice became a testbed where some new rules of the civic society were negotiated. For example, Greenpeace activists were involved in blocking the demolition and succeeded in preserving the church. However, as the major part of the village had vanished, the church standing alone in the landscape of mining lost its meaning and it finally disappeared without any media interest in 2002.

Conclusion

The concept of socialist heritage developed dynamically. Focusing on a relatively small area, it becomes evident in this chapter that the postwar socialist concept of heritage draws on earlier notions of heritage preceding World War II. In Northwest Bohemia, socialist concepts of heritage intersected with the tradition of solidarity among coal miners and traditions of remembering the dead. In the revolutionary atmosphere of the early 1950s, the grounds for a new form of relating to the past, and also for its public presentation, came into existence. The Duchcov viaduct, a site of conflict in the 1930s, became the focal point of authorized heritage discourse in the region during the 1950s, and this was ultimately manifested in its proclamation as a national cultural monument in 1962. This railway bridge embodied a new type of prominent socialist heritage site that commemorated important events in the official interpretation of recent history. In the case of Duchcov, the materiality of the bridge played an important role that expressed the event and legitimized heritage protection. In 1978, when a new series of national cultural heritage sites was declared, this materiality was not a necessary criterion for being granted protected status as the symbolic meaning of new built statues and memorials was sufficient.

During the socialist era, the cultural practice of visiting chateaus and castles (estate museums) enjoyed ever increasing popularity. Despite the official efforts to use these monuments in a socialist interpretation of history, the Romantic touch of the past attracted the attention of visitors the most. These examples show just how complex the legacies of socialist heritage preservation are. The main characteristic of heritage preservation, especially in the 1970s and 1980s, was an emphasis on the presentation of the act of preservation itself and the accessibility of cultural heritage to a broad working-class audience. Heritage preservation was supposed to be the last chapter of a narrative that argued that the victory of the working class made the preservation of artifacts from the past centuries necessary. But these historical artifacts were not supposed to refer to their previous owners from the nobility, the church, and the bourgeoisie. Instead, they were to function as an illustration of the skillfulness and mastery of the workers. This was how heritage was presented in public discourse in socialist Czechoslovakia with a focus on the labor invested in them by the creators of sites, buildings, and works of art.

There were more complicated processes under these layers, with some specialists in preservation trying to save as much from the past as possible, whatever its ideological significance, in complicated conditions. In the preservation of monuments of the working class, the discursive practices proved more significant and successful in the sphere of management and interpretation than in the sphere of tourism and leisure. Officials did not succeed in incorporating the new socialist memorials into cultural practices of visiting monuments. This could be one reason why after 1989 the consensus about socialist heritage dissolved so quickly. The significant rupture in preservation discourse and practice was particularly evident in the new types of socialist monuments, such as Duchcov viaduct whose heritage value was soon denied and reduced in 1989. Indeed, in the course of the transformation of heritage preservation in the 1990s, some processes rooted in socialist-era practices continued, leading to the destruction of some heritage sites (as in the case of Libkovice), while there clearly was continuity in the way the chateaus and castles (estate museums) were subsequently interpreted.

Socialist heritage preservation makes visible some structural changes in ways of relating to the past. The same kinds of changes occurred and continue across European societies. The case studies explored here illustrate how historical agents adopted and adapted concepts and practices in heritage preservation in local conditions, using the concept of socialist heritage for their own purposes. Socialist heritage sites were, on the one hand, a way of projecting a new identity onto a region that had undergone modernizing transformation and ethnic cleansing. On the other hand, heritage became a tool for preserving different heritage sites and different values to those intended by the state's authorized heritage discourse. This local focus is a relevant and important approach to the concept of heritage in other regions that also experienced such dramatic transformation in the twentieth century.

Čeněk Pýcha holds a PhD in History from the Faculty of Arts at Charles University in Prague. His dissertation project focused on the issue of the mediality of history in contemporary society. He works as lecturer and researcher at the Department of Education of the Institute for the Study of

Totalitarian Regimes. He conducts research in the fields of memory and media studies, and history didactics. He has contributed to several edited volumes and is a coauthor of several history education applications.

Notes

Work on this chapter was supported by the project "The Museum of Working Class Movement in 21st Century. Presentation of the Use of the Museum Collection Created in the Era of State Socialism and the Ways of Use of Its Materials for Professional and Wide Public" (DG18P02OVV045) and financed by the Ministry of Culture Czech Republic.

1. The Communist interpretation of Czechoslovak history is expressed in the work of one of the leading ideologists of the Communist Party, Zdeněk Nejedlý. See Nejedlý, *Komunisté, dědici*.
2. Glassheim, *Cleansing the Czechoslovak Borderlands*, 118–19.
3. Smith, *Uses of Heritage*.
4. On the history of Duchcov, see Wolf, *Duchcov*.
5. de Certeau, *The Practice of Everyday Life*. Besides Michel de Certeau, I have also drawn on the understanding of space developed by Karl Schlögel. See: Schlögel, *Im Raume lesen wir die Zeit*.
6. Industrial coal mining was developed there from the second half of the nineteenth century, although the first coal mines had opened in the eighteenth century already. Coal mining also changed the physical character of the landscape. From a cultural–historical perspective, the period of the Waldstein dynasty's reign in the seventeenth and eighteenth centuries had a significant influence on the region, giving the urban landscape its Baroque facade. In the nineteenth and twentieth centuries, industry (especially coal mining) developed quickly, and the character of the landscape became increasingly industrial.
7. Smith, *Uses of Heritage*, 13.
8. Some case studies are included in Stenning, "Placing (Post-)Socialism."
9. Glassheim, *Cleansing the Czechoslovak Borderlands*; Spurný, *Making the Most*.
10. See for example: Nowotny, Wranová, and Trevisan, "Heritage Protection."
11. See for example: Karous, *Vetřelci a volavky = Aliens and Herons*; Klíma, *Kotvy Máje*.
12. Lowenthal, "Fabricating Heritage"; Swenson, *The Rise of Heritage*.
13. Hall, "Whose Heritage."
14. Smith, *Uses of Heritage*, 29.
15. Randák, *V záři rudého kalicha*.
16. There was a project mapping heritage sites led by the Czech Academy of Science that began before World War I and continued during the First Czechoslovak Republic (*Soupis památek historických a uměleckých v království Českém*; *Soupis památek historických a uměleckých v Republice československé*—Lists of Historical and Art Monuments in the Bohemian Kingdom and the Czechoslovak Republic, respectively), but the volumes focused on Northwestern Bohemia were never completed or published.

17. Krejčí, "Možnosti a limity."
18. Uhlíková, *Národní kulturní komise*.
19. National Archive Prague, Kolegium ministra kultury, 15 September 1960, Návrh na využití a instalační zaměření hradů a zámků; Netková and Svatoňová, "Návštěvní řády."
20. Giustino, "Open Gates and Wandering Minds."
21. Muchka, "Vstupní historické a specializované expozice."
22. National Archive Prague, Kolegium ministra kultury, 29 November 1962, Za další rozvoj památkové péče v ČSSR.
23. Giustino, "Open Gates and Wandering Minds," 66.
24. Krejčí, "Ochrana památek."
25. For more on the terminology applied in heritage preservation from 1789 to 1914, see Astrid Swenson: "Historic preservation was not only one of the earliest forms of institutionalized preservation, but across languages the term 'monument' was also understood in a much wider way, than it is today. It was often applied to designate tangible but also intangible remains from the past much like 'heritage' is now." Swenson, *The Rise of Heritage*, 12–13.
26. "A canon is not a hit-list, it is instead independent of historical change and immune to the ups and downs of social taste. The canon is now built up anew by every generation, on the contrary, it outlives the generations who have to encounter and reinterpret it anew according to their time. This constant interaction with the small selection of artifacts keeps them in active circulation and maintains for this small segment of the past a continuous presence." A. Assmann, "Canon and Archive," 100.
27. Národní památkový ústav, archiv, spisy zámek Duchcov, inv. č. 2582, folder-files 1949–1973. Seznam památností okresu duchcovského, 1949.
28. Duchcov was a separate administrative district until 1960.
29. J. Assmann, "Communicative and Cultural Memory."
30. For more on this topic, see Hojda and Pokorný, *Pomníky a zapomníky*.
31. National Archive Prague, Statní památková správa 1946–1964 (State Heritage Administration). Fund number 864, file 152.
32. Czechoslovak law number 22/1958: Law about cultural monuments.
33. See Pýcha, "Duchcovský viadukt."
34. According to a letter to the sculptor from the municipal government, 23 May 1953. State district archive Teplice, ONV v Duchcově (District National Committee, Duchcov), collection 15A/4, 282.
35. Cach, *Duchcovský viadukt*.
36. Fučík, *Reportáže z buržoazní republiky*.
37. National Heritage Institute Ústí nad Labem, archive, writings concerning the Duchcov viaduct, folder Duchcov. Council of Duchcov, 4 April 1968, signed by Jaroslav Vrkoslav, secretary, and Josef Záda, chairman.
38. National Heritage Institute Ústí nad Labem, archive, writings concerning the Duchcov viaduct, folder Duchcov. National cultural monument Duchcovský viadukt—suggestion for abolition, 15 March 1968, National concern Doly Julia Fučíka.
39. Resolution of the government dated 30 March 1962, number 251. It refers to the declaration of some sites as national cultural monuments.
40. Resolution of the government n. 70/78 from day 24 February 1978. It refers to the declaration of some sites as national cultural monuments.

41. Svobodová, "Nové národní kulturní památky."
42. Especially Glassheim, *Cleansing the Czechoslovak Borderlands*, 123–46; Spurný, *Making the Most of Tomorrow*, 279–350.
43. Spurný, *Making the Most of Tomorrow*.
44. Ibid., 279–350.
45. National Archive Prague, Statní památková správa 1946–1964 (State Heritage Administration). Fund number 864, file 354, Most—územní plán (spatial planning).
46. The Waldstein family sold the chateau to the Czechoslovak state in 1920 while the hospital was sold to the Czech Building Cooperative in 1931. Hochel, *Valdštejnský Špitál*, 9.
47. Hochel, *Valdštejnský Špitál*.
48. Ibid., documents no. 1–40.
49. For a different perspective on the topic, see Giustino, "Open Gates and Wandering Minds."

Bibliography

Assmann, Aleida. "Canon and Archive." In *Cultural Memory Studies: An International and Interdisciplinary Handbook*, edited by Astrid Erll and Ansgar Nünning, 97–108. Berlin: de Gruyter, 2008.
Assmann, Jan. "Communicative and Cultural Memory." In *Cultural Memory Studies: An International and Interdisciplinary Handbook*, edited by Astrid Erll and Ansgar Nünning, 109–18. Berlin: de Gruyter, 2008.
Cach, Vojtěch. *Duchcovský viadukt: hra o 5 dějstvích*. Prague: Sešity divadelní žatvy, 1952.
de Certeau, Michel. *The Practice of Everyday Life*. Berkeley: University of California Press, 1984.
Fučík, Julius. *Reportáže z buržoazní republiky: Z let 1929–1934*. Prague: Státní nakladatelství politické literatury, 1953.
Giustino, Cathleen. "Open Gates and Wandering Minds: Codes, Castles and Chateaux in Socialist Czechoslovakia before 1960." In *Socialist Escapes: Breaking Away from Ideology and Everyday Routine in Eastern Europe, 1945–1989*, edited by Cathleen Giustino, Catherine Plum, and Alexander Vari, 48–72. New York: Berghahn Books, 2013.
Glassheim, Eagle. *Cleansing the Czechoslovak Borderlands: Migration, Environment, and Health in the Former Sudetenland*. Pittsburgh: University of Pittsburgh Press, 2016
Hall, Stuart. "Whose Heritage? Un-settling 'the Heritage,' Re-imagining the Post-Nation." *Third Text* 13, no. 49 (1999): 3–13.
Hochel, Marian, ed. *Valdštejnský Špitál a Reinerova Freska Nanebevzetí Panny Marie v Duchcově: obrazy a dokumenty*. Opava: Slezská univerzita v Opavě, 2014.
Hojda, Zdeněk, and Jiří Pokorný. *Pomníky a zapomníky*. Prague: Paseka, 1996.
Karous, Pavel, ed. *Vetřelci a volavky: atlas výtvarného umění ve veřejném prostoru v Československu v období normalizace (1968–1989) = Aliens and Herons: A Guide to Fine Art in the Public Space in the Era of Normalisation in Czechoslovakia (1968–1989)*. Řevnice: Arbor vitae, 2013

Klíma, Petr, ed. *Kotvy Máje: české obchodní domy 1965–1975*. Prague: Vysoká škola uměleckoprůmyslová v Praze, 2011.

Koura, Petr. "Die Visualisierung der Vernichtung: Das Dorf Lidice als tschechischer Erinnerungort." In *Krieg im Museum: Präsentationen des Zweiten Weltkriegs in Museen und Gedenkstätten des östlichen Europa*, edited by E. Makhotina, E. Keding, W. Borodziej, E. François, and M. Schulze Wessel, 183–201. Göttingen: Vandenhoeck & Ruprecht, 2015.

Krejčí, Marek. "Možnosti a limity meziválečné památkové péče." In *Věda a technika v českých zemích mezi světovými válkami*, edited by J. Kleinová, 347–56. Prague: Národní technické muzeum, 2014.

———. "Ochrana památek v 50. letech." In *Věda a technika v Československu v letech 1945–1960*, edited by M. Hořejší, 97–109. Prague: Národní technické muzeum, 2010.

Lowenthal, David. "Fabricating Heritage." *History and Memory* 10, no. 1 (1998): 5–24.

Muchka, Ivan. "Vstupní historické a specializované expozice na hradech a zámcích v ČSR." *Památky a příroda* 5 (1978): 257–66.

Nejedlý, Zdeněk. *Komunisté, dědici velikých tradic českého národa*. Prague: Okresní výbor Komunistické strany Československa, 1947.

Netková, Jarmila, and Jana Svatoňová. "Návštěvní řády a zpřístupňování hradů a zámků." *Památky a příroda* 5 (1984): 449–60.

Nowotny, Vojta, Alena Wranová, and Jitka Trevisan. "Heritage Protection Versus Individual Interests in a Post-Socialist Country: The Case of Mšeno, Czech Republic." *European Spatial Research & Policy* 21, no. 2 (2014): 83–96.

Pýcha, Čeněk. "Duchcovský viadukt. Socialistická politika paměti na regionální úrovni." In *Česká paměť: Národ, dějiny a místa paměti*, edited by Radka Šustrová and Luba Hédlová, 255–57. Prague: Academia, 2014.

Randák, Jan. *V záři rudého kalicha: Politika dějin a husitská tradice v Československu 1948–1956*. Prague: Univerzita Karlova Filozofická fakulta, 2015.

Schlögel, Karl. *Im Raume lesen wir die Zeit: über Zivilisationsgeschichte und Geopolitik*. Frankfurt am Main: Fischer-Taschenbuch-Verlag, 2009.

Smith, Laurajane. *Uses of Heritage*. London: Routledge, 2006.

Spurný, Matěj. *Making the Most of Tomorrow: A Laboratory of Socialist Modernity in Czechoslovakia*. Prague: Karolinum Press, 2019.

Stenning, Alison. "Placing (Post-)Socialism: The Making and Remaking of Nowa Huta, Poland." *European Urban and Regional Studies* 7, no. 2 (2000): 99–118.

Svobodová, Otilie. "Nové národní kulturní památky." *Památky a Příroda* 4 (1978): 193–203.

Swenson, Astrid. *The Rise of Heritage: Preserving the Past in France, Germany and England, 1789–1914*. Cambridge, UK: Cambridge University Press, 2015.

Uhlíková, Kristina. *Národní kulturní komise 1947–1951*. Prague: Artefactum, 2004.

Wolf, Jiří, ed. *Duchcov*. Prague: NLN, 2013.

CHAPTER 8

Socialism and the Rise of Industrial Heritage
The Preservation of Industrial Monuments in the German Democratic Republic

Nele-Hendrikje Lehmann

Industrial heritage has been considered a "neglected heritage" for a long time. At the end of the 1960s only a few countries, such as Great Britain, Poland, Sweden, the Federal Republic of Germany (FRG), and the German Democratic Republic (GDR) engaged in the preservation of industrial monuments.[1] However, within a decade the situation had changed significantly. Physical traces and remnants of the industrial past came to be accepted among national conservation bodies in many European countries as an important part of heritage. The number of specialists in the field grew rapidly and close international cooperation began.[2] The increasing interest in industrial heritage in the last third of the twentieth century has been the subject of extensive discussion.[3] Although the GDR and Poland are considered pioneers in the preservation of industrial monuments, the developments in these former socialist countries have received much less attention than those in the West.[4]

Focusing on the GDR, this chapter investigates the relationship between industrial heritage and socialist cultural policy. Historians have argued that the particular attention paid to the industrial monuments in the GDR was a result of the Marxist–Leninist understanding of history prescribed by the Socialist Unity Party of Germany (SED).[5] According to this argument, such monuments could easily fit with the state's propaganda policy.[6] At first sight, the argument seems convincing. In comparison to castles, mansions, and churches, industrial monuments at least constituted an ideologically unproblematic heritage for the government of the GDR. Hammer mills, tin buddles, and railroad bridges were easy to integrate into a Marxist-influenced history of productive forces and production relations.[7] Moreover, they could be used as an educational tool to illustrate the rapid development of the productive forces.

However, it is not enough to ascribe the success of industrial monument preservation in the GDR only to a Marxist–Leninist view of history. Such an approach would run the risk of ignoring the changing concepts of heritage and neglecting the fact that technical and industrial remnants were underrepresented in the GDR's inventory of monuments for a long time.[8] This chapter argues that the preservation of industrial monuments in the GDR was initially strongly influenced by concepts that had emerged already in the first third of the twentieth century, thus showing a tension between the propagated modernization and the necessity of accommodating the past in the 1950s. It presents the 1970s as a turning point and asserts that conceptual changes resulted from the SED's new cultural policy that guided the simultaneous internationalization and nationalization. This chapter examines the GDR's role in the emerging international debate and how this influenced the concepts of industrial monuments that emerged in East Germany and in international discourses. Thus, it presents the rise of industrial heritage as a result of multidirectional transfer processes.

Breaking with the Past?
Industrial Monuments in the GDR in the 1950s and 1960s

To show how the preservation of industrial monuments in the GDR was initially influenced by concepts of the 1920s and 1930s, I will first present a short historical outline. The preservation of technical artifacts began about 1900, when Germany emerged as one the most powerful industrial countries in the world. It was mainly initiated by the Association of German Engineers and was an expression of their growing self-confidence. In the nineteenth century, engineers in Germany had held a lower reputation than academics. Struggling for recognition and equal status, they started to use historical narratives to present technology as an intellectual and cultural achievement. The bourgeois concept of "culture" served as a criterion for social distinction.[9] It was used to draw a clear dividing line between the educated middle classes and those working with their hands. Since technology was associated more commonly with the hand than the mind, its cultural value was denied for a long time. In 1906, the engineers' efforts led to the foundation of the German Museum of Science and Technology in Munich. Its purpose was to show the "masterpieces" of science and technology and thus put them on an equal footing with art.[10]

In 1926–27, the first nationwide survey on industrial monuments was initiated by the German Museum, the Association of German Engineers, and the Bund Heimatschutz (Homeland Protection Society). While the German Museum managed only the central archive, the Bund Heimatschutz with its local and regional affiliations carried out the nationwide registration of industrial monuments.[11] At first glance, the interest of the Heimatschutz movement in industrial monuments may seem astounding. In its contemporary understanding, *Heimat* (homeland) formed a counterpoint to the industrialized society with its economic, political, and social tensions.[12] Thus, the Heimatschutz was a group that wanted to protect nature as well as the traditional way of life. Nevertheless, its program was not completely antimodern but tried to connect both sides, propagating an industrial architecture that was adapted to the landscape. A key figure in the movement was the architect Werner Lindner, who was later responsible for the integration of the Heimatschutz in the organizations of the National Socialists.[13] His interest in industrial monuments began in the early 1920s. He considered industrial monuments not only worthy of preservation but also a stimulus for good design in the future and thus as a means to reconcile tradition and modernization.[14] Lindner's close cooperation with Conrad Matschoß, director of the Association of German Engineers, had a major impact on the concept of industrial monuments, which was closely linked to the concepts of *Kultur* (culture) and *Heimat*. Their coauthored compilation, *Technische Kulturdenkmale* (Technical Cultural Monuments), which was published in 1932, focused mainly on pre- and early industrial monuments out of the fields of mining and metallurgy, power engines, construction, as well as crafts, trade, and peasant culture.[15]

After the war, a new legal basis was established in 1952 with the Ordinance for the Preservation of the National Cultural Monuments of the GDR. Beside art and architectural monuments, it also protected technical and industrial artifacts.[16] This offered new opportunities, which, however, were seized only by few preservationists. When in 1952 the five *Länder* were dissolved and replaced by fourteen districts (plus Berlin), the former Landesämter für Denkmalpflege (State Offices for Historic Preservation) were not broken up but incorporated as branch offices into a new central Institut für Denkmalpflege (Institute for Historic Preservation).[17] As Brian Campbell has shown, personal and institutional continuity "allowed the old offices to continue operating as they always had."[18] For this reason, the early activities almost exclusively concentrated on those parts of the GDR that already possessed a strong tradition in the care of industrial monuments, like Saxony. The foremost actor here was the architect Hans Nadler, chief conservator at the Dresden branch office. Under his direction, the branch office registered more than one thousand objects and restored several industrial monuments like the tin buddle at Altenberg.[19] Furthermore, Nadler stepped up efforts to raise the esteem of industrial monuments in the consciousness of the public.[20] In 1952, the exhibition *Technische Kulturdenkmale* (technical cultural monuments) based on drawings of the Dresden Institute was displayed at the Görlitz Municipal Art Collection.[21] Three years later, Nadler organized a touring exhibition on the same subject, which became a great success.[22] It was shown in twenty-three locations and attended by over four hundred thousand people.[23]

Nadler, who maintained the name *Technische Kulturdenkmale* for the touring exhibition, still felt obliged to emphasize in the introduction to the catalogue that technology should be seen as a part of the intellectual tradition of the people. Therefore, industrial monuments were to enjoy the same attention and care as the great works of architecture, sculpture, and painting.[24] A closer look at the conception of the exhibition reveals strong similarities with 1920s monument preservation. Like the publication *Technische Kulturdenkmale* by Matschoß and Lindner, the exhibition concentrated on pre- and early industrial monuments out of the fields of power engines, mining and metallurgy, construction, as well as crafts, trade, and peasant culture.[25] In particular, it focused on buildings that had shaped the landscape for centuries, such as those associated with ore mining in Saxony. Seeing the great achievements of the past would deepen people's love for their *Heimat*, argued Nadler.[26] Hence, industrial monuments should not only be regarded as culture, but also as a *wertvolles Stück Heimat* (precious piece of *Heimat*).[27]

At first glance, the similarities with the publication of Lindner and Matschoß as well as the references to the *Heimat* ideal may seem surprising. Due to their conservative attitude and regional orientation, the Heimatschutz groups were considered a danger to the state's efforts to build socialism.[28] Like all other associations, they were dissolved in 1949. The Party leadership, however, could not ignore the huge popularity of *Heimat* groups and practices among GDR citizens, and it therefore recognized the potential of the *Heimat* ideal for the construction of legitimacy.[29] Connecting the ideological concerns of the Party with the *Heimat* ideal was to help reconcile citizens with political, social, and economic transformation.

After the abolition of the independent associations, working groups for Natur- und Heimatfreunde (Friends of Nature and Homeland) were established within the Kulturbund (Cultural Association for the Democratic Renewal of Germany) to incorporate the members of the former *Heimat* groups. As many members of the former Heimatschutz joined, the Natur- and Heimatfreunde soon became the largest section of the Kulturbund, an organization that had been initially founded to overcome Nazism through a reappraisal of German classics.[30] Gerhard Thümmler, secretary of the Dresden District Administration for the Natur- und Heimatfreunde, initiated a close cooperation with the Dresden State Office for Historic Preservation, as had previously been the case with the Saxon Heimatschutz.[31] The cooperation resulted in joint publications, such as the journal *Natur und Heimat* (Nature and Homeland), which were intended to help convert the regional affiliation of the readers into loyalty toward the GDR.[32] With the socialist redefinition of *Heimat*, the *völkisch* and nationalist tendencies that existed within the *Heimat* groups before 1945 vanished.[33] However, the SED was not immediately able to alter cultural practices and traditions that persisted on a local level, as publications and exhibitions on industrial monuments in the 1950s show.[34] Subtly, they reflected the tensions between the pursuit of modernization and the necessity of accommodating the past. The conservation of industrial monuments was thus more a continuation of tradition than the radical new start that it was later presented as.

As the GDR still struggled to achieve economic consolidation at the end of the 1950s, science and technology began to play a crucial role in the policy of Walter Ulbricht, First Secretary of the Central Committee of the SED between 1953 and 1971. Both were considered decisive factors for industrial development and therefore also for the competition between the two rival political systems in East and West Germany.[35] In this context, technical education was introduced at schools and the foundation of technical museums was promoted. The fact that industrial monuments could not benefit from this development was probably due to the general situation of historic preservation, which changed drastically with the 1961 Decree on the Preservation of Historical Monuments. It paved the way for the final incorporation of historic preservation into the administrative structure of the GDR. The central Institut für Denkmalpflege, which was closed due to inefficiency in 1956, was reopened and given new responsibilities.[36] It was answerable to the Minister of Culture as a central scientific institution responsible for the preparation and guidance of the collection, protection, care, and development of monuments.[37] It had to advise the state institutions on the conception of monuments and monument preservation measures. The ultimate responsibility lay with the Ministry of Culture, which was able to independently direct the work on monuments of particular national importance.[38] Within the new centralized structure, the branch offices lost their autonomy. At the same time, historic preservation got a stronger national orientation as funding priorities were shifted to monuments that had national importance. Focusing on national achievements rather than on local traditions, the new preservation policy of the SED discouraged local groups from engaging in historic preservation.[39] For this reason, Hans Nadler and his colleagues from the other branch offices protested against these measures, but in vain.[40] The situation did not change until the 1970s, when major political changes led to a new concept of heritage.

International Cooperation and the Rise of "Industrial Heritage"

While in the 1950s and 1960s only a few countries engaged in the preservation of industrial monuments, interest increased rapidly in the 1970s. The reasons for this are not easy to discern, but most scholars agree that major changes in economic structures and cultural values provided a background for the emergence of an industrial heritage culture.[41] During the first two postwar decades, many European countries experienced unprecedented economic growth and modernization of the industrial sector. Plants expanded rapidly, as did residential areas together with road and transport infrastructure. Historic buildings and structures had to give way to reconstruction. This led to new challenges and realignments in the field of historic preservation that had abandoned its narrow focus on art history and become more involved in urban development planning.[42] The reorientation went hand in hand with a new concept of culture that focused less on elites and more on everyday life and ordinary people. At the same time, the economic crisis of the 1970s led to profound economic and social transformation in most Western European countries. As the textile industry and heavy industry declined, many plants and coal mines closed down with large-scale unemployment as a result.[43] While optimism and confidence in the future faded, historical heritage became more important as it promised consolation in the pride of a grand past.[44]

Nevertheless, there were huge differences in the economic and cultural trajectories between the individual countries. Since most existing studies relate to Western European countries, further research into the former socialist bloc countries will broaden our understanding of the emergence of an industrial heritage culture. Before I discuss the development in the GDR in more detail, I will focus on the transnational dimension of industrial heritage, in which international cooperation and transnational transfer processes constituted further important reasons for the rise of industrial heritage.

In 1973, the newly opened Ironbridge Gorge Museum hosted the First International Congress on the Conservation of Industrial Monuments (FICCIM). Scholars and monument conservators from the East and West were invited to present and discuss their respective national situations and working methods.[45] The congress at Ironbridge was a great success and led to further international conferences in the 1970s: the second (SICCIM) in 1975 in West Germany and the third (TICCIM) in 1978 in Sweden. The number of participants increased rapidly. While the first congress was attended by sixty delegates from eight countries, the congress in Sweden was already attended by over 140 delegates from nineteen countries.[46] Because the first congresses were mainly driven by personal engagement, the participants tried to foster an institutionalization of their collaboration. This resulted in the publication of congress transactions, which gained huge international attention.[47] A further step was the foundation of the International Committee for the Conservation of the Industrial Heritage (TICCIH) in 1978, which two years later became affiliated with UNESCO.[48] As representative of the GDR, Eberhard Wächtler was appointed to the board.

The congresses and the networks they created were the most important platforms for exchanging ideas and concepts across state borders and ideological divides. The regional reports on industrial archeology in particular provided a valuable summary of the state of preservation and research in various countries. At SICCIM, reports were presented by delegates from Austria, Italy, Belgium, the Netherlands, Czechoslovakia, Hungary, Poland, the USSR, Japan, Sweden, Norway, Denmark, Britain, the United States, the FRG, the GDR, and Canada. Because industrialization was regarded as a global phenomenon, the congresses were intended to help define which traces of the industrial past were to be considered indispensable "not only nationally but also from an international point of view—landmarks of the industrial history of the world."[49] This was not an easy task. As the Secretary of the first congress, Neil Cossons, remarked, "no unity of attitude resulted from the discussions of papers on conservation policies and legislation and the reviews or work carried out in various countries. Indeed, so varied were the themes of papers in these sessions that it was sometimes difficult at first to find areas of common concern and understanding."[50] Not only did the ideological backgrounds of the participants differ but so did their motivations, concepts, and methods.

The search for a common approach extended existing concepts, with industrial archeology probably the most prominent among them. It had been developed in Britain from the end of the 1950s to stop the ongoing decay and destruction of industrial buildings. Adopting methods of classical archeology and history, the new research field was intended to collect, preserve, and interpret the physical remains of past industries.[51] In the early years, however, the focus was mainly on the preservation of artifacts of the production process and the explanation of their technological functions. Moreover, due to the strong influence of amateur volunteers engaged in the field, the balance was tipped in favor of description.[52] In the 1960s, industrial archeology gained ground in other countries, including Sweden, the Federal Republic of Germany, and the United States.[53] Nevertheless, the approach employed by British industrial archeology was criticized for being too narrow, with some scholars like Ákos Paulinyi instead favoring the concept of "material culture" that had been institutionalized at the Polish Academy of Sciences in the 1950s.[54] It was conceived as an interdisciplinary research field between history, archeology, and ethnography that focused not only on the history of production but also on aspects of distribution and consumption.[55] Moreover, it was not limited to industry but also included agriculture and crafts. The most important enhancement, however, was the integration of social–historical issues, something to which most scholars consented. With the rise of social history and the influence of neo-Marxism, the history of the working-class movement, as well as the working and living conditions of the disadvantaged classes, had moved into focus likewise in Western countries. As a result, in West Germany the new concept of *Industriekultur* (industrial culture) emerged. It focused not only on industrial monuments but also on the history, present and future, of industrialized society.[56] However, the intention of some East and West German scholars to connect industrial monuments with current political issues was rejected by others, who criticized the growing politicization of the field and claimed scientific neutrality instead.[57]

Despite—or perhaps precisely because of—the ideological and methodological differences, some general trends emerged in the preservation and interpretation of industrial monuments. The study of industrial artifacts was conceived as an interdisciplinary research field that included both scholars and amateur volunteers. While at the beginning the "interest in the history of technology in its narrowest meaning"[58] had dominated, the focus shifted to the social aspects of industrialization like working and living conditions. Furthermore, the interest turned from individual monuments to industrial environments. These conceptual changes led finally to a semantic shift. After the third congress in 1978, the word "heritage" replaced the word "monuments" in the title. The new wording "industrial heritage" was enigmatic enough to accommodate the different approaches, methods, and political views.

Heritage and the Socialist Nation

Closer international cooperation in the 1970s was enabled by a policy of détente, which led to the Basic Treaty with the FRG and subsequently to growing diplomatic recognition of the GDR. In 1972, the GDR became a member of UNESCO, which adopted the World Heritage Convention the same year. The foreign policy of détente coincided with major changes in home affairs. With the Eighth Party Congress of the SED in 1971, the Walter Ulbricht era came to an end. His successor, Erich Honecker, initiated a radical change in social and economic policy.[59] Increasing the material and cultural living standards of the people became the central task of politics—hence, the government's new policy pushed the production of consumer goods and housing construction. This was intended, first and foremost, as a response to the increasing dissatisfaction of the population. Since material and cultural needs were seen as forming a single whole, these decisions also had a major impact on cultural policy and particularly on the concept of cultural heritage.[60]

In October 1974, a colloquium on cultural heritage was hosted in Weimar. Organized by the National Research and Memorial Sites of Classical German Literature in Weimar, the Academy of Sciences, the Academy of Arts, the Institute of Social Sciences at the Central Committee of the SED, the Friedrich Schiller University Jena, and the Kulturbund, the colloquium discussed the role of cultural heritage in the "developed socialist society." Two significant conceptual changes became apparent in the debate. First, the prevailing concept of cultural heritage was criticized as too narrow. Even in the GDR, as critics emphasized, it was limited to art and science while neglecting the creative heritage of the workers.[61] Horst Haase, Professor at the Institute of Social Sciences at the Central Committee of the SED, was particularly emphatic in demanding a broader concept of culture that would also include the working and living conditions of ordinary people. He claimed that the history of the productive forces should play a bigger part in the appropriation of heritage and emphasized the vividness of technical and agricultural monuments as a great advantage for the mass propaganda of working traditions.[62] Secondly, it became clear that the cultural heritage debate aimed at creating a national consciousness in the GDR that would be qualitatively different from that of the FRG.[63] Honecker, who followed Soviet policy on Europe and Germany, had abandoned the idea of an all-German nation at the Eighth Party Congress, as the intensification of relations between the two German states demanded concomitantly stronger demarcation.[64] Thus, he propagated the existence of two nations, a capitalist one and a socialist one.[65] The proclaimed "socialist German nation" needed historical legitimacy. Thus, the GDR had to determine its relationship to German history before 1945 and clarify what should be included in a national history. Concentrating on the history of the labor movement no longer seemed sufficient to create a national identity.[66] Rather, all of German history was seen as heritage. It included both the material–objective heritage and the totality of past economic, social, political, ideological, and cultural conditions.

Since German history contained elements that seemed unsuitable for appropriation, a distinction was made between heritage and tradition.[67] What fell under the definition of tradition were those historical lines of development on which the GDR was based, which it preserved and continued. Tradition was thus just one component of the entire heritage.[68] Kurt Hager, chief ideologist of the SED Politbüro, put it this way: "We must face the heritage we find in its entirety in order to develop a clear position on it. Traditions always entail valorization of heritage from the standpoint of a certain class and a certain *Weltanschauung* [worldview]. They are assessed and adopted to the extent that they contribute to solving current problems and offer an insight into the future."[69] Tradition was thus considered the legacy of those who contributed to "progress," regardless of their class affiliation. Consequently, previously neglected topics such as Prussian history or Martin Luther and the Reformation experienced a renaissance.[70] At the same time, the expanded concept of cultural heritage was well-suited to the existing *Heimat* practices and brought local and regional traditions back into focus.[71]

The reinterpretation of heritage provided new opportunities for the preservation of industrial monuments. However, it also entailed growing politicization and integration into a Marxist-influenced history of productive forces and production relations. This ideological framework produced Eberhard Wächtler, who became one of the most prominent figures within industrial monument preservation after 1970. Having studied history, philosophy, and political economy in Leipzig between 1948 and 1953, he then worked as a scientific assistant at the Institute of Economic History at the Berlin Academy of Sciences, until he became a professor at the Bergakademie Freiberg in 1962.[72] His interest in preserving industrial monuments began in the mid-1960s when he heard a lecture by the British economic historian William O. Henderson on the preservation of industrial monuments in Britain and the new discipline of industrial archeology.[73] After advocating the preservation of several industrial monuments in the GDR, Wächtler began to explore the subject more theoretically. He argued that the Marxist conception of history as well as the propagation of the history of the productive forces would necessarily require the maintenance of industrial monuments, which were part of the socialist tradition. The most difficult task, he argued, drawing on Lenin's words, was not the revolution itself but the further development of the productive forces.[74] Since new things could only be created by using or overcoming the old, Wächtler stated, progress would need tradition.[75] Hence, all traditions of creative power should be maintained and used as educational means. "We see the old technology as weapons, in which the experience of workers, technicians and scientists is incorporated, crystallized creative power. According to this historic experience, we see the old and new technology as weapons, which we have to develop further to complete the victory of socialism in the world . . . . Therefore, the preservation of technical monuments is a right and an obligation of the working class."[76]

The orientation toward a Marxist-influenced history and the international debate on industrial heritage changed the conception of industrial monument preservation in the GDR. First, the focus shifted from the technical to the social. The development of technology was seen as a social process that was not only scientifically and technically important, but also—and above all—had a significant impact on society.[77] Therefore, preservation, it was argued, should not just be concerned with technology, but also with labor traditions and the tradition of inventors. This drew attention to industrial sites with political significance, such as the Karl-Liebknecht-Shaft of the coal mine in Oelsnitz. In 1948, the hewer Adolf Hennecke was chosen by the SED to initiate an activist movement based on the Soviet model of Stakhanovites. In a thirteen-hour shift, Hennecke extracted three times more coal than the stipulated norm. The shaft buildings were therefore preserved after the cessation of coal mining in 1967. In the 1970s and 1980s they were converted into a museum as an example of the activist movement. By illustrating the great achievements of the working class in the past and its potential for power, industrial monuments thus corresponded to an important concern of the Eighth Party Congress of the SED.

Secondly, attention shifted from pre- and early industrial monuments to the period of industrialization. New branches of industry including machine tool manufacture, railway construction, and the textile and chemical industries were included. The presentation of past industrial achievements was intended to promote understanding of the development of industrial productive forces in the future. In this sense, the maintenance of industrial monuments under the condition of socialism was understood as "a unity of the historical and the contemporary."[78] Indeed, heritage was mobilized to serve the future, too.

A Socialist Obligation?
The Conservation of Industrial Monuments in the 1970s

The new understanding of cultural heritage resulted in increased funding for preservation and the passing of a Historical Preservation Law in 1975. It included the category *Denkmale der Produktions- und Verkehrsgeschichte* (monuments of the history of production and transport), which encompassed craft, commercial and agricultural production sites, industrial and mining facilities, machines and models, buildings, and means of transport.[79] According to the law, monuments had to be registered in three different lists. They were hierarchically ordered, but, unlike the 1961 formulation, preservation was to extend down to the district level.[80] The Ministry of Culture was still responsible for the *Zentrale Denkmalliste* (central monuments list) that included all monuments of national and international importance. The district councils created the *Bezirksdenkmallisten* (district monuments lists) that contained monuments of regional importance, whereas the monuments of local importance were registered in the *Kreisdenkmallisten*.[81] The *Zentrale Denkmalliste* was adopted by the Council of Ministers in 1979. It contained 37 industrial monuments, which corresponded to approximately 10 percent of the recorded monuments, while the *Bezirksdenkmallisten* contained 220 and the *Kreisdenkmallisten* 1,500 objects.[82] The high percentage of industrial monuments in all three lists was seen as a big success. More monuments were registered and placed under monument protection than ever before, stated for example the Gesellschaft für Denkmalpflege (Society for Historic Preservation.)

Historic preservation was conceived as a collaboration of state institutions and cultural mass organizations. The conservation of industrial monuments was only possible with the help of many volunteers, which were organized in the Kulturbund and mostly carried out the work on site. Within the Kulturbund, it was Otfried Wagenbreth who played a central role in the preservation of industrial monuments. He had studied mining at the Bergakademie Freiberg from 1946 to 1950. After being awarded a doctorate in 1958, he took up a position at the Geological Service in Halle. Starting in 1962 he worked as a lecturer in geology at the Weimar University of Architecture and Civil Engineering. In 1979, he gave up his post in Weimar and moved to Dresden University of Applied Sciences, where he worked as lecturer for history and documentation of the means of production.[83] Wagenbreth's interest in industrial monuments started in the early 1950s. In 1952, he took up an invitation from Hans Nadler to participate in training for volunteer monument conservators in Freiberg. Wagenbreth accepted the post as honorary commissioner for mining monuments in the Freiberg district and was soon appointed to the board of directors of the Natur und Heimat (Nature and Homeland) Section of the Kulturbund. He first met Wächtler in 1962 when both of them applied for the newly created chair for the History of Mining and Metallurgy at the Bergakademie Freiberg. The Ministry decided in favor of Wächtler, who had started his political career within the SED as a secretary in the Freie Deutsche Jugend (FDJ, Free German Youth) as early as 1946.[84] Despite personal differences, they began a close and successful cooperation, which resulted in numerous joint publications. The most important was certainly the book *Technische Denkmale in der Deutschen Demokratischen Republik* (Industrial Monuments in the German Democratic Republic), which helped to popularize the preservation of industrial monuments in the GDR.[85] It was reprinted seven times and became a basic textbook for many people working in the field of preservation and reconstruction of industrial monuments.[86] It was also widely recognized beyond the borders of the GDR.

Wagenbreth and Wächtler also advocated better organization of industrial monument preservation. Due to his connections to the highest Party functionaries, Wächtler succeeded in strengthening its position among the centralized cultural organizations. In 1972 he initiated the establishment of a Working Group on Industrial Monuments within the Zentraler Fachausschuss Bau- und Denkmalpflege (central expert committee for historic preservation) in the Kulturbund, supported by a member of the Politbüro, Günter Mittag. After its initial foundation as the Gesellschaft für Denkmalpflege, it was reestablished as Zentraler Fachausschuss für technische Denkmale (central expert committee for industrial monuments) in 1977. As a partner of the state authorities, the committee provided conceptual suggestions at a central, regional, and local level. Its members wrote expert reports and were involved in the creation of the Central Monument List of 1979.[87] Especially important were the thirty-eight factsheets on methodological questions on the conservation of industrial monuments published together with the Institut für Denkmalpflege. Through the leaflets the honorary officials in the counties, who were mostly neither technicians nor historians of technology, were to be empowered to establish, select, and evaluate industrial monuments.[88]

Several authors have considered the "effective and successful" cooperation of cultural mass organizations like the Kulturbund and state organizations, such as the Institut für Denkmalpflege, as a guarantor of success.[89] Their collaboration was codified in the Historical Preservation Law that described the preservation of monuments as an obligation concerning society as a whole. Nevertheless, the cooperation was difficult. As the main scientific institution, the Institut für Denkmalpflege had to explore the monument stock of the GDR and carry out research on the theory and methodology of monument preservation. For this reason, it also claimed responsibility for the conservation of industrial monuments. Two staff members of the Institut für Denkmalpflege were thus permanent members of the Zentraler Fachausschuss. Questions of authority were inevitable and already found expression during the drafting of the new law. Wagenbreth asserted that the Institut für Denkmalpflege had failed to develop a conceptual framework within the field of industrial monument preservation. He therefore argued for the creation of a new evaluation committee, while the function of the Institute should be reduced of the issue of "care."[90] His claims had no influence on the law, but an agreement was reached that later strengthened the role of the expert committee in the evaluation process. Despite the agreement, tensions between the Kulturbund and the Institute did not recede. The lack of support and information was a constant point of criticism. Furthermore, opinions about which objects were worth preserving differed widely. The Institute acted quite arbitrarily, deleting, for example, the saline in Bad Sulza from the central list of monuments without informing the Kulturbund about it.[91]

It was Wächtler's political networking that helped to counter the high-handedness of the Institute. At the same time, he was able to better institutionalize the preservation of industrial monuments. With the support of the Minister of Culture, Hans-Joachim Hoffmann, he succeeded in setting up the Technical Monuments Working Group at the Nationaler Rat für die Pflege und Verbreitung des Deutschen Kulturerbes (National Council for the Care and Dissemination of German Cultural Heritage) in 1980. No less important were his numerous international contacts. As cultural heritage was considered a crucial tool of foreign policy, international connections were convincing arguments when it came to the interests of industrial monuments.[92]

Conclusion

"The government of the GDR assigns the history of productive forces and the preservation of industrial monuments an important role in the development of society."[93] In this brief statement, Wächtler outlined the position of the socialist state toward its industrial heritage at the Second International Congress on the Conservation of Industrial Monuments in 1975. At the same time, he offered a simple interpretation for the success of industrial monument preservation in the GDR that has hardly been questioned by historians. In this chapter, however, I have argued that the meaning of industrial monuments shifted in different heritage discourses as the monuments offered diverse possibilities of interpretation and identification even in the GDR.

In the 1950s, the concept of industrial monuments was shaped less by Marxist ideology than by prewar concepts that were established by actors as diverse as the Association of German Engineers and the Bund Heimatschutz. Struggling for social recognition, engineers linked technical and industrial artifacts with the bourgeois concept of *Kultur*. The Heimatschutz, on the other hand, linked industrial monuments with architecture that was closer to the natural landscape and thus with the concept of *Heimat*. Both concepts still shaped the conservation of industrial monuments in the 1950s. This was mainly due to personal and institutional continuities. As the Landesämter were not broken up in the administrative reform of 1952, they could continue to work as they always had. Significantly, the early activities almost exclusively concentrated on those parts of the GDR that already possessed a strong tradition in the care of industrial monuments like the former Saxony. The Dresden branch office cooperated closely with the Natur- und Heimatfreunde of the Kulturbund. As many former members of the Heimatschutz had joined those groups, the concepts and traditions of the former Heimatschutz groups with their regional affiliations were retained.

The understanding of industrial monuments only changed in the 1970s. This resulted from two opposing but closely intertwined trends: the concomitant rise in both internationalization and nationalization of industrial monument preservation, with the latter rooted in major political changes after Honecker's accession. He initiated not only a radical shift in social and economic policy but also proclaimed the development of a socialist nation. Both sparked a debate that led to a new definition of heritage that now encompassed the whole German history. At the same time, the concept of cultural heritage was extended and focused less on art and science than on the living and working conditions of the population. This provided new opportunities for the preservation of industrial monuments that by then had come to be considered an important means for educating the working class according to a Marxist interpretation of history. Thus, heritage was mobilized to serve the future, too.

The redefinition of cultural heritage in the GDR mirrored an international trend in the 1970s. It was rooted in profound economic, structural, and cultural changes evident in many European countries, which led to increasing interest in industrial monuments and fostered a close international cooperation. Despite significant ideological and methodological differences between the individual countries, some general trends were evident in the preservation and interpretation of industrial monuments. It was conceived as an interdisciplinary research field that included both scholars and amateur volunteers. The focus shifted not only from individual monuments to industrial environments. Even more importantly, interest shifted away from a mere history of technology and toward the social aspects of industrialization like working and living conditions. These conceptual changes were significant and led to a new wording. "Industrial Heritage" was concurrently enigmatic enough to accommodate the different approaches, methods, and political views.

By the end of the 1980s, the GDR had created a broad institutional basis for the registration and preservation of industrial monuments. Retrospectively, Otfried Wagenbreth judged the preservation of industrial monuments in East Germany to have been more systematic than in West

Germany. The success, however, had been "diminished by the inadequate allocation of funds and the resulting deterioration of the monument substance."[94] This development was intensified by the political upheaval in 1989 that led to an unprecedented wave of deindustrialization in East Germany. This resulted in historically valuable industrial assets being demolished or decaying.[95] Furthermore, following reunification, the Kulturbund, the Gesellschaft für Denkmalpflege, and the Zentrale Fachausschuss were dissolved in the early 1990s.[96] The five *Länder* were reinstalled and adopted new preservation laws that were modeled on those of the western *Bundesländer*.[97] It is clear that further research on the transformation of historic preservation in the early 1990s is needed. Nevertheless, it is possible to state, at least for Saxony, that there were some continuities. The new Saxon preservation law of 1993 made provisions for the protection of industrial monuments as well as slagheaps and historical landscapes.[98] As Helmuth Albrecht emphasized, this enabled continuity in the preservation of industrial monuments.[99] Furthermore, in 1992, Wagenbreth took over Wächtler's chair in Freiberg, where he continued his work on industrial monuments.[100] The chair was renamed chair for the History of Technology and Industrial Archeology, thus becoming the first and only institution that offered the opportunity to study industrial archeology in Germany.

Nele-Hendrikje Lehmann is curatorial associate at the Deutsches Hygiene-Museum Dresden, where she recently cocurated the Fourth Saxon State Exhibition: Boom. 500 years of Industrial Heritage in Saxony. She received her degree in cultural studies at the Europa-Universität Viadrina Frankfurt/Oder and worked as a research associate at the Institute of Industrial Archeology, History of Science and Technology at the Technische Universität Bergakademie Freiberg. Her main research interests are the history of knowledge and the industrial heritage in Saxony.

Notes

1. Kierdorf and Hassler, *Denkmale des Industriezeitalters*, 123.
2. Nisser, "Preface," VI.
3. Itzen and Müller, "Industrial Heritage in Late Modern Industrial Societies," 3–9; Kierdorf and Hassler, *Denkmale des Industriezeitalters*, 123–26; Albrecht, "Technische Denkmalpflege in der DDR," XIV–XVI.
4. For an exception to this, see the work of Helmuth Albrecht.
5. Albrecht, "Zum Verhältnis von Industriearchäologie," 20; Waentig, "Denkmale der Technik und Industrie," 98.
6. Waentig, "Denkmale der Technik und Industrie," 98.

7. This issue is also addressed in the context of Czechoslovakia in the chapter by Čeněk Pýcha in this volume.
8. BArch (Bundesarchiv), SAPMO (Stiftung Archiv Partei und Massenorganisationen der DDR), DY 27/4354.
9. Daniel, *Kompendium Kulturgeschichte*, 444.
10. Trischler, "Zwischen Geschichte und Zukunft."
11. Kierdorf and Hassler, *Denkmale des Industriezeitalters*, 36.
12. Seifert, "Das Projekt 'Heimat,'" 13.
13. Banck, *Werner Lindner*, 198–200; Kierdorf and Hassler, *Denkmale des Industriezeitalters*, 36.
14. Banck, *Werner Lindner*, 175–77.
15. Matschoß and Lindner, *Technische Kulturdenkmale in Deutschland*; see also Albrecht, "Zum Verhältnis von Industriearchäologie," 17.
16. "Verordnung zur Erhaltung und Pflege der nationalen Kulturdenkmale der DDR."
17. Campbell, "Preservation for the Masses," 1; Brandt, *Geschichte der Denkmalpflege*, 25–26.
18. Campbell, "Preservation for the Masses," 1.
19. Wagenbreth and Wächtler, *Technische Denkmale*, 15.
20. Brandt, *Geschichte der Denkmalpflege*, 116–21.
21. *Ausstellung Technische Kulturdenkmale*.
22. *Technische Kulturdenkmale: Eine Wanderausstellung*.
23. Wagenbreth and Wächtler, *Technische Denkmale*, 15.
24. *Technische Kulturdenkmale: Eine Wanderausstellung*, 3.
25. Ibid., 7–9.
26. *Ausstellung Technische Kulturdenkmale*, 3.
27. *Technische Kulturdenkmale: Eine Wanderausstellung*, 5.
28. Schaarschmidt, "Sozialistische Heimat?," 18.
29. Palmowski, *Die Erfindung der sozialistischen Nation*, 73–74.
30. Ibid., 23.
31. Schaarschmidt, *Regionalkultur und Diktatur*, 355.
32. Schaarschmidt, "Sozialistische Heimat?," 18–19.
33. Palmowski, *Die Erfindung der sozialistischen Nation*, 42.
34. Bergner, "Die Alte Hoffnung Gottes bei Kleinvoigtsberg"; *Ausstellung Technische Kulturdenkmale*; *Technische Kulturdenkmale: Eine Wanderausstellung*; Brandt, *Geschichte der Denkmalpflege*, 111–12; for a more general discussion of the topic, see Palmowski, *Die Erfindung der sozialistischen Nation*, 73–75; Schaarschmidt, "Sozialistische Heimat?," 18–20.
35. Steiner, *Von Plan zu Plan*, 96.
36. Campbell, "Preservation for the Masses," 2; Magirius, "Zur Geschichte der sächsischen Denkmalpflege," 60.
37. "Gesetz zur Erhaltung der Denkmale in der DDR."
38. Magirius, "Zur Geschichte der sächsischen Denkmalpflege," 60.
39. See Campbell, "Preservation for the Masses," 2–3.
40. Ibid., 2.
41. Itzen and Müller, *The Invention of Industrial Pasts*, 6.
42. Kierdorf and Hassler, *Denkmale des Industriezeitalters*, 179–81.
43. Döring-Manteuffel and Raphael, *Nach dem Boom*, 52–53.

44. Mandler, "The Heritage Panic," 58.
45. Cossons, "First International Congress on the Conservation," 2; Kierdorf and Hassler, *Denkmale des Industriezeitalters*, 123.
46. Cossons, "First International Congress on the Conservation," 2; Nisser, "Preface," 5.
47. Kroker, "Zur Einführung," 15.
48. Kierdorf and Hassler, *Denkmale des Industriezeitalters*, 124.
49. Nisser, "The Industrial Heritage," 10.
50. Cossons, "First International Congress on the Conservation," 2.
51. Buchanan, "The Theoretical Basis of Industrial Archaeology," 147–49.
52. Stinshoff, "Between History and Heritage," 39.
53. Kierdorf and Hassler, *Denkmale des Industriezeitalters*, 123.
54. Paulinyi, "Industriearchäologie oder Geschichte der materiellen Kultur?," 158–59.
55. Kąkoleski, "A Would-Be Science?," 126; Paulinyi, "Industriearchäologie oder Geschichte der materiellen Kultur?," 158–59.
56. Albrecht, "Zum Verhältnis von Industriearchäologie," 27.
57. See the discussions at the Second International Congress on the Conservation of Industrial Monuments.
58. Nisser, "The Industrial Heritage," 8.
59. Malycha and Winters, *Geschichte der SED*, 203.
60. Haase, *Die SED und das kulturelle Erbe*, 366; Palmowski, *Die Erfindung der sozialistischen Nation*, 126–27.
61. Haase, *Die SED und das kulturelle Erbe*, 362.
62. Haase, "Sozialistische Lebensweise und Kulturelles Erbe," 12.
63. Meier and Schmidt, "Einleitung," 12–13; Kowalczuk, "Geschichte als Legitimationsinstanz," 35; Wollgast, "Bemerkungen zum Verhältnis von Tradition," 94–95.
64. Malycha and Winters, *Geschichte der SED*, 228, 203; Meuschel, "Auf der Suche," 79; Kowalczuk, "Geschichte als Legitimationsinstanz," 31.
65. Kowalczuk, "Geschichte als Legitimationsinstanz," 31.
66. Ibid, 34–35.
67. Wollgast, "Bemerkungen zum Verhältnis von Tradition," 90.
68. Bartel, "Erbe und Tradition in Geschichtsbild," 132–33.
69. Hager, "Tradition und Fortschritt," 523; cited in Meier and Schmidt, "Einleitung," 17. My translation.
70. Kowalczuk, "Geschichte als Legitimationsinstanz," 34–35.
71. Palmowski, *Die Erfindung der sozialistischen Nation*, 131–32.
72. Albrecht, "Technische Denkmalpflege in der DDR," VIII.
73. Wächtler, *Autobiografie eines aufrechten Unorthodoxen*, 268.
74. Wächtler, "Denkmale der industriellen Produktion," 121.
75. Wächtler, "Sozialistische Revolution und Technische Tradition," 165.
76. Wagenbreth and Wächtler, *Technische Denkmale*, 12. My translation of "Wir sehen in der alten Technik Waffen, in die Erfahrung und theoretisches Wissen von Arbeitern, Technikern und Wissenschaftlern eingingen, kristallisierte Schöpferkraft. Wir sehen in der alten und neuen Technik eingedenk dieser historischen Erfahrung Waffen, die wir weiter entwickeln müssen, um den Sieg des Sozialismus in der Welt zu vollenden."
77. Wagenbreth and Wächtler, *Technische Denkmale*, 10.

78. Wächtler and Wagenbreth, "Soziale Revolution und Industriearchäologie," 172. My translation.
79. "Gesetz zur Erhaltung der Denkmale in der DDR," § 3.
80. Campbell, "Preservation for the Masses," 3.
81. "Gesetz zur Erhaltung der Denkmale in der DDR," § 5. See also: Wagenbreth and Wächtler, *Technische Denkmale*, 20–21.
82. BArch, SAPMO, DY 27/4353, fol. 362.
83. Wagenbreth, *Das eigene Leben im Strom der Zeit*, 258.
84. Albrecht, "Technische Denkmalpflege in der DDR," VIII.
85. Although the official term for industrial monuments in the GDR was *Denkmale der Produktions- und Verkehrsgeschichte* (monuments of the history of production and transport), the older name *technische Denkmale* persisted. This resulted mostly from pragmatic reasons, as most people were used to the older terminology.
86. The first edition was in 1973, extended reprints followed in 1977, 1983, 1985, 1987, and 1989. See Albrecht, "Technische Denkmalpflege in der DDR," V.
87. Albrecht, "Geschichte, Stand und Perspektiven der Industriedenkmalpflege," 70.
88. See BArch, SAPMO, DY 27/4344, fol. 1.
89. Albrecht, "Technische Denkmalpflege in der DDR," IX.
90. BArch, SAPMO, DY 27/4354, fol. 125.
91. BArch, SAPMO, DY 27/4354, fol. 124.
92. BArch, SAPMO, DY 27/4354, fol. 85.
93. Wächtler and Wagenbreth, "Deutsche Demokratische Republik," 66.
94. Wagenbreth, "Industriedenkmalpflege," 57.
95. Albrecht, "Geschichte, Stand und Perspektiven der Industriedenkmalpflege," 78.
96. Wagenbreth, "Industriedenkmalpflege," 57.
97. Albrecht, "Geschichte, Stand und Perspektiven der Industriedenkmalpflege," 80.
98. "Gesetz zum Schutz und zur Pflege der Kulturdenkmale im Freistaat Sachsen."
99. Albrecht, "Geschichte, Stand und Perspektiven der Industriedenkmalpflege," 80.
100. Wagenbreth, *Das eigene Leben im Strom der Zeit*, 165–67.

Bibliography

Albrecht, Helmuth. "Geschichte, Stand und Perspektiven der Industriedenkmalpflege und Industriearchäologie in Sachsen." *Blätter für Technikgeschichte* 63 (2001): 61–97.

———. "Technische Denkmalpflege in der DDR—Eine historische Einführung." In *Technische Denkmale in der Deutschen Demokratischen Republik*, edited by Otfried Wagenbreth and Eberhard Wächtler, V–XXIV. Berlin: Springer, 2015 [1989].

———. "Zum Verhältnis von Industriearchäologie, Industriekultur und Industriedenkmalpflege in Deutschland." *Schriftenreihe der Georg-Agricola-Gesellschaft* 34 (2011): 15–30.

Ausstellung Technische Kulturdenkmale: Zeichnungen aus dem Planarchiv des Landesamtes für Volkskunde und Denkmalpflege und Modelle aus sächsischen Museen. Görlitz: Landesamt für Volkskunde und Denkmalpflege Sachsen, 1952.

Banck, Barbara. *Werner Lindner: Industriemoderne und regionale Identität*. PhD diss., Technische Universität Dortmund, 2007. Retrieved 22 September 2020. https://eldorado.tu-dortmund.de/handle/2003/25010.

Bartel, Horst. "Erbe und Tradition in Geschichtsbild und Geschichtsforschung der DDR." In *Erbe und Tradition in der DDR: Die Diskussion der Historiker*, edited by Helmut Meier and Walter Schmidt, 129–40. Cologne: Pahl-Rugenstein, 1988.

Bergner, Alfred. "Die Alte Hoffnung Gottes bei Kleinvoigtsberg." *Natur und Heimat* 8 (1952): 15–18.

Brandt, Sigrid. *Geschichte der Denkmalpflege in der SBZ/DDR: Dargestellt an Beispielen aus dem sächsischen Raum, 1945–1961*. Berlin: Lukas Verlag, 2003.

Buchanan, Robert Angus. "The Theoretical Basis of Industrial Archaeology." In *SICCIM. Second International Congress on the Conservation of Industrial Monuments*, edited by Deutsches Bergbaumuseum Bochum, 143–50. Bochum: Deutsches Bergbaumuseum Bochum, 1978.

Campbell, Brian. "Preservation for the Masses. The Idea of Heimat and the Gesellschaft für Denkmalpflege in the GDR." *kunsttexte.de* no. 3 (2004). Retrieved 22 March 2020. https://edoc.hu-berlin.de/handle/18452/7671.

Cossons, Neil. "First International Congress on the Conservation of Industrial Monuments." In *Transactions of the First International Congress on the Conservation of Industrial Monuments*, 2–3. Ironbridge: n.p., 1975.

Daniel, Ute. *Kompendium Kulturgeschichte: Theorie, Praxis, Schlüsselwörter*. Frankfurt am Main: Suhrkamp, 2002.

Döring-Manteuffel, Anselm, and Lutz Raphael. *Nach dem Boom: Perspektiven auf die Zeitgeschichte seit 1970*. Göttingen: Vandenhoeck & Ruprecht, 2008.

"Gesetz zum Schutz und zur Pflege der Kulturdenkmale im Freistaat Sachsen vom 03. März 1993." Retrieved 23 October 2020. https://revosax.sachsen.de/vorschrift_gesamt/5198.html.

"Gesetz zur Erhaltung der Denkmale in der DDR—Denkmalpflegegesetz—vom 19. Juni 1975." *Gesetzblatt der DDR*, 27 June 1975, Teil 1 Nr. 26.

Haase, Horst. *Die SED und das kulturelle Erbe: Orientierungen, Errungenschaften, Probleme*. Berlin: Kulturbund der DDR, 1986.

———. "Sozialistische Lebensweise und Kulturelles Erbe." In *Sozialistische Lebensweise und Kulturelles Erbe*, edited by Klaus Schnakenburg, 5–23. Berlin: Kulturbund der DDR, 1976.

Hager, Kurt. "Tradition und Fortschritt." *Einheit* 40 (1985): 516–530.

Itzen, Peter, and Christian Müller. "Industrial Heritage in Late Modern Industrial Societies: Britain and Germany in a Comparative Perspective." In *The Invention of Industrial Pasts: Heritage, Political Culture and Economic Debates in Great Britain and Germany, 1850–2010*, edited by Peter Itzen and Christian Müller, 3–13. Augsburg: Wißner, 2013.

———. *The Invention of Industrial Pasts: Heritage, political culture and economic debates in Great Britain and Germany, 1850–2010*. Augsburg: Wißner, 2013.

Kąkoleski, Igor. "A Would-Be Science? A History of Material Culture in Poland Before and After the Year 1989." In *Cultural History in Europe: Institutions—Themes—Perspectives*, edited by Jörg Rogge, 125–39. Bielefeld: transcript, 2011.

Kierdorf, Alexander, and Uta Hassler. *Denkmale des Industriezeitalters: Von der Geschichte des Umgangs mit Industriekultur*. Tübingen: Wasmuth, 2000.

Kowalczuk, Ilko-Sascha. "Geschichte als Legitimationsinstanz: Marxistisch-Leninistische Geschichtswissenschaft in der DDR." In *Elisabeth Charlotte Welskopf und die Alte Geschichte in der DDR*, edited by Isolde Stark, 12–41. Stuttgart: Steiner, 2005.
Kroker, Werner. "Zur Einführung." In *SICCIM. Second International Congress on the Conservation of Industrial Monuments*, edited by Deutsches Bergbaumuseum Bochum, 13–16. Bochum: Deutsches Bergbaumuseum Bochum, 1978.
Magirius, Heinrich. "Zur Geschichte der sächsischen Denkmalpflege." In *Denkmalpflege in Sachsen 1894–1994*, edited by Landesamt für Denkmalpflege Sachsen, 55–61. Weimar: n.p., 1997.
Malycha, Andreas, and Peter Jochen Winters. *Geschichte der SED: Von der Gründung bis zur Linkspartei*. Bonn: BpB, 2009.
Mandler, Peter. "The Heritage Panic of the 1970s and the 1980s in Great Britain." In *The Invention of Industrial Pasts: Heritage, Political Culture and Economic Debates in Great Britain and Germany, 1850–2010*, edited by Peter Itzen and Christian Müller, 58–69. Augsburg: Wißner 2013.
Matschoß, Conrad, and Werner Lindner. *Technische Kulturdenkmale in Deutschland*. Munich: F. Bruckmann, 1932.
Meier, Helmut, and Walter Schmidt. "Einleitung." In *Erbe und Tradition in der DDR: Die Diskussion der Historiker*, edited by Helmut Meier and Walter Schmidt, 7–25. Cologne: Pahl-Rugenstein, 1988.
Meuschel, Sigrid. "Auf der Suche nach Madame L'Identité. Zur Konzeption der Nation und Nationalgeschichte." In *Die DDR in der Ära Honecker: Politik—Kultur—Gesellschaft*, edited by Gert-Joachim Glaeßner, 77–93. Opladen: Westdt. Verlag, 1988.
Nisser, Marie. "The Industrial Heritage: The Nearest Future for Our Recent Past." In *Industrial Heritage '84: Proceedings. The Fifth International Conference on the Conservation of the Industrial Heritage*, edited by Helena E. Wright and Robert M. Vogel, 6–14. Washington: n.p., 1986.
———. "Preface." In *The Industrial Heritage: The Third International Conference on the Conservation of Industrial Monuments*, edited by Marie Nisser, V–VI. Stockholm: n.p., 1981.
Palmowski, Jan. *Die Erfindung der sozialistischen Nation: Heimat und Politik im DDR-Alltag*. Berlin: Ch. Links, 2016.
Paulinyi, Ákos. "Industriearchäologie oder Geschichte der materiellen Kultur?" In *SICCIM. Second International Congress on the Conservation of Industrial Monuments*, edited by Deutsches Bergbaumuseum Bochum, 151–59. Bochum: Deutsches Bergbaumuseum Bochum, 1978.
Schaarschmidt, Thomas. *Regionalkultur und Diktatur: Sächsische Heimatbewegung und Heimat-Propaganda im Dritten Reich und in der SBZ/DDR*. Cologne: Böhlau, 2004.
———. "Sozialistische Heimat? Der sozialistische Heimatbegriff und seine gesellschaftliche Aneignung." In *Heimat in der Diktatur*, edited by Joachim Klose, 15–30. Leipzig: Leipziger Universitätsverlag, 2014.
Seifert, Manfred. "Das Projekt 'Heimat'—Positionen und Perspektiven." In *Zwischen Emotion und Kalkül: Heimat als Argument im Prozess der Moderne*, edited by Manfred Seifert, 9–22. Leipzig: Leipziger Universitätsverlag, 2010.
Steiner, André. *Von Plan zu Plan: Eine Wirtschaftsgeschichte der DDR*. Berlin: BpB, 2007.

Stinshoff, Richard. "Between History and Heritage: The Debate about Industrial Archaeology in Britain." In *The Invention of Industrial Pasts: Heritage, Political Culture and Economic Debates in Great Britain and Germany, 1850–2010*, edited by Peter Itzen and Christian Müller, 36–57. Augsburg: Wißner, 2013.

Technische Kulturdenkmale: Eine Wanderausstellung, edited by Institut für Denkmalpflege. Dresden: n.p., 1955.

Trischler, Helmut. "Zwischen Geschichte und Zukunft: Ein neuer Museumstyp im Europa des frühen 20. Jahrhunderts." In *Erkenne dich selbst! Strategien der Sichtbarmachung des Körpers im 20. Jahrhundert*, edited by Sybilla Nikolow, 47–58. Cologne: Böhlau, 2015.

"Verordnung zur Erhaltung und Pflege der nationalen Kulturdenkmale der DDR vom 26. Juni 1952." *Gesetzblatt der DDR* 84 (1952): 514–15.

Wächtler, Eberhard. *Autobiografie eines aufrechten Unorthodoxen*. Essen: Klartext Verlag, 2012.

———. "Denkmale der industriellen Produktion." In *Sozialistische Lebensweise und Kulturelles Erbe*, edited by Klaus Schnakenburg, 121–28. Berlin: Kulturbund der DDR, 1976.

———. "Sozialistische Revolution und Technische Tradition." *Neue Museumskunde* 20, no. 3 (1977): 164–67.

Wächtler, Eberhard, and Otfried Wagenbreth. "Deutsche Demokratische Republik." In *SICCIM. Second International Congress on the Conservation of Industrial Monuments*, edited by Deutsches Bergbaumuseum Bochum, 66–70. Bochum: Deutsches Bergbaumuseum Bochum, 1978.

———. "Soziale Revolution und Industriearchäologie." In *SICCIM. Second International Congress on the Conservation of Industrial Monuments*, edited by Deutsches Bergbaumuseum Bochum, 160–76. Bochum: Deutsches Bergbaumuseum Bochum, 1978.

Waentig, Friederike. "Denkmale der Technik und Industrie: Definition und Geschichte." *Technikgeschichte* 67, no. 2 (2000): 85–110.

Wagenbreth, Otfried. *Das eigene Leben im Strom der Zeit: Lebenserinnerungen von Otfried Wagenbreth*. Freiberg: TU Bergakademie Freiberg, 2015.

———. "Industriedenkmalpflege in der DDR—ein Rückblick." In *Technik und Wissenschaft als produktive Kräfte in der Geschichte*, edited by Thomas Hänseroth, 49–60. Dresden: Technische Universität Dresden, 1998.

Wagenbreth, Otfried, and Eberhard Wächtler, eds. *Technische Denkmale in der Deutschen Demokratischen Republik*. Berlin: Springer, 2015 [1989].

Wollgast, Siegfried. "Bemerkungen zum Verhältnis von Tradition—Erbe—Philosophie." In *Sozialistische Lebensweise und Kulturelles Erbe*, edited by Klaus Schnakenburg, 89–96. Berlin: Kulturbund der DDR, 1976.

CONCLUSION

Transnational Heritage Networks in Socialist Eastern and Central Europe

Corinne Geering

The research presented in this volume has revealed the dynamics underlying the preservation of cultural heritage in socialist countries in the period following World War II. By looking at sites as different as a royal palace, a small railway viaduct, historical city centers, or a concentration and death camp, the chapters in this volume have demonstrated the broad spectrum of cultural heritage that found its way into official registries under socialism. In these vivid accounts, cultural heritage emerged as a field where experts, state authorities, and politicians, as well as tourists, visitors, and local residents, negotiated how state socialist societies related to and made use of the tangible past preceding the socialist revolutions. The historical built environment assumed a central role in socialist nation-building projects following destruction, ethnic cleansing, and displacement during and after World War II. As the new governments strived toward building communism, they rebuilt public spaces destroyed during the war to conform to the new needs of socialist society, nationalized property (including movable and immovable heritage), engaged in radical revisionist historiography, and devised new contents for public education. At the same time, the project of socialist modernity in many instances integrated objects and sites inherited from the prerevolutionary past, with their adaptation to fit socialist ideology involving discussion, negotiation, and sometimes even contestation.

Taken together, the stories told by the chapters have also shown that preservation of the past was a common endeavor across Eastern and Central Europe, not only due to shared ideologies, but also because of increasing international exchange from the 1950s onward. The decades after

World War II have entered the historiography of protection and preservation of cultural heritage as a period of intense internationalization through legislation and cooperation. The chapters have provided ample evidence of experts from socialist countries participating in international organizations, such as the United Nations Educational, Scientific and Cultural Organization (UNESCO) and the International Council on Monuments and Sites (ICOMOS). Whereas research has begun to provide more insight into international cooperation with Western Europe[1] and with the Global South,[2] relations among experts within the space of socialist Eastern and Central Europe have so far received very little attention. This lack of research on intrabloc relations has to some degree contributed to the flawed impression of a shared, monolithic position on cultural heritage in this region, determined by the political center in Moscow. Instead, as the chapters in this volume have revealed, it was the case that experts in other places were driving heritage policies in the Soviet Union; the Estonian SSR, for example, was the first Soviet republic to adopt a law on preservation in 1961. These experts also engaged in international exchange across the Cold War divide on methods of preservation, design of policies, and definition of core concepts.

This concluding chapter expands on the case studies explored throughout the volume to shed light on the transnational heritage networks in socialist Eastern and Central Europe. It thereby seeks to highlight two central themes that run through the contributions. First, it discusses the transnational dimension of preservation within Eastern and Central Europe, presenting the internationalization taking place primarily within the region during the postwar period. Second, this conclusion identifies nation-building as a central element of this internationalization, presenting a concise summary of the topics and questions that were of greatest concern to socialist countries in relation to cultural heritage. With a focus on the transnational level of interaction between people and the tangible past under socialism, this concluding chapter also inquires into the legacy of the socialist-era international cultural relations within Eastern and Central Europe. Finally, by discussing the limitations of the accounts presented in this volume, this conclusion also formulates perspectives for future research on heritage under socialism.

Transnational Exchange across Socialist Eastern and Central Europe

This volume has presented case studies from Poland, Romania, Czechoslovakia, the GDR, and Hungary, while also focusing on several Soviet republics separately, thus providing insights into the emergence of a new realm of transnational exchange in postwar Europe. The international relations between the countries discussed in this volume were consolidated by international agreements and regional meetings of states' representatives. After 1949–50, economic policies were regulated through membership in the Council for Mutual Economic Assistance (COMECON), and from 1955 on, membership in the Warsaw Pact governed the states' security policies. In a similar vein, international meetings governing the activities of socialist countries were established in the fields of culture and cultural heritage. This new realm of socialist internationalism in Eastern and Central Europe evidently did not emerge in a vacuum; experts in these countries had been trained earlier, while national policies as well as legislation relating to heritage had been adopted in the interwar and imperial periods. Elements of this legislation remained in place in the postwar period, and pre-World War II expertise contributed to shaping socialist policymaking.

Research on political transitions has highlighted repeatedly that whereas new governments employ a rhetoric of renewal and rejection of the past, there is often a high degree of continuity at the level of bureaucracy and everyday practices.[3] New scholarship has further revealed the structural continuity of nationalizing strategies from the Soviet era in urban development in post-Soviet cities in Kazakhstan and Belarus.[4] Most recently, research has demonstrated that one of the most prominent examples of national revival celebrated by a new political regime—the reconstruction of Warsaw Old Town after World War II—was rooted in reconstruction plans predating the destruction inflicted by Nazi Germany during the war.[5] Against this background, the chapters in this volume approached socialism in Eastern and Central Europe as a period neither marked by clear caesuras nor as detached from global historical processes. Instead, a picture emerges showing that as various actors tried to conceive of an officially sanctioned past compatible with state socialism, they continued to draw on existing historical layers, canons, and experiences of continuity and rupture.

Transnational exchange played a crucial role in finding answers to the questions of what constituted heritage under socialism and how it should be preserved. The establishment of new international organizations, adoption of international conventions and charters, professional travel and tourism, as well as international publications and translation of reports, provided a wide range of actors with opportunities to engage with heritage through a transnational lens. Exchanges involved both international visitors to socialist countries as well as experts, politicians, and practitioners from the region participating in restoration projects abroad and in international meetings in both socialist and nonsocialist countries. My chapter in this volume on cultural development in heritage policymaking has shown how, in these transnational exchanges, cultural heritage was intertwined with other political and economic interests, as the historical built environment was deployed by Soviet authorities as part of economic development through tourism. International visitors represented a valuable source of convertible currency, which is why state authorities together with experts devised tourist itineraries that prompted the restoration of historical buildings and sites. The presentation of restored cultural heritage was then combined with public lectures on a range of topics deemed of interest to the visitors, including the current five-year plan, agrarian policies, or the Soviet victory in the Great Patriotic War.

Iryna Sklokina's account in this volume has provided further insights into how international tourism shaped the national canon of Ukrainian heritage, with the encounters involving international tourists playing out at the local level while also feeding back into republic-wide policies. These encounters took place in a setting marked by frictions between the goal of disseminating propaganda among visitors, thus aligning them with state socialism, and providing them with entertainment, thus fulfilling their expectations of the tourist experience. In an encounter with a visitor from Canada who criticized the apparent lack of genuine Ukrainian folk traditions, Sklokina recounts how the tour guide made fun of the tourist's wish to see peasants and mud-huts in a country boasting dams and other large-scale modern constructions. The expectations of diaspora tourists who had come to visit their families' former homelands proved particularly challenging for tourist guides. Visitors from the bordering countries of Poland, Romania, Czechoslovakia, and Hungary with family roots in the Ukrainian SSR challenged the official historical account presented by tour guides that focused on Ukrainian history while ignoring those of other groups. The reports written by tourist guides provide insights into these contestations, but in some cases, they also included recommendations directed at their superiors to pay more attention to hitherto neglected parts of history.

International visits to heritage sites and centers of expertise by restorers, architects, and other preservationists were part of growing professional exchanges in the postwar period. Following the massive destruction inflicted during World War II, the countries in Eastern and Central Europe faced the challenge of reconstructing historical sites, urban districts, and villages. In several states, restoration workshops were established and made responsible for wartime and postwar reconstruction. One such agency was the PKZ State Workshops for the Conservation of Cultural Heritage (Polskie Pracownie Konserwacji Zabytków), established in 1945 by the Polish Ministry of Culture. The experts involved in PKZ participated in reconstruction projects not only in Poland but also in other socialist countries and in the Global South. The chapter on Estonian conservators' international contacts by Karin Hallas-Murula and Kaarel Truu addresses the restoration work by PKZ in Tallinn between 1978 and 1990, which resulted in negotiations and some frictions over restoration methods. Whereas both Polish and Estonian restorers agreed on the emphasis on the Old Town's medieval appearance, the Polish restorers added details to the Tallinn buildings copied from previous restoration work conducted in Poland. This decision, the authors argue, left a visible mark on Tallinn Old Town, but it did not have a lasting impact on Estonian restoration methods that instead drew inspiration from the Soviet republics of Lithuania and Latvia as well as from Finland and Sweden, with which existing pre-World War II networks were maintained.

The international acclaim of Polish restorers in the postwar years is also highlighted in Eszter Gantner's chapter on the reconstruction of the Royal Palace in Budapest. Hungarian restorers discussed Polish restoration work in professional journals, and a delegation of Polish experts visited the site of the Royal Palace in 1952 to advise on the reconstruction project. Jan Zachwatowicz, who had supervised the reconstruction of Warsaw Old Town and headed the delegation to Budapest, later remembered that the 1952 visit marked the beginning of regular collaboration of Polish preservationists with those in Hungary, Bulgaria, Czechoslovakia, Poland, Germany, Yugoslavia, Romania, the GDR, and the USSR. According to Zachwatowicz, it was only later that cooperation with preservationists from Western Europe intensified, with the International Congress of Architects and Technicians of Historical Monuments held in Paris in 1957 and especially the foundation of ICOMOS in Warsaw and Kraków in 1965.[6]

The same sequence of internationalization, with an initial intraregional phase involving socialist Eastern and Central Europe, can be observed in the memoirs of GDR restorers. Ludwig Deiters, General Conservator at the GDR Institut für Denkmalpflege (Institute for Historic Preservation), recalled very active transnational exchange between socialist countries, as conservation had been included in the states' cultural exchange programs. He traveled to Poland in 1957, followed soon after by Czechoslovakia and the Soviet Union where he visited Moscow, Leningrad, Kyiv, Yerevan, and Tbilisi, including Stalin's birth home as part of an official tour. His institute in the GDR also regularly received delegations from other socialist countries in order to examine possible procedures to assess the value of historical sites and to devise reconstruction plans.[7] These contacts between experts from socialist countries were institutionalized in the statutes of the Institute for Historic Preservation in 1976. As the central scientific institution for cultural heritage in the GDR, it was created to foster international cooperation, in the first instance with partner institutions in the USSR, other socialist countries, and with ICOMOS.[8] Deiters' account therefore confirms Zachwatowicz's understanding of ICOMOS as an extension and intensification of already existing international contacts within socialist Eastern and Central Europe.

Accounts like these demonstrate that processes of internationalization in socialist Eastern and Central Europe were neither uniform nor centralized, but instead involved multiple layers of interaction between people, places, and the built environment. Heritage sites received attention from several international bodies involving experts coming from socialist and nonsocialist countries. It was against this background that in 1978, the same year the ICOMOS General Assembly was held in Moscow and Suzdal', the Ninth Meeting of the Ministers of Culture of Socialist Countries also took place in Suzdal', a small town outside Moscow, where the topic of cultural heritage protection was also at the center of the agenda.[9] Around the same time, in Warsaw, the first meeting of the new Working Group of Socialist Countries for the Restoration of Monuments of History, Culture, and Museum Valuables took place. The meeting was attended by experts from Bulgaria, Hungary, Cuba, the GDR, Mongolia, Poland, Czechoslovakia, and the USSR, with the working group frequently collaborating with ICOMOS in the following years, thus attesting to the overlapping spheres of international organizations designed to fulfill the same tasks.[10] The ICOMOS General Assemblies, like other international meetings, were used by the authorities of socialist states to present their achievements in the field of heritage conservation to an international audience. The meeting in the Russian SFSR in 1978 displayed the restored ensemble of the new tourist center of Suzdal' and celebrated the adoption of the first all-union law titled "On the Protection and Use of Monuments of History and Culture" in the same year. The founding meeting of ICOMOS, held in Poland in 1965, had showcased the reconstruction of Warsaw Old Town and of Wawel Castle in Kraków. The decision to hold the third meeting in Budapest in 1972 was motivated by the celebration of the centenary of state monument protection in Hungary.[11] Finally, the meeting held in Rostock and Dresden in 1984 presented international experts with the reconstruction of destroyed cities that followed the principles outlined in the Declaration of Dresden on the "Reconstruction of Monuments Destroyed by War" that had been adopted two years prior.

Instances like this reveal that experts from socialist countries were neither excluded from nor merely bystanders in the articulation of international heritage policies that have guided preservation practices until the present day. They were coproducers of documents that incorporated their experiences and interests, thus extending the international discussion to include the region of Eastern and Central Europe. Julia Röttjer's chapter on Poland's contribution to the UNESCO World Heritage program provides ample evidence of how socialist interpretation of heritage was connected to both national and international interests in the postwar period. Adopted by UNESCO in 1972, the Convention Concerning the Protection of the World Cultural and Natural Heritage provided the basis for the World Heritage List. Poland was among the first states to submit nominations, with their selection of sites including the old towns of Kraków and Warsaw, as well as the former Nazi concentration camp Auschwitz-Birkenau. This led to controversies among international experts for different reasons. While the reconstruction of Warsaw Old Town was celebrated in the nomination documents as a symbol of the perseverance of the Polish people following the war, there were concerns over permitting onto the list a site representing "negative historical values." Julia Röttjer shows that the inclusion of Auschwitz-Birkenau as a UNESCO World Heritage site in 1978 was the result of a socialist interpretation of heritage that placed emphasis on events of national history connected to particular sites rather than material substance and appearance. The site's value was articulated in the framework of the People's Republic of Poland as a site of national martyrdom and served the socialist internationalist interest of commemorating the antifascist struggle. In this nexus between socialist, national, and transnational interests, heritage experts from Eastern and Central Europe also contributed to international standard-setting in preservation that remains in place today.

Heritage under Socialism

The protection, preservation, and restoration of heritage formed part of policies dealing with culture and were thus coordinated by the Ministries of Culture and specialized agencies that were established in the postwar period. In this institutional setting, not only the question of sanctioned historical accounts was of relevance but also what purpose heritage served in socialist culture overall. Whereas the answer to this question appeared to be comparably straightforward in the Stalinist period, over the course of almost four decades, it remained subject to ongoing discussions in publications, speeches, and official meetings until the end of state socialism in 1989–91. In states facing the transition to socialism after World War II, some authorities assumed a radical position and promoted a cultural revolution following the Soviet model, as Eszter Gantner's contribution outlines for cultural policy in socialist Hungary. In a speech at the Second Congress of the Hungarian Workers' Party in 1951, the Hungarian Minister of Culture, József Révai, claimed that this was not to be understood as a Russification of Hungarian culture, but rather as a strengthening of the national character that he believed was threatened by the homogenizing forces of capitalism.[12]

This idea of strengthening national culture was a crucial element of socialist ideology as elaborated by the Soviet Union, and it was promoted in the international context with regard both to Eastern and Central Europe and to national liberation movements in formerly colonial states in Africa and Asia. This position was also maintained by representatives of other socialist countries, notwithstanding the Soviet military interventions in the GDR in 1953, Hungary in 1956, and Czechoslovakia in 1968. The socialist governments did not operate with a conservative notion of national culture but rather one that strived toward far-reaching social transformation in line with the state ideology. This position was explained in the program of the Communist Party of the USSR that was adopted in 1961 and described the constant transformation of national cultures in socialist countries. As part of this process, they "freed themselves" from everything that was considered "outdated and contradicting the new conditions of life."[13] This understanding of national culture also framed the socialist approach to heritage that constituted one important issue to be addressed by cultural policies. According to contemporary socialist essays on cultural heritage, aspirations of social progress or social advance could only be realized by creating historical continuity through the careful selection and use of sites, buildings, and objects from the past for present socialist society.[14]

These ideas were not only articulated within state borders but also transnationally, as states' representatives increasingly engaged in exchanging views on cultural policies. In a similar vein to the "negative historical values" in the interpretation of UNESCO World Heritage, the debates on the role of the past in present societies found their way into international documents that transcended the socialist bloc. For example, the UNESCO Recommendation Concerning the Safeguarding and Contemporary Role of Historic Areas, adopted in 1976, was prepared by Krzysztof Pawłowski, a Polish architect-restorer who at the time worked for UNESCO as a conservation expert. The document recommended that the UNESCO member states adopt measures to safeguard heritage by identifying, protecting, restoring, and revitalizing it, and to "integrate it into the social life of our times."[15] The notion of socialism evidently did not figure into the recommendation; however, ideas underlying socialist policies were included, such as the equal importance ascribed to aesthetic and social values of historic areas.

In the 1960s and 1970s, the conservation of the historic city and its adaptation to present-day use was among the topics resulting in the most extensive participation by heritage experts from socialist countries in international scientific symposia organized under the umbrella of ICO-

MOS.[16] For example, in the course of a decade, the National Committee of Czechoslovakia alone organized two international symposia on the historic town—the first in 1966 in Prague and the second in 1973 in Vilnius together with the Soviet committee—and in 1976 they published the fourth issue of the *ICOMOS Bulletin* on the topic of "Protection and Restoration of Historic Towns in Czechoslovakia." The active involvement of experts from socialist countries in these debates provides the context for Liliana Iuga's discussion of the conceptualization of the historic town in Romania in the postwar national and international spheres. By tracing the legacy of interwar expertise, she reveals that the ideological change in the transition to state socialism did not entail a rupture in restoration principles that were still heavily influenced by Western European traditions. Moreover, Romanian experts were aware of postwar urban reconstruction principles in other countries through the international channels mentioned above. In this particular setting, the "preservation versus modernization" dilemma led to extensive methodological discussions on the built urban environment and the competing values of historical layers and contemporary civic functions. While the historic town in Romania was never the subject of national heritage protection, in contrast to other socialist countries, Iuga's account reveals the continuous efforts of heritage experts in Romania to expand the scope of preservation. At the same time, in a state associated with the large-scale destruction of the historical urban fabric, for example in Bucharest, Iuga's chapter points not only toward the international trends and debates over heritage preservation but also to those of destruction. Although the social function of heritage in the national cultures of socialist states followed the same guidelines articulated by socialist ideology, Iuga's account is illustrative of the fact that it took on different forms depending on the trajectories of the respective national histories.

The ways socialist ideological convictions were translated into heritage policies and preservation practices differed between countries in Eastern and Central Europe. In the 1970s and 1980s, UNESCO published a series titled *Studies and Documents on Cultural Policies* that outlined the content and objectives of members states' cultural policies. Written by experts from the states and aimed at an international readership, this source material provides a concise summary of the official understanding of "socialist culture" that consequently framed the notion of "socialist heritage" maintained by the authorities in the respective states. The Marxist–Leninist ideas guiding socialist policies on the material culture and built environment of the past and present were formulated most explicitly in the document on the USSR. By providing a general framework outlining the dependence of cultural development "on ethnical, national and class lines," the report concluded that "every ethnic group, nation and class creates, borrows, transforms and develops culture in the specific historical conditions."[17] Since, according to the ideology, socialist societies had overcome the class divide after the revolution, the defining factors for culture in socialist states were deemed to be ethnic groups and nations. Nations were considered the collective proprietor of cultural heritage in a state that had nationalized cultural institutions. The nationalization of property enforced by the Bolshevik regime after the October Revolution also provided the basis for declaring the preservation of cultural heritage to be the duty of the collective of all Soviet citizens in the 1977 Constitution of the USSR.[18]

Against this background, national traditions were integrated into a socialist culture that was believed to constitute the culmination of social progress. In accordance with the ideas expressed by the Cultural Revolution, the Hungarian report, for instance, explained that this social progress entailed a transformation of culture that eliminated "the harmful cultural heritage of the past," made cultural values public property, and enabled the broad masses to participate in it. [19] The Polish report stressed the fact that national cultural heritage was not rejected when creating the new socialist culture but was instead reviewed and approached in a new way in accordance with socialist ideology.[20] A special section in the report was dedicated to the protection of monuments, with the reconstruction of Warsaw characterized as "the most remarkable cultural achievement of the Republic of Poland,"[21] thus showing how adeptly the socialist authorities could draw on existing narratives of national martyrdom, infusing them with the sense of collective effort required in building communism. According to the report, foreign visitors were struck by the extent of the dedication of the state and the population to the restoration of old palaces and city districts, as well as to musical and theatre traditions. The nation's cultural heritage was not only preserved, the report claimed, but also perpetuated in contemporary social conditions, with the Polish cultural policy seeking to ensure access to and participation in it by the entire population.[22]

The close relationship between the heritage of the past and present social conditions that were tied to socialist ideology also broadened the understanding of heritage, taking it beyond artistic and cultural treasures. Under the heading "social exploitation of cultural monuments," the Czechoslovak report stressed the need to find new uses for historical and cultural monuments such as castles and palaces that now served as housing, artistic or cultural institutions, schools, offices, old people's homes, or health institutions.[23] By looking at a particular location in Northwest Bohemia, Čeněk Pýcha's chapter in this volume has shed light on this process of heritage-making under socialism. His account shows how a railway viaduct whose architectural design bore no particular significance and was located in a small town was attributed the same value as Prague Castle, since both were included in the list of national monuments of Czechoslovakia. The small viaduct was the site where a strike was crushed and four workers were killed in 1932, thus lending itself well to being made a place to commemorate "the heroes of class struggle" by the new communist elites. This example reflected the inclusion of objects into socialist heritage that were valorized through their association with historical events, such as World War II or socialist revolutions, even as their material substance were of no particular historical or aesthetic value.

The extension of heritage to include monuments from the workers' movement, among others, reveals the relevance of public education for preservation in state socialist societies. In the GDR report on cultural policy, the author Hans Koch, Director of the Institute of Cultural and Art Studies at the Academy of Social Sciences, emphasized the state's intention to turn the interest in cultural heritage into a "vast mass movement"[24] that would use historical sites for educational purposes. Large groups of people were encouraged to visit sites connected to the memory of events that marked the history of the GDR, which Koch defined primarily through the lens of the German workers' movement. The emphasis on "the revolutionary traditions of the German working class"[25] as the historical foundation of the GDR provided the context for many industrial sites and buildings to be recognized as national heritage, a theme touched upon in Čeněk Pýcha's chapter and discussed in more detail in Nele-Hendrikje Lehmann's contribution. Her chapter traces the reinterpretation of industrial heritage in the GDR in the 1970s, with the focus shifting from technical to social aspects, after new policies were introduced that worked toward the development of a socialist nation. Industrial monuments were important means for public education that served the purpose of a Marxist interpretation of history and emphasized the role of the broad masses not only as consumers of culture but also as its producers. At the same time, Lehmann's account also highlights that the national interpretations were inseparably linked with internationalization, as international congresses on the conservation of industrial monuments were initiated in the 1970s.

Whereas most examples in this volume emphasize transnational transfer and exchanges of practices and ideas, they also reveal limits of such networks. Heritage experts in socialist countries were subject to severe travel restrictions and could face repercussions if their relations were strained with the Communist Party. Moreover, the scarcity of resources (personnel, material, foreign publications) was a continuous topic among employees of institutions responsible for preservation. In many cases, the restrictions and isolation experienced during the socialist period are more prominent in today's memory than the exchanges facilitated by the socialist regimes that this volume has addressed. While the postsocialist transition has been assessed by many heritage experts as a positive change because it removed barriers, other issues persist until today, such as the relative scarcity of resources, lack of transparency in decision-making, and the competition between different state authorities overseeing preservation and construction in public spaces. In particular, nongovernmental organizations and civil society have been facing difficulties in participating in the protection of cultural heritage in postsocialist states, as evidenced by several conferences on the topic held since around 2010.[26] Postsocialism also involved negative experiences for some heritage experts and restorers owing to the rapid transition to a market economy and the institutional instabilities resulting from their reorganization after 1989–91. For example, the strength of state authorities in the Soviet Union meant that preservationists employed by state institutions were equipped with procedures to halt or delay decisions to redevelop historical sites; however, once they started facing privatized businesses and extractive industries, new challenges emerged from the need to navigate between the public sector and a considerably larger private sector when promoting issues of preservation.

The transnational dynamics within Eastern and Central Europe revealed by this volume in the postwar period also raise the question of the legacy of socialist internationalism in this region. It is only recently that scholarship has started exploring the multiple global entanglements of socialist Eastern and Central Europe that might change the ways that postwar histories of culture and the built environment are written.[27] Efforts toward European integration after the demise of state socialism—with the formation of the Visegrád Group in 1991 and in particular since the 2004 enlargement of the European Union—have dramatically reshaped the landscape of international relations for the former Warsaw Pact states. However, as the contributions in this volume have revealed, the dominance of the Soviet Union's political center in Moscow was not necessarily felt in the field of preservation by individual Soviet republics or the other socialist states. While the socialist internationalist bodies and forums of exchange evidently ceased to exist with the fall of state socialism, several other international organizations established during the Cold War period, ranging from UNESCO to ICOMOS and ICOM, continue to provide central platforms of transnational exchange for experts in Eastern and Central Europe. Within these organizations, experts from postsocialist countries continue the international exchange that emerged in the postwar decades, while contact with Russian colleagues was never predominant even during the socialist period, as evidenced by personal correspondence by Polish heritage experts.[28] The transnational framework of this book, with its focus on transfers and exchanges between actors, sites, and objects, may help bring to light continuities that are sometimes overshadowed by accounts that place political caesuras center stage.

Future Research Perspectives

The historical accounts in the chapters in this volume have revealed that heritage under socialism was shaped through continuous transnational exchange both within the socialist bloc and with experts from capitalist countries. As a result, this volume has considerably broadened the scope of historical sites, buildings, and objects that would be readily associated with socialist states, such as modernist architecture, industrial towns, and large-scale constructions made of steel and concrete. The case studies presented in this volume show how socialist interpretations of royal palaces, historic city centers, Cossack military bases, and the concentration and death camp in Auschwitz-Birkenau were carved out, as they were all included in the official heritage canon of the respective socialist countries. On the other hand, the discussion of industrial heritage, comprising sites more readily associated with socialist ideology, demonstrates the legacy of interwar interpretations, the changing meanings during the socialist period, and the relevance of transnational networks transcending the socialist bloc. The evidence provided in the contributions to this volume also point to the need to pay closer attention to overlaps of historical legacies and spaces of interaction under socialism that continue to inform heritage practices and discourses in post-socialist countries today. Therefore, by uncovering debates and efforts that were not translated into practice or were forgotten during the political transition of 1989–91, this volume has also highlighted the ways historiography has come to remember the socialist period in Eastern and Central Europe.

Based on these insights, there are a number of questions that emerge from the discussions in the chapters that could inspire further research on the topic of heritage under socialism. Some of these questions, as briefly outlined here, could deepen our understanding of the role played by the material culture of the past in socialist societies. First of all, the locations discussed in this volume have confirmed the need for further studies that provide more insights into regional dynamics beyond the national centers. While there is already a considerable amount of research on larger cities like Saint Petersburg, Warsaw, Bucharest, and Berlin, research on smaller towns and rural regions is still lacking to a significant extent. For instance, Čeněk Pýcha's chapter in this volume on Northwest Bohemia and the small town of Duchcov has shown how a local perspective may inform on processes unfolding on other scales, as the values associated with sites changed over time. His account also highlights the relevance of the state's peripheries for symbolic nation-building and thus sheds light on the interaction between local, regional, national, and transnational spaces in heritage-making.

A more decentered perspective on heritage in socialist states would also benefit inquiries into the participation of the general population in preservation activities. From the 1960s, in several Soviet republics as well as other socialist states, mass voluntary organizations had an officially sanctioned function in the preservation of cultural heritage. For example, the All-Russian Society for the Protection of Historical and Cultural Monuments (VOOPIiK) acquired millions of members after its foundation in 1965. Reflecting the inseparable bond of past and present meanings of heritage, the source material relating to local and regional branches show that restoration of historical buildings was combined with erection of new monuments to Lenin and to the memory of the so-called Great Patriotic War. While the fascinating story of VOOPIiK has been addressed in passing by several studies, there is so far no comprehensive historical account that would shed light on the activities on the ground and the dynamics across the vast space of the Russian SFSR. Similarly, the relations between the Russian voluntary society to those of other Soviet republics, especially in the Caucasus where they first emerged, have received little scholarly attention. The chapters in this volume on the Ukrainian and the Estonian SSR show that inquiries into activities beyond the political center in Moscow yield fascinating insights that offer a clearer understanding of national culture, institution-building, and international cooperation in the Soviet Union and during the socialist period at large.

The transnational heritage networks discussed in this volume that have focused on cultural heritage and the region of Eastern and Central Europe could be expanded to include actors connecting research on heritage to other issues. Iryna Sklokina's chapter has highlighted the role of the Ukrainian diaspora in the construction of the national heritage canon through tourism. Members of the diaspora also promoted preservation in socialist states through participation in voluntary associations like the New York-based American Society for the Preservation of Russian Monuments established in the late 1970s. Moreover, the archival collections of international organizations include hundreds of appeals written by individuals or organizations that called attention to the neglect or destruction of cultural heritage in the respective socialist countries.[29] The topic of activism by individuals also connects cultural heritage to larger movements promoting international peace and disarmament or environmental issues that both operated with notions of conservation. Through the establishment of peace committees, the movement promoting international peace and disarmament was officially sanctioned by the socialist governments. Julia Röttjer's chapter on Auschwitz-Birkenau mentions such a peace demonstration that was organized on behalf of the ruling Polish United Workers' Party, with more than one million participants descending on the site of the former concentration camp. On the other hand, the history of environmental protection in socialist states is still characterized to a large extent by a focus on devastation and pollution. Due to the separation of responsibilities in institutions, research on natural and cultural heritage has remained separate for the most part, although particular sites provide evidence of interaction between the two groups. Moreover, the diverse activities of the Soviet Union in the Man and the Biosphere program under UNESCO (launched in 1970) that made it the program's most active participating state, remain virtually unexplored, even though the very notion of biosphere was coined by Russian scientists.[30]

Generally, research examining the different trajectories of conservation theories and methodologies in Europe remains at an early stage. While this has become a salient question in research focusing on postcolonial states, due to the articulation of approaches that seek to overcome Eurocentrism, research on heritage has not yet diversified Europe as the location where most international conservation policies were articulated until the last decades of the twentieth century. The contributions to this volume have highlighted the different influences that shaped the national policies of socialist states, thus attesting to the need to differentiate more strongly the traditions of heritage conservation in Europe. Several chapters have provided insights into the legacy of imperial and interwar practices for socialist states after World War II. The chapter by Karin Hallas-Murula and Kaarel Truu has also revealed the various regional influences on national heritage-making under socialism. The Estonian SSR was the recipient of and interacted with expertise exported from the well-connected Polish restoration company PKZ. At the same time, exchange among experts in the Baltic Soviet republics intensified and trips to nearby Finland and Sweden that did not form part of the socialist bloc ensured a steady flow of information from those countries. Such changing regional dynamics counter narratives that emphasize Moscow's apparent unparalleled influence and present a static and monolithic understanding of the way institutions worked in socialist states. The kinds of insights offered in this volume also deepen the understanding of institutions in postsocialist states, especially in the cultural sphere, that represented a continuation of bodies established during the socialist period.

Finally, this as well as many other accounts dealing with heritage are concerned with documentation, protection, conservation, or revitalization of the tangible past, ranging from architecture, public infrastructure, and sites to other cultural artifacts. This focus has been complemented by inquiries into willful destruction and heritage protection in the event of armed conflict that fostered international cooperation and policies on conservation.[31] While this volume contributes to a transnational history of preservation, similar transnational histories of neglect, decay, and destruction remain to be written. In particular, this concerns practices of urban planning and large-scale redevelopment that are today often associated with radical socialist modernization projects, like the Novyi Arbat depicted on the cover of this volume. The chapter by Liliana Iuga in this volume on the redevelopment of the historic town in Romania has already illuminated the potential of adopting a transnational historical perspective that goes beyond the socialist bloc to explore destruction. A comparison of practices involving disregard of historical buildings and sites in socialist and nonsocialist countries, rather than comparing those practices involving care, would further deepen our understanding of the focus and the limits of ideology that shaped particular socialist understandings of heritage. Consequently, a transnational history of heritage under socialism could also revisit the connections of practices unfolding in socialist Eastern and Central Europe to those in Western Europe. Such research could reassess large-scale urban redevelopment and the conversion of sacral buildings into clubs and other social facilities in postwar Europe outside the ideological framing of socialism.

The transnational history of preservation in this volume has contested a monolithic understanding of the so-called socialist bloc and instead revealed the relevance of transnational heritage networks that, in some cases, had roots in the interwar period but in others emerged from new international organizations that reached across the Iron Curtain. The multifaceted nature of the examples examined by the contributions to this volume reveals the roles of actors and sites at local, national, and transnational levels, thus enabling discussion of the overlapping and divergent spheres that shape general historical accounts on socialist Eastern and Central Europe. The fields and questions for future research that I have outlined in this concluding chapter could contribute to further diversification of the concepts used in the history of socialism and to emphasizing the agency of a variety of historical actors. Taken together, the chapters in this volume have shown that the region of Eastern and Central Europe was neither peripheral to global processes nor exceptional when viewed against the developments in a wider postwar Europe.

Corinne Geering leads a junior research group at the Leibniz Institute for the History and Culture of Eastern Europe (GWZO) in Leipzig. She received her PhD from the University in Giessen in 2018, where she was a doctoral fellow at the International Graduate Centre for the Study of Culture (GCSC). She has published on material culture, cultural politics, international cooperation during the Cold War, and the use of the past for regional development. She is the author of *Building a Common Past: World Heritage in Russia under Transformation, 1965–2000*.

Notes

1. For a general overview on East–West relations in Europe during the Cold War, see Mikkonen and Koivunen, *Beyond the Divide*; international heritage cooperation in this context is discussed in Gfeller, "Preserving Cultural Heritage."
2. For a general overview on global East–South relations during the Cold War, see Calori, Hartmetz, Kocsev, Mark, and Zofka, *Between East and South*. The ways heritage experts were engaged in these relations have been explored in Gzowska, "Exporting Working Patterns"; Telepneva, "A Cultural Heritage for National Liberation?"; Cowcher, "The Museum as Prison."
3. See my own research on the disintegration of the Soviet Union in Geering, *Building a Common Past*. The project "1989 after 1989: Rethinking the Fall of State Socialism" based at the University of Exeter has shown the longer history and the connection to global processes of the end of state socialism in Eastern Europe. Mark, Iacob, Rupprecht, and Spaskovska, *1989*.
4. Bekus, "Ideological Recycling."
5. Popiołek-Roßkamp, *Warschau*.
6. Zachwatowicz, *Ochrona zabytków*, 141.
7. Deiters, "Das Institut für Denkmalpflege," 43–44.
8. Ibid., 20–31.
9. "Shorthand report on the Ninth Meeting of Ministers of Culture of Socialist Countries in Suzdal´ for the problems of the protection of historical and cultural monuments and the adoption of final documents of the meeting for the development of cultural relations," 1978, Russian State Archive of Literature and Art (RGALI), f. 2329, op. 35, d. 150.
10. A. V. Chekmarev, I. P. Gorin, and L. A. David, "Report on the First International Meeting of the Working Group of Socialist Countries for the Restoration of Monuments of History, Culture and Museum Valuables, on the work of the Soviet delegation and suggestions for the organization of further activities," 1978, RGALI, f. 2329, op. 29, d. 937, ll. 10–16.
11. Andràs, "The Third General Assembly of ICOMOS," 17.
12. James, "Envisioning Postcommunism," 161.
13. Kommunisticheskaia Partiia Sovetskogo Soiuza, *Programma Kommunisticheskoi Partii*.
14. See Baller, *Kul'turnoe nasledie i kommunizm*. For a Polish example, see Chałasiński, "Integracja idei klasowej i narodowej."
15. UNESCO, *Recommendation Concerning the Safeguarding*, Art. 2.
16. See Geering, *Building a Common Past*, 143–53.
17. Zvorykin, Golubtsova, and Rabinovich, *Cultural Policy*, 11.
18. USSR, "Konstitutsiia (Osnovnoi Zakon)," Art. 68.
19. Hungarian National Commission for Unesco, *Cultural Policy in Hungary*, 11.
20. Balicki, Kossak, and Żuławski, *Cultural Policy in Poland*, 15.
21. Ibid., 61.
22. Ibid., 13
23. Šimek and Dewetter, *Cultural Policy in Czechoslovakia*, 49.
24. Koch, *Cultural Policy in the German Democratic Republic*, 30.

25. Ibid., 13
26. See, for example, the international conference "Non-governmental organizations in the protection of World Heritage sites" (*Nepravitel'stvennye organizatsii v zashchitu ob"ektov vsemirnogo naslediia*) held in Saint Petersburg on 22–24 June 2012: Mezhdunarodnyi Forum NPO, *International NGOs Forum*; see also the contributions in Doempke, *The UNESCO World Heritage*.
27. See Stanek, *Architecture in Global Socialism*; Bach and Murawski, *Re-Centring the City*.
28. Geering, *Building a Common Past*, 224.
29. This is the case, for example, in the collections held in the UNESCO Archives in Paris. In some cases, these appeals also resulted in official UNESCO missions, as discussed by Demeter, "Transnational Activism."
30. An overview attesting to the wide-ranging nature of Soviet participation in this program is provided in Geering, *Building a Common Past*, 214–20.
31. For instance, I have shown elsewhere how the Cold War promoted the understanding of a heritage of humanity: Geering, "Protecting the Heritage of Humanity."

Bibliography

Andràs, Roman [sic]. "The Third General Assembly of ICOMOS—1972." *ICOMOS Scientific Journal* 5 (1995): 17–21.

Bach, Jonathan, and Michał Murawski, eds. *Re-Centring the City: Global Mutations of Socialist Modernity*. London: UCL Press, 2020.

Balicki, Stanisław Witold, Jerzy Kossak, and Mirosław Żuławski. *Cultural Policy in Poland*. Paris: UNESCO, 1973.

Baller, È. A. *Kul'turnoe nasledie i kommunizm*. Moscow: Izdatel'stvo "Znanie," 1968.

Bekus, Nelly. "Ideological Recycling of the Socialist Legacy: Reading Townscapes of Minsk and Astana." *Europe-Asia Studies* 69. no. 5 (2017): 794–818.

Calori, Anna, Anne-Kristin Hartmetz, Bence Kocsev, James Mark, and Jan Zofka, eds. *Between East and South: Spaces of Interaction in the Globalizing Economy of the Cold War*. Berlin: de Gruyter, 2019.

Cowcher, Kate. "The Museum as Prison and Other Protective Measures in Socialist Ethiopia." *International Journal of Heritage Studies* 26, no 12 (2020): 1,166–84.

Chałasiński, Józef. "Integracja idei klasowej i narodowej." In *Odzyskanie młodości: Pamiętniki. Młode pokolenie wsi polski ludowej 9*, edited by Bronisław Gołębiowski, Zdzisław Grzelak, and Franciszek Jakubczak, 5–14. Warsaw: Ludowa Spółdzielnia Wydawnicza, 1980.

Deiters, Ludwig. "Das Institut für Denkmalpflege in der DDR—Erinnerungen und Reflexionen." In *Denkmalpflege in der DDR: Rückblicke*, edited by Jörg Haspel and Hubert Staroste. Berlin: nicolai, 2014.

Demeter, Laura. "Transnational Activism against Heritage Destruction as a Human Rights Violation in Romania before and after 1989." *Revue d'études comparatives Est-Ouest* 2-3, no. 2–3 (2020): 121–50.

Doempke, Stephan, ed. *The UNESCO World Heritage and the Role of Civil Society: Proceedings of the International Conference Bonn 2015*. Berlin: World Heritage Watch,

2016. Retrieved 24 November 2020. https://world-heritage-watch.org/wp-content/uploads/2020/10/2015-WHW-Bonn-Conference-Proceedings.pdf.

Geering, Corinne. *Building a Common Past: World Heritage in Russia under Transformation, 1965–2000*. Göttingen: Vandenhoeck & Ruprecht, 2019.

———. "Protecting the Heritage of Humanity in the Cold War: UNESCO, the Soviet Union and Sites of Universal Value, 1945–1970s." *International Journal of Heritage Studies* 26, no. 12 (2020): 1,132–47.

Gfeller, Aurélie Elisa. "Preserving Cultural Heritage across the Iron Curtain: The International Council on Monuments and Sites from Venice to Moscow, 1964–1978." In *Geteilt—Vereint! Denkmalpflege in Mitteleuropa zur Zeit des Eisernen Vorhangs und Heute*, edited by Ursula Schädler-Saub and Angela Weyer, 115–21. Petersberg: Michael Imhof Verlag, 2015.

Gzowska, Alicja. "Exporting Working Patterns: Polish Conservation Workshops in the Global South during the Cold War." *ABE Journal* 6 (2014). Retrieved 13 April 2020. https://journals.openedition.org/abe/1268.

Hungarian National Commission for Unesco [*sic*]. *Cultural Policy in Hungary*. Paris: The Unesco Press, 1974.

James, Beverly. "Envisioning Postcommunism: Budapest's Stalin Monument." In *Rhetorics of Display*, edited by Lawrence J. Prelli, 157–76. Columbia: University of South Carolina Press, 2006.

Koch, Hans. *Cultural Policy in the German Democratic Republic*. Paris: The Unesco Press, 1975.

Kommunisticheskaia Partiia Sovetskogo Soiuza. *Programma Kommunisticheskoi Partii Sovetskogo Soiuza priniata XXII s′′ezdom KPSS*. Moscow: Pravda, 1961.

Mark, James, Bogdan C. Iacob, Tobias Rupprecht, and Ljubica Spaskovska. *1989: A Global History of Eastern Europe*. Cambridge, UK: Cambridge University Press, 2019.

Mezhdunarodnyi Forum NPO. *International NGOs Forum "Protection of World Heritage Properties."* Retrieved 13 January 2021. https://spbforum.wordpress.com/.

Mikkonen, Simo, and Pia Koivunen, eds. *Beyond the Divide: Entangled Histories of Cold War Europe*. New York: Routledge, 2015.

Popiołek-Roßkamp, Małgorzata. *Warschau: Ein Wiederaufbau, der vor dem Krieg begann*. Paderborn: Ferdinand Schöningh, forthcoming.

Šimek, Milan, and Jaroslav Dewetter. *Cultural Policy in Czechoslovakia*. Paris: UNESCO, 1970.

Stanek, Łukasz. *Architecture in Global Socialism: Eastern Europe, West Africa, and the Middle East in the Cold War*. Princeton: Princeton University Press, 2020.

Telepneva, Natalia. "A Cultural Heritage for National Liberation? The Soviet-Somali Historical Expedition, Soviet African Studies, and the Cold War in the Horn of Africa." *International Journal of Heritage Studies* 26, no. 12 (2020): 1,185–1,202.

UNESCO. *Recommendation Concerning the Safeguarding and Contemporary Role of Historic Areas*. 1976. Retrieved 17 April 2020. http://portal.unesco.org/en/ev.php-URL_ID=13133&URL_DO=DO_TOPIC&URL_SECTION=201.html.

USSR. 1977. "Konstitutsiia (Osnovnoi Zakon) Soiuza Sovetskikh Sotsialisticheskikh Respublik. Priniata na vneocherednoi sed′moi sessii Verkhovnogo Soveta SSSR deviatogo sozyva 7 oktiabria 1977 g." Historical Faculty of the Lomonosov Moscow State University. Retrieved 30 March 2020. http://www.hist.msu.ru/ER/Etext/cnst1977.htm.

Zachwatowicz, Jan. *Ochrona zabytków w Polsce*. Warsaw: Polonia, 1965.

Zvorykin, A. A., N. I. Golubtsova, and E. I. Rabinovich. *Cultural Policy in the Union of Soviet Socialist Republics*. Paris: UNESCO, 1970.

Index

A
Albania, 135
Alexander Leopold of Austria, Archduke, 131
All-Russian Society for the Protection of Historical and Cultural Monuments (VOOPIiK), 43, 111, 230
Altenberg tin buddle, 198
American Society for the Preservation of Russian Monuments, 230
antifascist struggle, 8, 16, 62, 70, 92, 179, 185, 223
Architects Union
    in Estonia, 110, 113–14
    in Romania, 150, 156
Architectural Planning Company KÖZTI, 130
Association of German Engineers, 196–97, 208
Association of United Ukrainian Canadians, 81
atheism, 1, 10, 12, 89, 108
Auschwitz-Birkenau (heritage site), 16, 23, 56–62, 64–71, 223, 229–30
Austria, 121n40, 171, 201
Austria-Hungary, 80, 131, 149–50, 171
authorized heritage discourse, 21, 170, 172–74, 177–80, 184–85, 189–90

B
Babyn Yar, 17, 95
Bad Sulza, 208
Baliasna, Riva, 95
Baller, Ė. A., 40–41
Baltic states, 18, 105, 107, 154, 231
Baroque, 85, 90, 130, 134, 139, 149, 184, 187–88, 191n6
    neo-Baroque, 131, 134, 139
Battle of Mohács, 130, 142n14
Belarus, 35, 120n1, 219

Belgium, 112, 115, 201
Bergakademie Freiberg, 204, 206
Berlin, 149, 163n39, 197, 204, 229
Białowieża National Park, 58, 62–63, 68, 70
Bilciurescu, Virgil, 156–57
Bistrița (Bistritz/Beszterce), 150
Böckler, Teddy, 115
Bohemia, 21, 169–71, 173–74, 186, 189, 226, 229
Bolsheviks, 2, 38, 86, 226
Borobudur Temple, 42
Brasilia, 155
Brașov (Kronstadt/Brassó), 150–52, 156, 158, 162n82
Braun, Matyáš Bernard, 187
Britain. See United Kingdom
Broggio, Ottavio, 187
Brokoff, Ferdinand Maximilian, 187
Bruns, Dmitri, 111, 117
Bucharest, 21, 145–46, 151–52, 160, 225, 229
Buchenwald (concentration camp), 93
Budapest, 20, 131, 134, 136, 140, 150, 221
    1972 ICOMOS meeting in, 13, 111, 222
    Buda Castle in, 19–20, 127–41, 221
    National Gallery in, 132, 139–41
Budimex, 117
Bukovina, 91
Bulgaria, 43, 68, 92, 111–12, 135, 221–22

C
Călinescu, G., 152
Canada, 58, 81, 86, 88, 96, 98n21, 201, 220
capitalist countries, 12, 35, 41, 79, 81, 93, 105–6, 110, 112–13, 118, 135, 203, 229
Caucasus, 83, 230
Ceaușescu, Nicolae, 21, 145, 160

Central Asia, 38
Central-Commission zur Erforschung und Erhaltung der Baudenkmale, 174
Charter 77, 11
Chernivtsi, 83
Chernobyl, 11
civilizing mission, 38, 86
class struggle, 108, 169–70, 175–76, 179, 183, 186, 227
Cold War, 6, 11–13, 15, 36–37, 44, 79, 96, 153, 218, 228
collective farm, 82–83, 88
colonialism, 36, 173
Communist party, 10, 227
    of Czechoslovakia, 173–74, 184
    in the German Democratic Republic (GDR), 195, 199, 203–6,
    in Hungary, 129, 139–40, 142n8, 223
    in Poland, 57, 61–62, 70, 230
    of the Ukrainian Soviet Socialist Republic, 79, 83, 87
    of the Union of Soviet Socialist Republics (CPSU), 39–41, 44, 109, 138, 224
communist society, construction of, 1, 3, 35, 38, 40–41, 44, 48, 217, 226
concentration camp, 7, 59, 61, 64, 66, 69, 93, 223, 229–30
consumer culture, 9, 13, 79–80, 84, 87–88, 92, 203
Cossack, 17, 85, 87–88, 96–97, 100n57, 229
Cossons, Neil, 201
Council for Mutual Economic Assistance (COMECON), 3, 219
Council of Europe, 37, 47
Crimea, 85–86, 94
Crimean Tatars, deportation of, 82
Cuba, 11, 111, 222
cultural policy, 12, 15, 35–36, 38, 40–41, 44–48, 132, 195–96, 199, 203, 223–27
cultural revolution, 7, 132–33, 141, 223, 226
cultural sovereignty, 44–45
Curinschi, Gheorghe, 21, 145–47, 150, 153–56, 161n2

Czechoslovakia, 21–22, 79, 83, 89, 111–14, 134–35, 140, 148, 169–75, 178, 180, 184–86, 188, 190, 220–22, 225–27
    1968 Soviet military intervention in, 11, 224
    First Czechoslovak Republic, 174, 179, 184–85

D
Deiters, Ludwig, 221
Denkmale der Produktions- und Verkehrsgeschichte, 205, 213n85
Denmark, 112, 114, 201
de-Stalinization, 11, 82, 138
destruction, 130, 137, 145–47, 153, 160, 178, 186–90, 201, 210, 217, 225, 230–32
    of church buildings, 1, 108, 145, 187, 189
    during World War II, 2, 7–9, 20, 39, 62, 65, 70, 86, 127–28, 131, 134–35, 148, 217, 219–20, 222
détente, 11, 79, 202–3
development aid, 42, 44
Dniprohes, 87–88
Donetsk, 85, 94
Dresden, 197–99, 206, 209, 222
Duchcov (Dux), 21, 170–71, 176–87, 189–90, 229

E
Ecuador, 58
education, 8, 16, 35–36, 38–45, 48–49, 59–60, 107, 133, 199, 217, 227
Entz, Géza, 134–35
Estonia, 15, 17–18, 105–119, 218, 220–21, 230–31
    Republic of Estonia (interwar period), 107–8
Estonian Heritage Society, 18, 119
Ethiopia, 58, 112
Europe, idea of, 3, 14
European Union, 2004 enlargement of, 228

F
Faro Convention, 47

Federal Republic of Germany (FRG), 58, 69, 81, 92, 94, 114–15, 195, 201–3
Finland, 18, 106, 110, 112–13, 115, 118, 221, 231
five-year plan, 44, 87, 220
Fláje, 188
folk culture, 82, 84–85, 88–89, 91, 93, 96–97, 99n33, 220
France, 81, 112, 136, 153, 160
Franz Joseph I of Austria, Emperor, 131
Freiberg, 206, 210. *See also* Bergakademie Freiberg
Freie Deutsche Jugend (FDJ), 206
friendship of peoples, notion of, 81, 86, 92, 110
Furtseva, E. A., 45

G
Galicia-Volhynia, Principality of, 90–91
garden town movement, 152, 157
Gazzola, Pietro, 111
Gdańsk, 136
Gerevich, László, 134
German Democratic Republic (GDR), 8, 13, 19, 22, 69, 81, 87, 92, 111–14, 129, 135, 156, 195–210, 221, 224, 227
German Museum of Science and Technology in Munich, 196–97
Gerő, László, 134–36
Gierek, Edward, 62
Glemža, Jonas, 111
Gorée Island. *See* Senegal
Gothic, 90, 107–8, 114, 130, 137, 149, 151
Gottwald, Klement, 184
Granasztói, Pál, 139
Great Patriotic War. *See under* World War II
Greenpeace, 189

H
Haase, Horst, 203
Habsburg Empire. *See* Austria-Hungary
Hager, Kurt, 204
Hauszmann, Alajos, 131, 134
   Hauszmann style, 134, 138
   National Hauszmann Program, 141

Heimat, concept of, 22, 197–99, 204, 208
Heimatschutz movement, 197–99, 208–9
Helsinki, 110
Henderson, William O., 204
Hennecke, Adolf, 205
Hidasi, Lajos, 139
Hiroshima, 57, 67
Historicism, 82, 90, 134
historic town, 43, 62–63, 111, 115, 145–50, 153–54, 156, 158–60, 224–25, 227, 232
Hoffmann, Hans-Joachim, 208
Holocaust, 16, 69, 90, 95
Honecker, Erich, 203, 209
Horthy, Miklós, 131
Hungarian Socialist Workers' Party (MSZMP). *See* Communist party: in Hungary
Hungarian Working People's Party (MDP). *See* Communist party: in Hungary
Hungary, 13, 127–141, 160, 201, 218, 223–24
   1956 uprising and Soviet intervention in, 11, 20, 139, 224
   diaspora, 17, 20, 81, 89, 220
   and exchange between restorers, 20, 111–15, 135–38, 153, 201, 221–22
   Kingdom of, 129, 131, 142n14
   See also Austria-Hungary
Hussite movement, 174

I
Iancu, Marcel, 152
ideology, of socialism, 8, 10–12, 19–23, 35–36, 38, 40, 48–49, 57, 70, 81, 91, 95–96, 106–8, 128–30, 132–33, 137–38, 140–41, 153, 169–70, 175, 178, 185–86, 195, 198, 204, 217, 224–26, 229, 232. *See also* Marxism
industrial heritage, 7, 19, 21–22, 63, 115, 195–210, 227, 229
   and technical monuments in the GDR, 197–98, 206–7, 213n85
industrial archeology, 201–2, 204, 210

industrialization, 87, 147–48, 153, 160, 169, 172, 201–2, 205, 209–10
Institut für Denkmalpflege, 197, 199, 207–8, 221
International Auschwitz Committee (IAC), 59, 64
International Bank for Reconstruction and Development. *See* World Bank
International Campaign to Save the Monuments in Nubia, 42
International Centre for the Study of the Preservation and Restoration of Cultural Property (ICCROM), 112
International Committee for the Conservation of Industrial Heritage (TICCIH), 201
International Congress of Architects and Technicians of Historical Monuments, 221
International Congress on the Conservation of Industrial Monuments, 22, 200, 208, 227
International Council of Museums (ICOM), 12, 111, 228
International Council on Monuments and Sites (ICOMOS), 12, 13, 15, 39, 43, 58, 64–65, 68, 105, 111–14, 116, 118, 218, 221–22, 225, 228
International Fund for the Promotion of Culture, 45
interwar period, legacy of, 12, 14, 18–22, 128, 147–48, 151–52, 160, 184–85, 187, 219, 221, 225, 229, 231–32
Inturist, 80–83, 85–86, 92, 96, 110
inventory, of monuments, 6, 12, 21, 59, 90, 108, 115, 149–50, 177–79, 184–85, 196–98, 206–9, 217, 227
Iorga, Nicolae, 151–52
Israel, 69, 81–82, 94
Italy, 43, 114, 136, 153, 160, 201
Ivanov, Vladimir, 111
Izmail (city), 85

J
Janáky, István, 134, 138–39
Japan, 201
Jewish World Congress, 66

K
Kaljundi, Yevgeny, 115
Karling, Sten, 107, 114
Karlštejn Castle, 179
Katyń massacre, 8
Kazakevich, V. M., 42–43
Kazakhstan, 120n1, 219
KGB. *See under* Union of Soviet Socialist Republics (USSR)
Khalturin, A. G., 43
Kharkiv, 80, 84–85, 93
Khrushchev, N. S., 40. *See also* Union of Soviet Socialist Republics (USSR): Krushchev Thaw in
Koch, Hans, 227
Korotkevich, V. B., 35
Kossowski, Jerzy, 58
Kotka (city), 110
Kotsis, Iván, 134
Kraków, 16, 58, 62–64, 68, 70, 91, 221–23
    Kazimierz, 59, 63, 136, 162n20
    Wawel Castle in, 63, 137, 222
Krušné hory (Erzgebirge), 172
Kulturbund, 198, 203, 206–10
Kyiv, 17, 80–83, 88–89, 92–93, 95, 221

L
Laar, Mart, 119
Lahošť (Loosch), 179
Lahti, 110
Latvia, 221
Lăzărescu, Cezar, 156, 159
League of American Ukrainians, 81
legislation, on heritage, 4, 6, 9, 11–12, 14, 47, 128, 201, 218–19
    in Czechoslovakia, 162n16, 172, 175, 177, 179
    in Estonia, 105, 109, 120n4
    in the GDR, 197, 205–7, 210
    in Romania, 149–50, 160, 162n15, 165n87
    in the USSR, 17, 39, 41, 120n1, 165n86, 218, 222
Leipzig, 204
Lenin, V. I., 35, 184, 204, 230
Leningrad. *See* Saint Petersburg
Libkovice, 188–90

Lindner, Werner, 197–98
Liptice, 188
Lithuania, 18, 64, 109, 111, 221
Lopès, Henri, 46
Louis I of Anjou, King, 130
Lviv, 80–84, 90–92

M
Mączeński, Zdzisław, 137
Maiste, Juhan, 112
Malinowski, Kazimierz, 136
Maria Theresia, Empress, 127, 130
Marxism, 208
    notion of bourgeois culture in, 19–20, 108, 129, 139, 152, 162n9, 190, 196, 208
    notion of feudalism in, 129, 153–55
    and historical materialism, 148, 153, 159
    on historiography, 57, 61, 154, 195–96, 204–5, 209, 227
    Marxism-Leninism, 35, 38, 40, 47–48, 195–96, 225
    neo-Marxism, 202
Matschoß, Conrad, 197–98
Matthias Corvinus, King, 130, 137, 139
Mauritius, 57
M'Bow, Amadou, 64, 66
Mediaș (Mediasch/Medgyes), 150
memory, 1, 2, 4, 8, 16, 24, 66, 69–70, 90–91, 119, 131, 145, 177–79, 186, 227, 230
    politics of, 57, 61–62, 70, 129, 133, 184
Middle Ages, 112, 117, 129, 131, 134–35, 137–38, 150, 153, 172
    urban structure from, 9, 62–64, 71, 105, 107–9, 114, 127, 148–52, 154, 156–59, 187, 221
Mihályfi, Ernő, 139
Mikhalkov, N. S., 47
mining, 22, 172, 178, 180, 183, 186–89, 197–98, 205–6
Mittag, Günter, 207
modernism, 2, 7, 20–21, 97, 134, 147–48, 152, 155–57, 229
modernization, 1–3, 22, 80, 145, 148, 153, 155, 160, 173, 196–97, 199–200, 225, 232

Moldova, 91, 149–50, 158
Mongolia, 111, 222
Montréal, 199
Morris, William, 155
Moscow (city), 8, 13, 15, 46, 68, 83–85, 87–88, 93, 111–12, 116, 118, 120, 221–22
    1980 Summer Olympics in, 18, 116
    Church Christ the Savior in, 1
    Church of the Venerable Simeon Stylites on the Povarskaia in, 1–4, 12
    Kremlin, 127, 134, 136
    Novyi Arbat (Kalinin Prospekt) in, 1–4, 12, 232
Most (city), 186–87
    Church of the Assumption of the Virgin Mary, 187
Mostar, 57

N
Nadler, Hans, 197–99, 206
national history, 6, 20, 57, 62, 64, 70, 87, 127–28, 130, 132, 135, 137, 140–41, 174, 223
national identity, formation of, 24, 78, 81–82, 88, 119, 127, 131, 203
nationalism, 9–10, 17, 24, 36, 78, 80, 88, 141, 161, 199
nationalization, of property, 10, 38, 129, 217, 226
National Socialism, 59, 62, 64, 197
nation-building, 9, 15, 17, 19–20, 22, 78–79, 96, 128, 217, 229
Neoclassicism, 85, 138, 149–50
Netherlands, 121n40, 201
Neuwirth, Carl, 131
Norway, 112, 201

O
October Revolution, 2–3, 7, 9, 38, 112, 226
Odesa, 80, 85, 92–93, 95
Oelsnitz, coal mine in, 205
Orbán, Viktor, 127, 141
Orthodox church (architecture), 1, 90, 157

Ottoman Empire, 20, 130, 137, 142n14, 149–50

P
Parent, Michel, 64, 67, 112
patriotism, 2, 8, 41, 79, 87, 95, 119, 148
Paulinyi, Ákos, 202
Pawłowski, Krzysztof, 58–59, 63, 68, 224
peace, promotion of, 60, 66, 70, 93, 230
perestroika, 11, 17, 40, 44, 46–47, 85–86, 90
Petergof, 128
Piskarevo cemetery, 93
Pitești, 156–57
Piwocki, Franciszek Ksawery, 136
Poland, 8, 11–12, 15–17, 22, 45, 56–71, 89–91, 111–14, 117, 128–29, 135–37, 140, 148, 153–54, 160, 195, 201, 220–23, 226
Polish State Workshops for the Conservation of Cultural Heritage (PKZ), 18, 20, 106, 116–18, 220–21, 231
Polish United Workers' Party (PZPR). See Communist party: in Poland
Polish Workers' Party (PPR). See Communist party: in Poland
Prague, 148, 179, 184, 187
    1966 ICOMOS symposium in, 225
    Hradčany (Prague Castle) in, 21, 127, 179–80, 226
    Lidový dům (People's House) in, 184
    U Kaštanu house in, 184
propaganda, 8, 12, 63, 81–82, 91, 94, 97n4, 98n7, 133, 195, 203, 220

R
Raam, Villem, 107, 113–15, 119, 121n35
Rákosi, Mátyás, 128, 133–34, 138
    government of, 127, 129, 134, 137
Reformation, 22, 204
Reiner, Václav Vavřinec, 187
Renaissance, 63, 90, 130–31, 137, 139
restoration, 2, 3, 5–6, 20, 23, 43, 63, 68, 107–12, 115–19, 136, 141, 149, 153–56, 158–60, 219–21, 225–26, 230
    workshops, 39, 108, 110, 113–14, 135, 220–21 (*see also* Polish State Workshops for the Conservation of Cultural Heritage [PKZ])
Révai, József, 133, 223
Riegner, Gerhart, 66
Riga, 107, 118
Říp, 179
Rivne, 84
Robben Island, 67
Romania, 11, 17, 19–21, 85, 89, 91, 114, 129, 135, 145–60, 220–21, 225, 232
Rome, 42, 113
Rostock, 13, 222
Russian Culture Fund, 47
Russian Empire, 40, 80–81, 85
Russian Soviet Federative Socialist Republic (RSFSR), 8, 12–13, 43, 109, 222, 230

S
Saint Petersburg, 40, 92–94, 110, 117, 221, 229
Saxony, 197–99, 209–10
Scandinavia, 18, 118–19
Second International Congress of Architects and Specialists of Historic Buildings, 12, 58, 146
Senegal, 56, 58, 67
Serov, Valentin, 89
Sfințescu, Cincinat, 152, 163n39
Shevchenko, Taras, 84–85, 88
Sibiu (Hermannstadt/Nagyszeben), 151–52
Sighișoara (Schäßburg/Segesvár), 150, 152
skansen, 82, 89
Smoleń, Kazimierz, 59
Sneyers, René, 115
socialist bloc, 3, 6, 11, 14–15, 17–18, 68, 79, 106, 116, 128, 140, 147, 178, 200, 224, 229, 231–32
socialist internationalism, 10, 12, 14, 16, 41, 128, 133, 219, 223, 228
Socialist Unity Party of Germany (SED). See Communist party: in the German Democratic Republic (GDR)
Soiuzvneshstroiimport, 117
Solidarność, 11

souvenirs, 44, 83–85, 88–89
Stalin, I. V.
  birth home of, 221
  cult of, 128, 138
  death of, 11, 106, 110, 114, 138
  regime of, 106, 113–14, 119, 139
strike, 170, 179–80, 183, 186, 227
Sudeten Germans, expulsion of, 21, 169–71, 178
sustainable development, 42, 46
Suvorov, A. V., 85
Suzdal′, 13, 23, 43, 49, 111, 222
Sweden, 18, 114–15, 118, 195, 201–2, 221, 231

T
Tallinn, 18, 20, 23, 105–10, 112–14, 116–20, 221
  Niguliste (St. Nicholas) Church in, 112, 115
Târgoviște, 151, 157, 159
Tartu, 107–8
  Church of St. John in, 115–16
Tbilisi, 221
Teplice (Teplitz), 171
Ternopil, 81, 83, 92
Thümmler, Gerhard, 199
Timișoara, 152
Tomps, Fredi, 111, 116–17
Toss, Hain, 115
Toulouse, 68, 155
tourism, 12–13, 15–17, 37, 40, 42–44, 48–49, 63, 78–97, 105, 156, 190, 220, 222
  diaspora tourists, 17, 23, 80–84, 86, 96, 220
  travel abroad by Soviet citizens, 9, 106, 109–10, 113–14
  visiting castles and chateaus, 19, 98n7, 174–75, 189–90
Transylvania, 142n14, 147, 149–50, 152, 157–58
  German colonists in, 150, 154, 162n4
Tsarskoe Selo, 128
Tunisia, 58
Turku, 110
Tuulse, Armin, 114

U
Ukrainian Soviet Socialist Republic (SSR), 7, 15, 17, 78–97, 109–10, 230
Ukrainka, Lesia, 86
Ulbricht, Walter, 199, 203
UNESCO, 2, 3, 12, 15, 36–37, 39, 42, 44–47, 111, 115, 158, 201–2, 218, 224–25, 228, 231
  World Heritage, 16–18, 56–71, 202, 222–24
Union of Soviet Socialist Republics (USSR), 2–3, 8–9, 11, 13, 15, 17–18, 36, 38–49, 79–81, 83, 87–90, 92–93, 95–96, 105–12, 115–17, 128–29, 136, 138, 221, 224–25, 228, 230–31
  1977 Constitution of, 226
  Committee for State Security (KGB), 106, 108, 121n35
  ICOMOS-USSR, 111–14, 116, 118
  literacy campaigns in, 38
  memorandum between UNESCO and, 46–47
  nationality policy in, 38, 82, 91, 99n25
  Khrushchev Thaw in, 11, 84, 106
United Kingdom, 22, 46, 160, 136, 153, 195, 201–2, 204
United Nations, 35, 40, 42, 44–48, 82
  World Decade for Cultural Development, 16, 36, 44, 46–47
United Nations Educational, Scientific and Cultural Organization. See UNESCO
United States (US), 46, 58, 81, 86, 94, 96, 112, 201–2
Üprus, Helmi, 107, 109, 111, 113–15, 119
Uranov, G. V., 46
urban development, 1, 6, 12, 37, 149, 152, 200, 219
urban planning, 20, 37, 43, 131, 145, 147–48, 154, 160, 171, 232
Ústí nad Labem (Aussig), 171, 175, 177
Uzhhorod, 80, 82, 84

V
Vali, Jaan, 115

Venice Charter. *See* Second International Congress of Architects and Specialists of Historic Buildings
Vienna, 130, 140, 150, 174
Vietnam, 111–12
Vilnius, 109, 111, 118, 225
Visby, 114
Visegrád Group, 228
Vítězný únor, 185
Vladimir Oblast, 43–44
VOOPIiK. *See* All-Russian Society for the Protection of Historical and Cultural Monuments

W

Wächtler, Eberhard, 201, 204, 206–8, 210
Wagenbreth, Otfried, 206–7, 209–10
Wallachia, 149–51, 157–58, 163n26
Warsaw, 16, 23, 57–58, 62, 65–66, 68, 70, 116, 135–36, 222–23, 229
    ICOMOS founding meeting in, 12, 111, 221
    postwar reconstruction of, 63, 65, 137, 148, 162n15, 219, 221–23, 226
    Royal Castle in, 63, 128
Warsaw Pact, 3, 13, 219, 228
Weimar, 203, 206
Weiss, Josef, 131
Wieliczka Salt Mine, 16, 58, 62–64, 68, 70
wine, 85–86
workers' movement, 21, 183–86, 202, 205, 227
Working Group of Socialist Countries for the Restoration of Monuments of History, Culture, and Museum Valuables, 111–12, 222
World Bank, 37, 45
World Commission on Culture and Development, 47
world conferences on cultural policies, 36, 45–46
World War II, 2, 7–8, 41, 61–62, 64, 70, 85–87, 91, 179, 217, 227, 230
    Great Patriotic War, 2, 8, 44, 92–93, 220, 230
    memorials and sites relating to, 92–96, 108, 185
    reconstruction after, 2, 7–8, 20, 39, 137–141, 148, 153–54, 219–22 (*see also* Warsaw)
    See also destruction
Wrocław, 136

Y

Yalta, 80, 86, 94
Ybl, Miklós, 131
Yerevan, 221
Yugoslavia, 43, 113, 221

Z

Zachwatowicz, Jan, 137, 221–22
Zápotocký, Antonín, 184
Zagreb, 115
Zamość, 68
Zaporizhia, 17, 23, 80, 83, 87–88, 101n62, 110
Zatiahan, Yosyp, 88–89

www.ingramcontent.com/pod-product-compliance
Lightning Source LLC
Chambersburg PA
CBHW071338080526
44587CB00017B/2876